Contents

NINE
CONTEMPORARY POETS

A critical introduction

NINE CONTEMPORARY POETS

A *critical introduction*

P. R. King

METHUEN
London and New York

First published in 1979 by
Methuen & Co. Ltd
11 New Fetter Lane, London EC4P 4EE

Published in the USA by
Methuen & Co.
in association with Methuen, Inc.
733 Third Avenue, New York, NY 10017

© 1979 P. R. King

Phototypeset by
Western Printing Services Ltd, Bristol

Printed in Great Britain by
Richard Clay (The Chaucer Press) Ltd, Bungay

ISBN 0 416 71850 7 (hardback)
ISBN 0 416 71860 4 (paperback)

British Library Cataloguing in Publication Data

King, Peter R
  Nine contemporary poets
  1. English poetry – 20th century – History
    and criticism
  821'.9'1409   PR601

  ISBN 0 416 71850 7 (hardback)
  ISBN 0 416 71860 4 (paperback)

Preface

In talking to and teaching a variety of groups of people interested in contemporary poetry (A-level students, undergraduates, members of adult education classes and general readers enjoying modern literature) I have been made aware of a widespread need for a simple and systematic introduction to the more important postwar English poets. This book came to be written in order to go some way towards filling that need. I hope it will be found to be of some help to those who are reading contemporary poetry for the first time and who seek some signposts to this well-populated and fascinating terrain. But this is not a historical survey, nor an attempt to map out the whole territory. It is intended as a guide to some of the major features of the landscape, giving sufficient information to provide the newcomer with the ability to go on to find his own way and to explore his own interests.

In contemporary matters there is always a lack of consensus concerning who should be considered important and who should not. I am aware that my selection of poets for discussion is personal but I have tried to prevent it from being eccentric. In making my choice I have borne in mind the following points:

1   I have selected poets whom I believe to be writing work of lasting value and of these only those whose literary reputation has been established since 1960. All of them have published their first collections since 1945 and published first with English publishers (which explains the inclusion of an American, Sylvia Plath).

This principle of selection excludes poets like Dylan Thomas and Edwin Muir whose work was first published before 1945, although some of their important poems appeared after that date.

It also excludes a poet like Robert Graves who still continues to produce important poetry but whose first book appeared many years ago.

2   I have selected only those poets who seem to me to have appealed to a fairly wide reading public and whose work is, to some extent, appreciated by sixth-formers. This explains why I have not discussed the work of a poet of the stature of Geoffrey Hill whom I felt had a less wide appeal because of the allusive and complex nature of his poems.

3   I have selected those poets about whom I personally have something to say. Negative criticism seems to me to be a trivial occupation. That is not to say that I have not allowed myself to be evaluative in my remarks. This also explains the absence of a discussion of the so-called 'pop' poets (such as Adrian Henri, Roger McGough and Brian Patten) who enjoy a wide readership.

Nevertheless there always remain poets, like R. S. Thomas and Peter Porter, whose work I would like to have discussed if space had permitted.

This is not a scholarly academic work and makes no pretence of originality. I believe that a synthesis of a number of ideas scattered among the pages of recent writing about contemporary poetry is of particular value to the reader new to such poetry. I am indebted to a number of critics for the background to my own views and I have acknowledged them in the best way I know, by including them in the select bibliography.

If this book helps in some small part to encourage readers to make their own assessment of these poets or, more importantly, encourages them to read or reread their poetry, I shall consider my task worthwhile.

I wish to acknowledge the helpful advice of Roger Hubank and Ernest Frost who read an earlier draft of parts of this book. I am also grateful to Douglas Dunn, Tom Paulin and Paul Mills for their co-operation in compiling Chapter 7; and I wish to thank my wife for her unfailing support. Where such help has been unable to prevent any errors of judgement, the fault remains entirely my own.

January 1979

Acknowledgements

The author and publisher would like to thank the following for permission to reproduce copyright material:

Faber and Faber Ltd for 57 lines from *The Whitsun Weddings* and 28 lines from *High Windows*, and The Marvell Press for 117 lines from *The Less Deceived*, all by Philip Larkin; Charles Tomlinson and Oxford University Press for 76 lines from *Seeing Is Believing* (© Charles Tomlinson 1960), 24 lines from *The Way of A World* (© Oxford University Press 1969), 20 lines from *The Shaft* (© Charles Tomlinson 1978), 13 lines from *A Peopled Landscape* (© Oxford University Press 1963), 16 lines from *American Scenes* (© Oxford University Press 1966), all by Charles Tomlinson; Faber and Faber Ltd for 19 lines from *The Sense of Movement*, 'To His Cynical Mistress' from *Fighting Terms*, 23 lines from *Touch*, and 15 lines from *My Sad Captains*, and Farrar, Strauss and Giroux, Inc. for 15 lines from *Moly and My Sad Captains*, all by Thom Gunn; Faber and Faber Ltd and Harper and Row, Publishers, Inc. for 17 lines from *The Hawk in the Rain*, 8 lines from *Lupercal*, 30 lines and additional short extracts from *Wodwo*, 20 lines from *Crow* and 9 lines from *Gaudete*, and Faber and Faber Ltd and Olwyn Hughes for 9 lines from *Season Songs*, all by Ted Hughes; Ted Hughes and Harper and Row, Publishers, Inc. for 46 lines from *Ariel*, Ted Hughes for 38 lines from *The Colossus*, and Alfred A. Knopf, Inc. for 38 lines from *The Colossus and Other Poems*, all by Sylvia Plath; Faber and Faber Ltd for 76 lines from *Death of a Naturalist*, 8 lines and 'The Forge' from *Door into the Dark*, and Faber and Faber Ltd and Oxford University Press, New York, for 56 lines from *Wintering*

Acknowledgements

Out, 20 lines from *North* and additional short extracts, all by Seamus Heaney; Faber and Faber Ltd for 'A Removal from Terry Street' from *Terry Street* by Douglas Dunn; Faber and Faber Ltd for 'Settlers', 'States', 'A Just State', 'Newness' and 6 lines from 'Fin de Siècle' from *A State of Justice* by Tom Paulin; Carcanet Press Ltd for 'Cape Cornwall' and 'The Green Room' from *North Carriageway* and 'Procris' from *Third Person*, all by Paul Mills.

1

Without illusion

The poetry of Philip Larkin

Poetry and sanity

Philip Larkin enjoys a high reputation among contemporary poets. As long ago as 1965 one critic talked of him as 'the best poet England now has'[1] and ten years later this opinion was reaffirmed by Alan Brownjohn when he claimed that 'Larkin has produced the most technically brilliant and resonantly beautiful, profoundly disturbing yet appealing and approachable, body of verse of any English poet in the last twenty-five years'.[2]

Larkin's first volume of poetry appeared as long ago as 1945. *The North Ship* (revised in 1966) was quickly followed by two novels, *Jill* (1946) and *A Girl in Winter* (1947). The remaining volumes have been collections of poetry and have appeared at widely separated intervals: *The Less Deceived* (1955), *The Whitsun Weddings* (1964) and *High Windows* (1974). Larkin has also edited *The Oxford Book of Twentieth-Century English Verse* (1973) and a collection of his own essays on jazz, *All What Jazz?* (1970). His total number of published poems does not exceed much more than 100 (of which nearly 30 are regarded by him as juvenilia). He has said he feels lucky if he writes more than one or two poems a year. This reflects the fact that Larkin has never been a full-time writer; but it also shows a high degree of self-criticism.

This somewhat slender output is a result of the scrupulous awareness of a man who refuses to be taken in by inflated notions of either art or life. Larkin is keenly aware of all aspects of the pretentious. In his introduction to *Jill* he accounts for this by the fact that he grew up just before and during the Second World War. He writes: 'at an age when self-importance would have been normal, events cut us ruthlessly down to size'. Ever since then his poetry has been very much concerned with the ways in which man's dreams, hopes, ideals and pretensions are relentlessly diminished by the reality of life.

This refusal to overestimate the value of things extends to his resolute avoidance of literary self-aggrandizement and to the attitude he displays towards the writing of poetry. He believes that a poet must write only about that which he feels deeply. Inflated feelings or rhetoric are to be avoided; for Larkin, poetry is a way of being honest. It is the record of the poet's recovery of his authentic response to experience, and his muse is the muse of memory. He has written of poetry as an act of preservation, a way of defeating time:

> I write poems to preserve things I have seen/thought/felt (if I may so indicate a composite and complex experience) both for myself and for others, though I feel that my prime responsibility is to the experience itself, which I am trying to keep from oblivion for its own sake. Why I should do this I have no idea, but I think the impulse to preserve lies at the bottom of all art.[3]

It is characteristic of Larkin that he should claim no part of that tradition of the poet as visionary or seer.

His demand for fidelity to experience is supported by his insistence that poetry should both communicate and give pleasure to the reader. Indeed, it is only by truth to experience that the poet is enabled to communicate. It is his belief that many modern artists have ignored this need to communicate and give pleasure that leads to his castigating of the 'modernist' movement in the arts. Larkin seems to have in mind the abstract movement in twentieth-century painting, some of the more esoteric poetry of this century and non-traditional jazz music. He sees in it only a deliberate attempt to obfuscate and bewilder, to mystify and outrage. He feels that the result of this has been increasingly to reduce the audience for the arts to a disastrously narrow group of academics and professionals. Larkin believes that poetry must regain a wider audience and that, 'at bottom poetry, like all art, is inextricably bound up with giving pleasure, and if a poet loses his pleasure-seeking audience he has lost the only audience worth having.'[4]

It would be a mistake to dismiss this attitude as a form of simple literary conservatism. Larkin is not so much expressing an anti-intellectualism as attacking a particular form of artistic snobbery.

With this insistence that good poetry results from honesty to feeling and the desire to communicate, it is hardly surprising to discover that Larkin found his poetic identity after a close reading of the poetry of Thomas Hardy. Hardy antedates the modernist movement and his poetry blends traditional forms (which are nevertheless kept flexible enough for him to express his unique perspective) with very personal pressures of feeling. Larkin speaks of Hardy having given him 'a sense of relief that I didn't have to try and jack myself up to a concept of poetry that lay outside my own life'.[5] Hardy taught him that a modern poet could write about the life around him in the language of the society around him. He encouraged him to use his poetry to examine the reality of his own life – an encouragement that led him to the view that 'poetry is an affair of sanity, of seeing things as they are'.[6] As a result Larkin abandoned the highly romantic style of *The North Ship*, which had been heavily influenced by the poetry of Yeats, and set out to write from the tensions that underlay his own everyday experiences. Hardy also supported his employment of traditional forms and techniques, which Larkin has gone on to use with subtlety and variety.

These attitudes to poetry are similar to those held by The Movement poets of the mid-1950s with whom Larkin was associated for a time. The Movement was a loosely connected group including Kingsley Amis, John Wain, Robert Conquest, John Holloway, D. J. Enright, Elizabeth Jennings, Donald Davie and Thom Gunn. Subsequently these poets developed their work in very different directions, but at the time that they were all contributing to the anthology *New Lines* (1956) they shared some similar opinions concerning the kind of poetry that ought to be written. They rejected both the politically committed poetry of the 1930s (of the young Auden, Spender and Day Lewis) and the neo-romantic surrealism of the poetry of the 1940s. To a generation that had grown up under the shadow of war it seemed that there had been altogether too much rhetoric and not enough rationality. They looked for poetry which expressed the ordered, rational self, that had 'a suspicion of large rhetorical gestures, a belief that the intellect and moral judgement must play a decisive part in the shaping of a poem',[7] and which made use of traditional forms, a conversational idiom and adopted a strongly ironical tone of voice.

With the passage of time The Movement may be seen as of much less literary importance than previously, its chief claim to fame being as a nursery for the early growth of a number of talented poets. But it would be a mistake to see Larkin as one of these. Although he had sympathy with many of the attitudes to poetry represented by The Movement, his work is generally more robust and wider-ranging than most of the poetry of *New Lines*. Certainly he has links with The Movement, as Peschmann has pointed out:

> What particularly links Larkin with The Movement in *The Less Deceived* is its fundamental honesty to experience: a clear-eyed, unillusioned view of contemporary living and its problems, and a refusal to sentimentalize them; the whole couched, for the most part, in a language instantly recognizable as the colloquial idiom of our day, free from pedantry, grandiloquence, or the recherché phrase.[8]

Larkin's relationship with The Movement was casual, not causal. His view of the poet's task owes more to his discovery of Hardy and antedates the formation of The Movement.

From the three major volumes of poetry Larkin has so far published there has emerged a consistency of poetic identity. It is the identity of a detached yet careful observer of the behaviour of himself and others. In many poems he seems to turn away from the society of others and to take up a solitary stance implying a purer vantage point from which to survey life in his 'humorous, self-deprecatory and observant'[9] way. The adoption of this role and a frequently ironic tone should not mislead the reader into assuming he is unmoved by his feelings and response to what he observes. The detachedness appears to be the necessary concomitant of his view of the artist's role. He observes and remains apart as a result of his commitment to an art which is to record and preserve life rather than to enact or transcend life. He sees this commitment as demanding above all an honesty about his own nature and, if this requires him to be on the outside looking in, it must be accepted. This is made plain in 'Reasons for Attendance', where art is seen as his way of remaining true both to himself and to what he observes. The person in the poem is looking through a lighted window to watch people dancing inside. He realizes he prefers to remain outside and he asks himself why this should be so:

> Why be out there?
> But then, why be in there? Sex, yes, but what
> Is sex? Surely, to think the lion's share
> Of happiness is found by couples – sheer
>
> Inaccuracy, as far as I'm concerned.
> What calls me is that lifted, rough-tongued bell
> (Art, if you like) whose individual sound
> Insists I too am individual. . . .
>
> Therefore I stay outside,
> Believing this; and they maul to and fro,
> Believing that; and both are satisfied,
> If no one has misjudged himself. Or lied.

Although the dedication to his art is insisted upon, the final two words make it clear there is no room for self-congratulation. Larkin is aware that even this commitment of his may finally be as much an illusion and self-deception as those he exposes elsewhere in so many of his poems. Larkin seems anxious not to be taken in even by his own commitments.

The voice of this poetic identity has many tones and a variety of diction and idiom. It can be sharp and satirical ('Vers de Société'), quiet and almost plaintive ('Broadcast'), conversational and meditative ('Church Going'), even lyrical and mysterious ('Coming') and occasionally resentful and bitter ('Send No Money'). In all these tones and moods the same tension is at work: the conflict between our dreams, hopes and expectations, and the various ways in which reality serves to make them collapse. Larkin records the various ways in which man pulls the wool over his own eyes in being tempted to believe that he can achieve a paradise of money, or fame, or sex, or close relationships with others. He explores the way we 'pick up bad habits of expectancy' which is only to be destroyed eventually by that 'solving oblivion' which runs just under everything we do. He is concerned to expose our illusions and evasions so that we may stand naked but honest, 'less deceived' by ourselves before the reality of life and death.

It is this underlying concern which provides the constancy of the relatively small number of themes in Larkin's poetry: the passage of time, memory and the past, the illusory visions of man (especially the failure of the promise of love) and old age and death. But this continuity of theme should not blind the reader to the variety of tone, form and intention in the poems. The central poetic identity remains constant but does not become dull. Larkin's poetry may not develop in the sense of going through any sudden alterations of theme or style, but it rather has continued to deepen and refine his chosen concerns. He has said, 'I don't think I want to change; just to become better at what I am.'[10] This has led some critics to be suspicious of his achievement, as if development in its meaning of change was the *sine qua non* of greatness in poetry. Since he found his mature style in *The Less Deceived* Larkin has not sought this kind of development and therefore it is not necessary to pursue a chronological approach in introducing his poetry. The remaining part of this chapter will consider a number of individual poems in the light of Larkin's main themes, characteristic voices and variety of tones.

Time's fool

At the heart of Larkin's poetry lies a constant awareness of the passing of time and a belief that man is always in thrall to time. Time strips us of illusions and is the bearer of realities which we would prefer to avoid. In 'Reference Back' he writes,

> Truly, though our element is time,
> We are not suited to the long perspectives
> Open at each instant of our lives.
> They link us to our losses.

Time is a chain that binds us to our earlier hopes and dreams which, as we grow older, we realize will never become reality. This sense of loss, of hopes blasted and ideals destroyed, pervades the poetry. In many of the poems Larkin looks over his shoulder at his own past, or indirectly considers that past by observing the youth around him, and rubs his nose in the fact that memory is cruel enough to remind us that the adult life we now experience as mundane and drab is that very same life that in our childhood and youth we invested with all possible excitement and meaning. There is a double cruelty in time: it both reminds us of what we *might* have had, and turns what we *do* have into a sense of disappointment. The 'long perspectives'

> ... show us what we have as it once was,
> Blindingly undiminished, just as though
> By acting differently we could have kept it so.

Although others might claim man can assert his will to prevent such diminishing of his hopes, the *persona* in many of these poems rules that out. He adopts a deterministic view of life whereby 'something hidden from us' destroys all attempts we make consciously to control our lives and seize our happiness. This attitude may be seen at work in 'Triple Time', 'Next, Please', 'I Remember, I Remember', 'Dockery and Son' and 'Arrivals, Departures'.

Time (as the inexorable servant of decay and death) destroys us and corrodes any meaning we attach to our lives by its insidious attack upon purpose and intention. Yet we are also time's accomplices in the sense that we ourselves employ time as an instrument with which to deceive ourselves. It is *we* that use time as a comfort, it is we who allow ourselves the hope that in *time* all shall be well, that in *time* all our purposes will be accomplished. In 'Triple Time' this is exposed as a threefold illusion.

In this poem the poet assumes, without argument or evidence, that the present is colourless and empty, 'a time unrecommended by event' in which no important or meaningful occurrence may be anticipated to add a significance to our dreary existence. What makes this situation worse is the realization that this dull present was once a future, as seen from childhood, bright with possibilities. Our childhood gave the future 'an air lambent with adult enterprise'. This choice of 'lambent', a somewhat archaic and mysterious word, stands out in a poem with a diction that elsewhere is unspectacular and catches perfectly that sense of the romantic projections which the young place on an adult future. In fact the complete phrase has an air of preciousness (particularly in the use of 'enterprise') which gives the feel of adulthood as being serious and important, as it appears to a child.

But in the last stanza a final illusion is exposed when the present, which will soon become our past, is seen in the light of so many missed opportunities. It is 'a valley cropped by fat neglected chances / That we insensately forbore to fleece'. This image suggests opportunities heavy with possibilities. The last lines, 'On this we blame our last / Threadbare perspectives, seasonal decrease', have an air of inevitability in their insinuation of a seasonal, cyclical decline and combine with the previous image to insist that life is a series of missed chances and that our present opportunities will pass untaken before we are even aware of their existence. This poem declares that we deceive ourselves into imagining that the past or the future will give our present a sense of meaning.

'Next, Please' takes an even more sombre look at time. 'Triple Time' used image and metaphor to flesh out its central idea, but this poem is built up from a single image or extended metaphor after the initial generalization:

> Always too eager for the future, we
> Pick up bad habits of expectancy.
> Something is always approaching; every day
> *Till then* we say. . . .

This generalization is developed in the image of our keeping watch from a cliff, looking out to sea at the approaching 'sparkling armada of promises'. Our emotions range from the irritation we feel at the apparent slowness with which the armada approaches, through the great hope we place upon it ('each one will heave to and unload / All good into our lives'), to our self-satisfaction when we consider how much we deserve such beneficence. But such a weight of hope and selfishness is doomed to dissatisfaction. The ships pass by and we are left 'holding wretched stalks / Of disappointment'. Up to this point the poem proceeds in the simplest of ways: the central metaphor springs no surprises – indeed it is rather conventional (a variant on the old saying 'when your boat comes in') – but in the last stanza the language rises to a more sinister and harder-hitting climax in which the ship image takes on a ghostly, mysteriously dangerous quality. The ship turns out not to be heavily laden and not to be hauling a grand future towards us. It is empty and its decks deserted. Immediately our mind is taken back to that opening stanza with its 'something is always approaching' and we suddenly realize that what always approaches us – the only part of life that we can anticipate with certainty – is death:

> Only one ship is seeking us, a black-
> Sailed unfamiliar, towing at her back
> A huge and birdless silence. In her wake
> No waters breed or break.

Through the image in this extract of the birdless silence and the blank expanse of waters death becomes a sterile emptiness that extends across nature itself. The familiar theme and metaphor are infused with a new texture in this stanza. In the earlier lines the attitude that there will be an inevitable and continuous frustration of all our hopes is merely an assertion that rises from the poet's personal conviction. This final stanza of 'Next, Please' spreads beyond the personal and partakes of a common reality whose very impersonality is part of its shattering truth.

For Larkin in these poems time 'brings no comfort'. Even his happy memories are tainted and lose their power to console when he becomes aware of their 'pastness', their everlasting loss, and contrasts them with a present which can only seem the more drab the longer the contrast is made.

'Arrivals, Departures' has similarities to 'Next, Please' in its handling of a related theme. It too develops a comment on time and the frustration of our expectations by means of a metaphor connected with ships. In this poem we are in a channel port watching the continuous traffic of the cross-channel steamers and hearing the ever-present wail of ships' sirens. This sound of the sirens 'lowing in a doleful distance' winds its way throughout the poem and serves to suggest some insistent call to a wider experience of life, an invitation to journey beyond our everyday existence. The vaguely disturbing call of these sirens with their hint of distant places hidden in the rather melancholy note is an apt motif for that obscure inner feeling most of us experience from time to time and which suggests to us that it is time we made a change in our lives, seeking out new challenges. It is a sound that brings 'horny dilemmas at the gate once more' and calls upon us to make decisions about the direction our life should take. The inbound ships call 'Come and choose wrong', the outward-bound reply 'O not for long' and thus serve between them to imply both the perennial human need to follow our experience wherever it may lead us and the continuous danger that we thus run of making the wrong decisions. Timms[11] suggests that the siren is the sound of desolation. If it is, it is so because it expresses at one and the same time the emptiness of a life which refuses to respond to the possibilities of new experiences and the inevitable disappoint-ments we face when we do respond and the risks we then run of making the wrong choice. We are reminded of 'Next, Please' and remember particularly the possibility that the ship which carries us on our journey may also be the ship of death, its siren luring us on with a call we can neither ignore or command. A sense of inevitable disappointment, even disaster, echoes through the play of sounds (the repeated 'or', 'on' and 'oing') which is heard throughout the poem and culminates with the final doubt as to whether we ever know 'if, this night, happiness too is going'.

Two of the best poems concerning the relationship between the past, memory and the possibilities of hope are 'I Remember, I Remember' and 'Dockery and Son'. Each is concerned with the memories of the poet's own past and they succeed in convincing the reader of his honesty to his feelings.

In 'I Remember, I Remember' the poet is travelling by train with a companion when they pass through the city in which the poet was born. In this poem Larkin seems determined to avoid any sentimentalizing of his own childhood through holding romanti-cally inflated notions of the significance of a writer's childhood. This is brought out further by the direct contrast to the nostalgia and sentimentality of the famous nineteenth-century poem by Thomas Hood which shares the same title as Larkin's poem. His travelling companion asks him if the town they are passing through, his home town, is where he has his roots. Before replying the poet recalls all those childhoods described as so important in the popularized biographies of writers, or in a novel like *Sons and Lovers*. In a series of satirical thrusts he casts aside any idea that his own past has a particular significance that marked him out at an early stage as someone special:

> Our garden, first: where I did not invent
> Blinding theologies of flowers and fruits . . .

> And here we have that splendid family
> I never ran to when I got depressed,
> The boys all biceps and the girls all chest . . .

> The bracken where I never trembling sat,
> Determined to go through with it when she
> Lay back, and 'all became a burning mist'.

This irony turns into a more serious note of disenchantment in his own thoughts of a reply, 'No, only where my childhood was unspent'. That 'unspent' carries a world of disillusion. His honest recognition of the ordinariness of his childhood is a deliberate defiance of all the romantic self-aggrandizing gestures of the artist and his fawning public. By the time the actual reply of the last lines is reached, this attitude is generalized from his own life to embrace the life of thousands of ordinary people who cannot escape the mundane lot of a perfectly ordinary life:

> 'You look as if you wished the place in Hell,'
> My friend said, 'judging from your face.' 'Oh well,
> I suppose it's not the place's fault,' I said.

> 'Nothing, like something, happens anywhere.'

The final line stands naked, isolated from the body of the poem, as an honest response to life which takes on the tone of authority of a proverb – a summary of a whole way of looking at life and not just a passing comment. It throws its shadow back across the whole poem. It implies that man is always tempted to twist his memories of his past under the pressure of self-justification or self-glorification. The appeal of the poem lies in the poet's self-exposure, his own refusal to compensate for his own sense of ordinariness by sentimentalizing his past. But the reader carries away from the poem an after-feeling that someone who can so confidently assert the omnipresence of 'nothing' is unlikely to be the one to escape a sense of the dullness and futility of life.

The price that the individual may have to pay for his refusal to be under any illusions about life is the theme of 'Dockery and Son'. It is a poem that is central to any understanding of Larkin's mixture of honesty and self-doubt which is so much a part of his best poems. Like many of these poems, the total effect of 'Dockery and Son' is only to be understood by an appreciation of the careful manipulation of tone. It begins in a calm, unruffled manner which is soon broken by a realization of the passage of time and opportunities, and it culminates in an acceptance that our lives are ultimately controlled by powers beyond those we may influence.

These thoughts are prompted by a visit that the poet pays to his former college where the Dean tells him that the son of Dockery, one of the poet's college contemporaries, is studying there. This announcement is what leads the poet on to consider the very different ways in which individuals carve out their lives. He tries, in this mood, to visit his old rooms but finds the door locked. He returns home on the train 'ignored' and as he dozes through the journey tries to recall Dockery. The locked door and lack of recognition emphasize his outsider status in a place where he once felt very much at ease, and this is further underlined by his inability to remember Dockery very clearly after all these years.

It is on the train that the poet begins to awaken to the fact of his middle age and to the distance not only of time but of differing life choices between himself and someone like Dockery who must have chosen marriage and family life at an early age. The poet's own bachelorhood and lack of settled conviction about his life become prominent reminders of this gap between himself and Dockery. This growing awareness is carried through in the imagery of the railway tracks as they move him further and further away from his visit and his past: 'the ranged / Joining and parting lines reflect a strong / Unhindered moon'. The concrete particulars of the journey, especially the eating of 'an awful pie' after 'waking at the fumes / And furnace glare of Sheffield', give both a solidity to the narrative and imply the growing sense of unease, even disappointment, failure and loneliness.

A further tone change follows on from these musings as to the difference between himself and Dockery. Dockery, the poet assumes, must have been a man who knew early what he wanted

12

from life. The poet finds it difficult to understand Dockery's desire for paternity,

> Convinced he was he should be added to!
> Why did he think adding meant increase?
> To me it was dilution.

This leads him to speculate on the source of our assumptions about the way our lives should be lived and his answer to this question suggests a determinism about life. It is not our ideals nor our selfishness that control our life ('Those warp tight-shut, like doors') but rather that our habits, never consciously chosen, harden with the passage of time into the only life we have. Thus Dockery's paternity and the poet's bachelorhood are equal destinies: they are both results of neither choice nor desire but simply the fact of life happening, as it were, behind their backs before they had time to realize the situation they were in. It appears that choice is one of life's major illusions. Larkin has revealed elsewhere that it is a deception that man regularly plays on himself to believe that, had we acted differently at some crucial point in our past, our present would have been changed. There is here a strong suggestion that our lives are beyond our control and that we are being continually displaced from our own possibilities by a force stronger than ourselves, or at least by the unwilled habits of a lifetime binding us into a straitjacket that denies us any freedom to change, like the young mothers in 'Afternoons' for whom 'Something is pushing them / To the side of their own lives'. The conclusion of this poem is not just a description, but is also a warning of the ultimate fatuity in believing life has any choice for us:

> Life is first boredom, then fear.
> Whether or not we use it, it goes
> And leaves what something hidden from us chose,
> And age, and then the only end of age.

This bleak conclusion and the preceding meditations have been bound together in regular eight-line stanzas rhyming abbcaddc and moving forward on a steady iambic rhythm. This solid frame is upheld by a colloquial diction and imagery drawn from everyday experiences. These combine to set the keynote of ordinariness which convinces the reader of the authenticity of the experience. The success of the poem lies in its precise rendering of the changing tones of voice and the tension between the idea of divergent paths in people's lives and the poet's personal conviction that our lives are determined by powers outside our control. The poem betrays a strong feeling that it is time which decides all in a man's life and that the best a man can do is not to delude himself into thinking it can be otherwise. Yet that final stanza remains an assertion. It may result from the poet's being honest to his own experience, but it cannot be generalized except as a dogmatism. Finally the poem is valuable rather for its creation of a distinct and powerful sense of a personality brooding over the facts of his experience, than for its sweeping generalization.

Being less deceived

A desire not to be fooled by time leads to a concern to maintain vigilance against a whole range of possible evasions of reality. It is partly this which makes Larkin's typical stance one of being to one side of life, watching himself and others with a detached eye. The privilege of such an outsider's role is that it allows him to expose the illusions of those who remain too close to their experience ever to stand back and take an objective view of themselves. In many poems the *persona* expresses an acute awareness both of his own limitations and of the illusions of those he sees around him. These poems record his refusal to be deceived into evading reality. We have already seen this in relation to time and love, but there are a variety of other evasions and deceptions and Larkin's exposure of them can often be humorous and witty.

One of the realities of life, for most people, is the need to work. In 'Toads' Larkin displays a lively fun as well as self-awareness in his picture of the ever-present demands of the routine of work. He sees work as a huge and dirty toad squatting on our lives:

> Six days of the week it soils
>   With its sickening poison –
> Just for paying a few bills!
>   That's out of proportion.

The possibility of avoiding this dull routine is raised. Perhaps he can use his 'wit as a pitchfork' to toss the toad away,

> Lots of folk live on their wits:
> Lecturers, lispers,
> Losels, loblolly-men, louts –

(The lumping together of such disparate types in this excessive alliteration is both amusing and a sly jibe at the 'professions' referred to.) The speaker of the poem laments not being 'courageous enough / To shout *Stuff your pension!*' But he knows the toad cannot be so easily driven off because he realizes it is part of his own psyche: he can see that he is unable to break away from the security which regular employment offers him.

> For something sufficiently toad-like
> Squats in me, too;
> Its hunkers are heavy as hard luck,
> And cold as snow,
>
> And will never allow me to blarney
> My way to getting
> The fame and the girl and the money
> All at one sitting.

The poem is lightly handled, the lines alternate in a tripping rhythm of trimeters and dimeters; the rhymes are slant ('wits/louts') with a wit of their own; the language is idiomatic and lively; the toad image is amusing, and all these characteristics add up to a humorous light verse with a serious underlying self-awareness.

'Toads Revisited', published in a later volume, expands the same subject. But this poem has a darker mood. It describes the poet enjoying a day off from work. He walks in the park and observes all the others there who have managed to free themselves from the toad of work. But, in contrast to the previous poem in which people used their wits to free themselves from work, the people he sees in this poem are old, ill or outcast – they are the witless:

> Palsied old step-takers,
> Hare-eyed clerks with the jitters,

Waxed-fleshed out-patients
Still vague from accidents.

This expresses the other side of the idea of work. The in-tray, the secretary, the busy routines of work are seen here as a necessary barrier to keep out loneliness, boredom and meaninglessness. Ultimately, however, even work cannot put off the inevitable, and in the poem's final couplet (which has the only full rhyme in the poem and therefore pulls the reader up with a jolt) work is seen as a mask worn to hide ourselves from death. But the poet knows no such hiding is possible:

Give me your arm, old toad:
Help me down Cemetery Road.

'Poetry of Departures' is heavily ironical. It considers this possibility of freeing ourselves from the enervating routines of a dull life. It examines the response of admiration, even approval, that we often have when we hear of someone who has really made the break and got away from it all.

Sometimes you hear, fifth-hand,
As epitaph:
He chucked up everything
And just cleared off,
And always the voice will sound
Certain you approve
This audacious, purifying,
Elemental move.

But the poet points out that for most of us this is an easy, unthinking reaction that is part of a purely fantasy revolt against our situation.

A double use of irony is at work in this poem. The first target for it is the unthinking, escapist romanticism in our response. The third stanza aims at this target by allying our responses to the inauthentic and exaggerated world of 'pulp' fiction:

He walked out on the whole crowd
Leaves me flushed and stirred,
Like *Then she undid her dress*
Or *Take that you bastard.*

16

The second target of the irony is the poet's own 'ordered life' from which he has launched his first attack on the dishonest romanticizing of those who evade their responsibilities by just clearing off. Admitting to a feeling that he detests his room at times, 'its specially-chosen junk, / The good books, the good bed, / And my life, in perfect order', the poet turns on himself and in the last stanza attacks his overdeveloped notion of an orderly and conventional life – 'Books; china; a life / Reprehensibly perfect'.

The title 'Poetry of Departures' is intended to suggest the fond illusion that some kind of liberation is to be discovered in throwing up the life we know for some vaguely imagined alternative. But to the poet this is an evasion. Yet the double irony works to suggest that his own refusal to be taken in by the romantic cliché may itself be another evasion. The well-ordered life might be a cowardice in the face of different ways of living. It is a cliché of another kind. The irony is a weapon against the artificial perfections of both responses to life, and it creates a self-knowledge and honesty characteristic of Larkin as a poet.

'Deceptions' begins as a response to the description of a girl drugged and raped in an attic in nineteenth-century London given by H. Mayhew in *London Labour and the London Poor* (1861). It opens with the poet's sympathy for the girl and a calling up of the unfeeling, unpitying life of the nineteenth-century capital which 'bows the other way'. The poet can 'taste the grief' the rapist made her 'gulp' along with the drug he gave her, and yet Larkin knows his sympathy can in no way be a meaningful consolation:

> Slums, years, have buried you. I would not dare
> Console you if I could. What can be said,
> Except that suffering is exact . . .

What does remain to be said, for the poet, is that suffering is of more than one kind. There is the obvious pain of the victim, no less painful for being obvious, but there is also a suffering to be understood in the nature of her assailant. Although the girl may appear the more deceived, the rapist is also to be understood as being deceived into thinking that the gratification of his desire would bring him a fulfilment. The poet denies that there could be any such fulfilment. Thus it is the girl who is less deceived, although the poet has the human sympathy to realize this brings her no consolation:

> For you would hardly care
> That you were less deceived, out on that bed,
> Than he was, stumbling up the breathless stair
> To burst into fulfilment's desolate attic.

This attic image reveals the extent of man's delusions. The poem's implication is that the only value in a world of suffering lies in the individual divesting himself of any illusions including the illusion that being the less deceived can bring any comfort. There is no complacency in this paradox, and it is this exposure of the illusion concerning fulfilment that is a constant feature of Larkin's poetry.

'Mr Bleaney' (the very name suggests both bleakness and meanness, according to Timms[12]) begins as a study of a middle-aged, lonely bachelor who was the previous tenant of the dingy lodging room the poet now occupies. The narrow meanness of Bleaney's life is conveyed by a series of small, particular details: 'His preference for sauce to gravy, why / He kept on plugging at the four aways'; 'Christmas at his sister's house in Stoke', etc. While he occupies the same room as Bleaney did, it is inevitable that the poet should ask himself how far they are alike. Does he share the same dull life and mediocrity? The only reminder that Bleaney has left behind is the television set he persuaded the landlady to buy. In the final lines 'hired box' refers both to this set and to the rented room which might be seen as either a prison or a coffin:

> But if he stood and watched the frigid wind
> Tousling the clouds, lay on the fusty bed
> Telling himself that this was home, and grinned,
> And shivered, without shaking off the dread
>
> That how we live measures our own nature,
> And at his age having no more to show
> Than one hired box should make him pretty sure
> He warranted no better, I don't know.

This convincing evocation of a dull, dispirited bachelor life rises to poignancy in that final 'I don't know' when we realize it refers not only to Bleaney but to the poet's uncertainty as to how far he shares his fate. The poem is a wry grimace of self-recognition built round the notion that if the previous occupant 'warranted no better' then perhaps neither does the tenant who follows.

This rather grim reminder of possible self-deception shares a similar theme, but contrasts sharply in tone, with the poems in which Larkin employs satire and a heavy irony to expose some of the fatuities and pretensions of various attitudes.

A favourite target for satire is the cynically ambitious literary academic. In 'Naturally the Foundation Will Bear Your Expenses' it is the jet-setting, name-dropping, trendy literary academic who is satirized for his reduction of the pursuit of truth and knowledge to no more than a hunt for the quickest means to advance his career. The speaker of the poem is just such an academic who is sitting in his plane waiting to fly on a new lecture tour. The irony of the poem stems from the speaker's assumption that the reader will share his point of view when he expresses his annoyance that the taxi carrying him to the airport had been held up by the crowds attending the Armistice Day Remembrance Service. He is contemptuous of the memorial service, that 'solemn-sinister / Wreath-rubbish in Whitehall', and dismisses the crowds as 'colourless and careworn', of no importance except in so far as they impede his progress. The satire is directed not only at the superficiality and self-seekingness of the academic but also at anyone's contemptuous dismissal of the memorial for the fallen which cannot but be a dismissal of the fallen themselves.

In 'Posterity' the wry tone of the earlier poem has become distinctly more cynical. This time the poet imagines the young postgraduate student in America who might have chosen to write about the poet as his way to secure tenure as a university lecturer. The student has no sympathy for his chosen subject and would, apparently, have preferred to study the far trendier topic of Protest Theatre, but the need to support a young family demands he complete a safe Ph.D. Jake Balokowsky (a suitably ludicrous name) is impatient with the poet's dull life. He does not even have the compensation of discovering the hidden secrets of wild bohemian living. The poem catches perfectly the tone of barely suppressed anger and cynicism in Balokowsky's utterance:

'I'm stuck with this old fart at least a year;

I wanted to teach school in Tel Aviv,
But Myra's folks' – he makes the money sign –
'Insisted I get tenure. When there's kids –'

The callous, empty trendiness of Balokowsky is evident, but the poem is not without a self-criticism in the final line which speaks of the poet being 'one of those old-type *natural* fouled-up guys'. The poet might not be able to live up to his biographer's hopes for an extravagant mess but he knows that his life is nevertheless not without its disasters.

One of the best of the satirical poems is the early 'Sunny Prestatyn'. It describes a railway station poster advertising the pleasures of Prestatyn through the alluring image of a girl in a swimsuit:

She was slapped up one day in March.
A couple of weeks, and her face
Was snaggle-toothed and boss-eyed,
Huge tits and fissure crutch
Were scored well in, and the space
Between her legs held scrawls
That set her fairly astride
A tuberous cock and balls.

The deliberately coarse language underscores both the unreality of the original picture ('she was too good for this life') and the half-conscious anger of the despoiler whose graffiti might be taken as a comment on the falsity of the advertisement. It represents another aspect of the tension between fact and fantasy, reality and illusion. The advertisement's cliché sex symbol is part of the advertisers' untruths, a dream world of perfection which contrasts starkly with the real world most of us live in. As 'Essential Beauty' puts it, the advertisements rise

Serenely to proclaim pure crust, pure foam,
Pure coldness to our live imperfect eyes
That stare beyond this world, where nothing's made
As new or washed quite clean, seeking the home
All such inhabit.

The graffiti artist's response in 'Sunny Prestatyn' is the response of an inhabitant of the real world who has been deprived of true feeling by the advertisers' contemptuous exploitation of the human desire for the illusion of perfection. The defacing of the poster is an act of angry rebellion and the rough language of the poem (as it is elsewhere in Larkin's satirical poems) is an expression of a self-deflation which guards against any possibility of self-pity. In this poem's last line, in typically Larkin fashion, reality reasserts itself when the poster is replaced by one carrying a 'Fight Cancer' slogan. Larkin has said that he intended this poem to be both funny and horrid and its effect is just this. The poem forms part of his campaign against the untruth of romantic gestures as well as being a wittily accurate description of a common occurrence.

Another strongly satirical poem is the recent 'Vers de Société'. This attacks the conventional notion that being sociable is one of the highest virtues, and it explores the tension between solitariness and sociability, truth and hypocrisy. The poet receives an invitation to cocktails whose hypocrisy is expressed in his scornful interpretation of its real meaning:

> *My wife and I have asked a crowd of craps*
> *To come and waste their time and ours: perhaps*
> *You'd care to join us?* In a pig's arse, friend.

Yet, even after seeing the truth of it, the poet finally accepts. This gulf between the manifest relations of the poet and the sender of the invitation and their true, hidden relationship leads the poet to speculate about the general connection of sincerity and social relations. The poet admits that he finds it difficult to be alone and seeks companionship even when he knows it to be a charade. He would prefer the courage to remain solitary but knows he lacks it. This self-awareness gives him an insight into society's attitude towards solitariness. Society hides its fear of loneliness under the guise of a false morality when it utters the clichés 'All solitude is selfish' or 'Virtue is social'. This stems from a self-centredness the very opposite of the one acknowledged: 'the big wish / Is to have people nice to you, which means / Doing it back somehow'. Being sociable is so often just playing at being interested in others. Nevertheless, having admitted all this, the poet suggests that perhaps after all the charade may in fact hint at what *should* be the reality. But, for the middle-aged poet, the truth is that it is neither loneliness nor some altruistic desire to be interested in others that provides the motive for his final acceptance of the invitation. It is his admission of a wholly human weakness:

> Only the young can be alone freely.
> The time is shorter now for company,
> And sitting by a lamp more often brings
> Not peace, but other things.
> Beyond the light stand failure and remorse
> Whispering *Dear Warlock-Williams: Why, of course* –

This is a poem which begins in a satirical spirit but which, through the exercise of a subtle change of tone reflecting the inquiringly self-critical mind of the poet, finally becomes a penetrating analysis of a common human situation.

'That much-mentioned brilliance, Love'

In Larkin's poetry is one of the supreme illusions of man. When love is present in his poems it is something either hopelessly longed for (as in 'Faith Healing') or cynically dismissed as just another evasion of reality (as in 'Love Songs in Age'). 'An Arundel Tomb' and 'Faith Healing' make it clear that, although man clutches at his instinctive belief that only love will comfort, console and sustain him, such a hope is doomed to be denied. A lover's promise is an empty promise and the power to cure suffering through love is a tragic illusion:

> In everyone there sleeps
> A sense of life lived according to love.
> To some it means the difference they could make
> By loving others, but across most it sweeps
>
> As all they might have done had they been loved.
> That nothing cures.

Even a poem like 'If, My Darling' – which at first appears to be a lover's invitation to his beloved to get to know him better – turns out not to be quite the invitation we expect. The tone and images

of the poem take the form of a lively and imaginative free-verse
fantasy which admits the lover to the deeper recesses of his
personality:

> If my darling were at once to decide
> Not to stop at my eyes,
> But to jump, like Alice, with floating skirt into my head . . .

What she would find are not the traditional lover's protestations
of deepest devotions but 'delusions that shrink to the size of a
woman's glove / Then sicken inclusively outwards'. The lover in
this poem can see nothing but 'an adhesive sense of betrayal', a
phrase whose sharp economy both suggests that the lover's loyalty is frail and hints at the physically repulsive nature of the act of
love itself, a denigration continued in the brusque bawdy of the
ensuing lines: 'A Grecian statue kicked in the privates, money, / A
swill-tub of finer feelings'. Here 'the past is past and the future
neuter' and the slightly supercilious lilt of that phrase is typical of
the poem as a whole. It evades any possibility of true commitment
between lovers.

'Self's the Man' is about marriage and contrasts that state –
through the family life of one Arnold – with the bachelorhood of
the poet. Arnold, the poet allows, 'is less selfish than I' because he
got married and is providing for a family. But we are soon left
with little doubt as to the price poor Arnold pays. He works all
day to hand his money over to his wife to buy 'the kiddies' clobber
and the drier / And the electric fire' and he cannot get away from
his wife's constant demands to do this and that,

> He has no time at all,

> With the nippers to wheel round the houses
> And the hall to paint in his old trousers
> And that letter to her mother
> Saying *Won't you come for the summer*.

Any apparent sympathy for Arnold is soon lost by the insistence
on the fact that 'He married a woman to stop her getting away'
and that he is not really any less selfish than the bachelor because
'He still did it for his own sake / Playing his own game'. The one
important difference seems to be that the poet considers himself to
be better at knowing what will keep him sane:

Only I'm a better hand
At knowing what I can stand
Without them sending a van –
Or I suppose I can.

It is a comic yet cruel portrait of marriage. Even that last line, implying that in the end the poet is not completely confident that his is the best deal after all, does not wholly overcome a rather sneering quality in the poem. It leaves a suspicion that self-justification may be stronger than any self-doubt.

'Self's the Man' and 'If, My Darling' can begin to look like rationalizations of an inability to sustain a genuinely close relationship. 'Wild Oats' gives support to this judgement to some extent. It records how the poet met two girls, one beautiful and one plain, and how he courted the plain girl, became engaged to her and then broke it off, while all the time it was really to the other girl that he had lost his heart. Finally he gains neither. He puts the loss down to his shyness and inability to declare his true love, but the real reason for his disappointment goes deeper than that: it is a result of his dishonesty to his true feelings.

'No Road' and 'Talking in Bed' appear to claim that love, in any case, has little room for honesty and genuine closeness. They express an inability to draw near to someone else. In 'No Road' the breakdown of a relationship is seen as willed by the poet, a renunciation which, it is implied, is inevitable given his kind of personality. He is unable to commit himself to a relationship. This meaning is borne by the metaphor of a road running between the lovers which the poet lets fall into disuse. The core of the poem is contained in its imagery rather than in comment. The images suggest that only slowly will the possibility of relationship pass away and that it is more than time which destroys it – it is the lovers' own action:

Leaves drift unswept, perhaps; grass creeps unmown;
No other change.
So clear it stands, so little overgrown,
Walking that way tonight would not seem strange.

What kills the love is the refusal to make that contact while it remains a real possibility. Beginning with a tender melancholy,

24

the poem ends, as so often in a Larkin poem, with a final stanza expressing a realistic self-awareness which amounts almost to a stoical acceptance of his limitations. But we should not ignore the fact that the limitation is self-imposed, stemming from the poet's personality more than from the situation: 'Not to prevent [the building of a barrier] is my will's fulfilment. / Willing it, my ailment.' It is a personal ailment that in other poems is unfairly universalized as a failure in love itself.

'Talking in Bed' describes a situation that should epitomize the closeness of a relationship. It ought to be the 'emblem of two people being honest', as the poet admits, but it is seen here as an impossibility. Natural images express the couple's response, as in the previous poem:

> . . . the wind's incomplete unrest
> Builds and disperses clouds about the sky.

> And dark towns heap up on the horizon.
> None of this cares for us.

The uneasy movement of the wind and sky reflects the inability of the couple to settle to a close and honest relationship:

> At this unique distance from isolation

> It becomes still more difficult to find
> Words at once true and kind,
> Or not untrue and not unkind.

The inability to achieve even the compromised conditions of those last lines is the final sad defeat.

In these poems Larkin's lover is an individual who is either afraid of love or has been made powerless to love by his corrosive honesty and self-awareness. He believes that 'that much-mentioned brilliance, love' which is 'still promising to solve, satisfy, / And set unchangeably in order' ('Love Songs in Age') is totally false in the hopes it raises. Love is one of man's self-deceptions: it cannot bear all the weight of the dreams we place upon it.

Larkin's most moving expression of the relationship between love, time and truth is 'An Arundel Tomb'. The immediate subject of this is a monument of a medieval knight and his lady recumbent upon their grave in Chichester Cathedral. The description of the monument focuses on the fact that the stonemason has carved the couple as if holding hands. The remainder of the poem argues that what was carved as no more than a simple reminder of their marital status has been taken by our generation as a powerful symbol of undying love. It seems that because the stone has endured so long the onlooker is inclined to attribute similar endurance to the husband's and wife's love, an attribution that the poet sees as a misrepresentation of reality brought about by our too eager willingness to use the mere passage of time to uphold our sentimental hopes:

> Time has transfigured them into
> Untruth. The stone fidelity
> They hardly meant has come to be
> Their final blazon, and to prove
> Our almost-instinct almost true:
> What will survive of us is love.

The economy and beauty of this conclusion reveals Larkin's craftsmanship. 'Transfigured', 'fidelity' and 'blazon' give a tone of courtly courtesy and stateliness appropriate to the monument and its reminder of a medieval world. The break at the end of the first line emphasizes in its run-over the sudden realization of the inappropriateness of regarding this as a monument of loyalty and love. The unexpected 'untruth' has the same effect as 'not untrue and not unkind' noted in 'Talking in Bed' – a less forceful word than 'lie' and yet a negative that penetrates and stains all associations of the word 'true'. 'Stone fidelity' in this context refers us back to the second line of the poem where the pun 'lie in stone' is now made explicit and dispossesses the monument of any further connection with fidelity. Finally, 'almost-instinct almost true' suggests both the desire to believe in love and the poet's refusal (as he sees it) to be taken in by sentimentality. Nevertheless the phrase implies that the joined hands may almost be a true statement because the mason's instinct for what would best represent his subject merges with the modern observer's example of a perennial human need to believe in love – a need the poet here acknowledges even while refusing to give his assent to it.

The sheer expressive power of this poem may also be observed in the lightness of touch with which Larkin handles the images of snow and light to suggest the passing of time in some of the most beautiful lines he has yet written:

> Snow fell, undated. Light
> Each summer thronged the glass. A bright
> Litter of birdcalls strewed the same
> Bone-riddled ground. And up the paths
> The endless altered people came,
>
> Washing at their identity.

The two themes this poem links are quintessential Larkin: that the passage of time may be used by man to destroy or deny the truth as he struggles to redefine his past; and that love, as one of man's supreme attempts to live an ideal, cannot support the expectations we have of it.

Possibilities of meaning

There are two groups of poems among Larkin's published work which strike a more positive note than many of the poems so far discussed. In the first there is a small number of poems that express a sense of fulfilment unusual to Larkin; and in the second group, a group that contains his most ambitious and successful poems, there are several which tentatively explore the possibility of positive meaning in life.

The short lyrical poems of the first group make frequent use of images drawn from nature to celebrate a sense of power and purpose, as in 'Wedding-Wind', 'Coming', 'For Sidney Bechet', 'Water' and 'Solar'.

'Wedding-Wind' is a very early poem (written in 1946) and is a dramatic monologue expressing the feelings of a new bride on waking the morning after her wedding night on the farm she is to share with her new husband. To her it seems as if the whole of nature echoes to the rush of happiness and energetic fulfilment that she now experiences. The success of this poem lies in the way the mood of the woman washes over the whole landscape and, in particular, invests the wind with a joyful force whose power to overcome all resistance even the woman can hardly dare to believe:

                    All is the wind
        Hunting through clouds and forests, thrashing
        My apron and the hanging clothes on the line.
        Can it be borne, this bodying-forth by wind
        Of joy my actions turn on, like a thread
        Carrying beads?

The immediacy of her happiness is felt in the movement, the
'thrashing' energy, but the simile of the wind carrying her happiness like a thread carrying beads hints at the frailty of the experience: a thread may easily snap. But, for once, the final image
implies a hope of sustaining the dream of happiness, although
even so the interrogative leaves a slender doubt:

        Can even death dry up
        These new delighted lakes, conclude
        Our kneeling as cattle by all-generous waters?

There is a spirit of humble gratitude borne along with the great joy
which is rare in this poetry.

   But perhaps it is the brief and beautiful lyricism of 'Coming'
that is the most delicate expression of Larkin's rare 'epiphanies'
(as John Bayley – employing a term used by James Joyce – has
called these poems which celebrate the poet's infrequent moments
of delight). It is brief enough to quote in full.

            On longer evenings,
            Light, chill and yellow,
            Bathes the serene
            Foreheads of houses.
            A thrush sings,
            Laurel-surrounded
            In the deep bare garden,
            Its fresh-peeled voice
            Astonishing the brickwork.
            It will be spring soon,
            It will be spring soon –
            And I, whose childhood
            Is a forgotten boredom,
            Feel like a child
            Who comes on a scene

Of adult reconciling,
And can understand nothing
But the unusual laughter,
And starts to be happy.

It is a perfect evocation of a mood in which every aspect of the
poem contributes to its articulation. The momentary gasp of
delight at the reaffirmation of spring, of the possibility of new
growth – the short intermission of positive meaning – is like a
sudden visitation of grace to the poet to allow him to enjoy the
scene and season without his fully understanding the reasons for
such an unexpected accession of delight. In the carefully selected
details of description, the translucency of the images and the
power of particular key words, the whole poem moves towards
the simple spontaneity of that last line. The poem is in two parts
which pivot on the repeated middle lines. In the first part the scene
is described in such a way as to present the mood and feelings of
the speaker. The second part, which is one sentence, catches up
that mood and sweeps it through the commentary explaining its
quality and importance in relation to that speaker. In the description of the lengthening evening and birdsong, the emphasis falls
on the light and sound refreshing the senses – the houses are
bathed in a cool serenity of light which suggests a washing clear of
winter and the old moods of care being surrendered to the naked,
open, raw new mood of joy suggested by 'fresh-peeled'. This sense
of newness and surprise is caught up in the middle lines, which are
repeated both to suggest the bird's reiterated call and the astonishment of the speaker who can hardly believe in his mood. These
lines are the pivot on which the whole harmony of the mood is
delicately poised and they effectively underline the importance of
the preceding 'astonishing' which collects to itself the whole
weight of the poem. A word which normally applies to a human
response is here transferred to the inanimate 'brickwork' which
has the effect of completely drenching the scene in the speaker's
feelings. Both the unexpectedness and the transitoriness of the
experience are expressed in the final image which likens the
speaker's mood to his childhood moments of brief and inexplic-
able encounters with adult happiness. The reference to his childhood as 'a forgotten boredom' reminds us of the reference to an

'unspent' childhood in 'I Remember, I Remember', and we are thus made more strongly aware of the unusual joy and meaning exhibited in this poem. That final image of 'adult reconciling' retrospectively throws a hesitancy over the earlier mood, however, which leaves an increased impression of the fleeting nature of this whole experience.

Listening to the jazz player in 'For Sidney Bechet', the speaker of the poem experiences another moment of affirmation and happiness in which the music is 'greeted as the natural noise of good / Scattering long-haired grief and scored pity'. But the choice of 'scattering' and 'scored' creates a submerged ambiguity in its suggestion that, although the music has the power to overcome grief and express pity, it nevertheless also expresses the suffering which is the source of blues music and is therefore *scattered* in the notes that are *scored* for the player (and the experience which is their source is also *scored* in the player's personality). It is as if the affirmative mood must not be allowed to escape the realities of life.

Only in 'Solar' does Larkin appear to express an unequivocally positive note. This poem is a brief hymn to the sun that is a 'suspended lion face / Spilling at the centre / Of an unfurnished sky'. This exuberant image with its almost physical force (a reading aloud draws attention to the alliterated sibilants which give a sense of the overflowing flood of energy and light) is typical of the complete poem. In its final part the lion-faced sun (an image born of the sun's appearance but also suggesting its fierce heat and its ruling over the whole of life) becomes a source of both delight and awe, two responses almost unique in Larkin's poetry.

The second group of poems, which could be said to represent a search for a more positive view of life, is composed of poems less wholeheartedly affirmative than these. The two most successful of this and any other group of Larkin's poems, 'Church Going' and 'The Whitsun Weddings', are rather tentative examinations of meaning and hope. Together with later poems like 'To The Sea', 'Show Saturday' and 'Livings' they represent Larkin's most balanced response to life.

'Church Going' begins with the concrete experience of the poet, which lends an air of personal conviction to the whole poem through its carefully chosen details of scene and behaviour:

Philip Larkin

Once I am sure there's nothing going on
I step inside, letting the door thud shut.
Another church: matting, seats, and stone,
And little books; sprawlings of flowers, cut
For Sunday, brownish now; some brass and stuff
Up at the holy end; the small neat organ;
And a tense, musty, unignorable silence,
Brewed God knows how long. Hatless, I take off
My cycle-clips in awkward reverence. . .

The changing tones and emotions of the remainder of the poem
are all subtly prefigured in this stanza. The initially detached and
unresponsive pose of the visitor is suggested in the careless lumping together of 'some brass and stuff / Up at the holy end'; the
almost abandoned condition of the church is called up in the
description of the neglected flowers and the musty smell; the
impossibility of not experiencing a sense of the unusual peace and
strange power of the place is revealed in the 'tense' and 'unignorable silence', and, finally, the visitor's change of mood (his waver-
ing detachment and move towards a hint of respect for commitment to what this building might stand for) is captured in the
action of removing his cycle-clips in 'awkward reverence'.

In the second stanza the apparently agnostic observer considers
the building at first merely as a piece of architecture, idly speculating as to whether the roof is cleaned or restored, then standing at
the lectern boyishly imitating a vicar's voice and finally leaving
after making a small, unconsidered donation. As he goes out he
reflects 'the place was not worth stopping for'. But stop he frequently does. Why?

The answer lies in the fact that the empty church is a subtle
prompt for him to consider the purpose of church and religion in
an agnostic age. The remaining two-thirds of the poem develops
into a meditation upon this idea and the change is marked by the
move from the first person singular to the second person plural.
This move from perception and individual observation to a
generalized contemplation of meaning is typical of many of Larkin's poems (as we have seen in 'Deceptions' and will see in 'The
Whitsun Weddings'). In this way personal experience is used to
give credence to the universalized meanings that follow.

31

These first two stanzas describe an actual visit made by the poet, his own church-going. In the remaining part of the poem it is the other side of the title's meaning that is explored – the implications of the church in decline and the underlying meaning of what the church has traditionally stood for and might be made to stand for in a secular future.

The third stanza begins these speculations, wondering whether churches will become merely museums, 'A few cathedrals chronically on show, / Their parchment, plate and pyx in locked cases', or will be left to moulder as ruins, 'let . . . rent-free to rain and sheep', or will become haunted places, avoided as unlucky or the secret centre of superstitious cults, or will be ravaged by 'Some ruin-bibber, randy for antique'. The poet assumes that religion is in decline and that we shall soon see the last church-goer to seek out the church for its original purpose. In the final two stanzas the ironic catalogue of possible future visitors is replaced by serious questioning. Will there always be some who, like the poet himself, cannot help but stop because although they are 'bored, uninformed' and know the old institutionalized religion is dead, nevertheless come

> . . . to this cross of ground
> Through suburb scrub because it held unspilt
> So long and equably what since is found
> Only in separation – marriage, and birth,
> And death, and thoughts of these – for which was built
> This special shell?

For modern agnostic man this church is an 'accoutred frowsty barn' whose worth he cannot judge. This unusual phrase serves to underline its own meaning in that it points by its own uncommonness to the oddity that the church has become. The preceding image of suburban scrubland and the suggestion of the church traditionally holding 'unspilt' the sense of the importance of those moments in our life which dedicate us to a greater goodness together imply the bare, desolate landscape of modern spiritual life and the metaphorical spilling of our precious lifeblood. Without the church, it seems, our lives lack a focus for our most serious concerns. By the last stanza a case has been asserted (not argued for), suggesting that, despite the desire of this rational age to debunk all religious impulses, human nature will continue to require some kind of focus for those most serious and deeply felt times in our life (such as birth, marriage and death). The language of the last lines soars to an elevated and solemn realm:

A serious house on serious earth it is,
In whose blent air all our compulsions meet,
Are recognised, and robed as destinies.
And that much never can be obsolete,
Since someone will forever be surprising
A hunger in himself to be more serious,
And gravitating with it to this ground,
Which, he once heard, was proper to grow wise in,
If only that so many dead lie round.

There is no longer any of the earlier tone of belittlement but instead (as the thrice-repeated 'serious' suggests) a calm, solemn and dignified conclusion. The language is almost stately (note 'robed as destinies', 'gravitating', 'proper to grow wise in') and the cadence and rhythm give a supporting solemnity, strength and seriousness. It is a remarkable development from the colloquial idiom and concrete particulars of the opening description and is effected without the slightest strain. This conclusion is an affirmation of the importance of the central events of our lives and the need for them to be celebrated by some centre for a community with its rituals and traditional memorials.

It is not a religious poem unless the word 'religion' is interpreted very broadly. It is a recognition that in the past the church has ministered to a perennial human need which cannot be brushed aside in a secular society. The narrator's role is to exemplify this in his own need and discovery of that 'hunger in himself to be more serious'. He is modern man who truly does not know the worth of this 'accoutred frowsty barn' but who is pulled towards it almost despite himself. The value of this poem is that it does two things at once, both of which summarize the basic dilemma of an age without faith: it reveals that age's desire to dismiss what it considers to be the spurious crutches of superstition and religion; and it reveals our continuing need to recognize and symbolize our deepest nature. It does not resolve the tensions between this scepticism and this desire to believe. The difference between them is caught in the contrasting language of the opening and closing stanzas, although the subtly achieved movements from the language of the one to that of the other through the voice of the same narrator might point to the possibility of some form of resolution.

'The Whitsun Weddings' may also be seen as a comment on this 'hunger to be serious' and is a poem that similarly moves from personal experience and observation, eventually to speak with the voice of a whole society. The subject of the poem is the narrator's observations of the several wedding parties that he sees boarding his train at the different stations on the way down to London one Whitsun Saturday. This situation is archetypal Larkin – several of his poems take place on journeys – because the passenger role allows the narrator to remain detached, uninvolved in the action, and yet to enter into the lines of those he carefully observes and to embrace them in a universalized meditation. His detachment does not mean he is unmoved; rather, it gives him the opportunity to 'see things as they are'.

The first two stanzas are a wholly successful evocation not only of a train journey but of a complete panorama of English rural and city landscapes. The Whitsuntide heat, the holiday mood, the sights and smells of a hot afternoon journey – even the reek of the hot carriage cushions – are caught in a series of snapshot details taken from the train window. The very movement of the train is caught as the scene flows from 'the backs of houses', 'a street / Of blinding windscreens' and the smell of the fish-dock in the city, through the 'level drifting breadth' of Lincolnshire farmland, to the 'canals with floatings of industrial froth'. The 'slow and stopping curve southwards' is perfectly realized in a description of scenes which capture the variety of English landscape, from the terraced housing, suburbs and industrial buildings of old cities, the featureless faces of new towns ('approached with acres of dismantled cars') with their own particularly English life ('An Odeon went past, a cooling tower, / And someone running up to bowl'), to the farms of rural England.

In the third stanza the observer's keen eye is caught by one especial scene: the wedding parties that he realizes are occurring on several station platforms and which are gathered to see off the newly married couples. The details to which his eye is drawn

embody the whole gamut of emotions these weddings create in the
guests:

> . . . grinning and pomaded, girls
> In parodies of fashion, heels and veils,
> All posed irresolutely, watching us go,
>
> As if out on the end of an event
>   Waving goodbye
> To something that survived it.

The attitudes and feelings of younger sisters and girlfriends of the
bride are deftly sketched in – their mixture of sharing the bride's
happiness and the re-aroused anticipations of their own mar-
riages – together with the innocent but clumsy attempts to look
fashionable and their unsureness on such a formal occasion.
Similarly, the fathers' hearty attempts to make things go with a
swing, the mothers' proudly shouted joys and the relations'
smutty jokes are captured in the fourth stanza. They give the scene
a solidity and reality. The poet watches with fascination but his
commentary on these ordinary family scenes is detached, distant.
Indeed, it verges on the patronizing with its stress on the vulgarity
of the occasion ('seamy foreheads', 'loud and fat', 'grinning and
pomaded', 'parodies of fashion', 'the perms, / The nylon gloves
and jewellery-substitutes'), and yet it is in fact an attempt 'to show
things as they really are and if they appear shoddy and second-rate
to say so', according to one critic.[13] To the fathers the success is
'huge and wholly farcical', to the mothers it is a secret shared 'like
a happy funeral' and to the unmarried girls it is like 'a religious
wounding'. The poet's eye may be detached but his understanding
of the feelings of the participants is clear. At one and the same time
he expresses the meaning of the occasion for its participants and
places his own interpretation upon the scene.

In the final lines his personal interpretation of events becomes
dominant. As the various newly married couples are blended into
a shared harmony in their brief journey, their common hopes of
fulfilment are blessed by the narrator's affirmation. His early tone
of detached amusement modulates into an earnest yet unsolemn
prayer for their future. As the train approaches London he thinks
of the city 'spread out in the sun, / Its postal districts packed like

squares of wheat' (the boundaries of the boroughs on a map look like cornfields seen from the air). 'This frail / Travelling coincidence' (which is all any of us ever have) is nearly over. The journey symbolizes the change that is taking place in the lives of the couples, and as the train finally decelerates it creates a sense of falling which suggests to the poet the image of an arrow-shower. It is an image suggesting the new lives of the couples shooting forth into London and falling upon a life of new hope and happiness like a shower of rain bringing forth new stalks of wheat:

> We slowed again
> And as the tightened brakes took hold, there swelled
> A sense of falling, like an arrow-shower
> Sent out of sight, somewhere becoming rain.

Larkin's instructions as to how this poem should be read aloud – a 'level, even a plodding, descriptive note, until the mysterious last lines, when the poem should suddenly "lift off the ground"'[14] – suggest the affirmative ending.

This poem may be read as dealing with English society as a whole through its panorama of scenes and the couples who suggest the recurring life of a whole community, together with the traditional journey image as a symbol for life itself. In this way it becomes almost a muted prayer for the continuously revitalizing power of change in society – a forward impetus and hope of fulfilment, even if such fulfilment still remains 'out of sight'. It is perhaps as positive a view as is possible for a poet who finds such difficulty in believing in the fruition of dreams and ideals.

'Church Going' refers to the need for some symbolic focus for life's most serious moments, and one of these moments with its attendant rituals is the subject of 'The Whitsun Weddings'. In some ways, it seems that Larkin can see all sorts of social rituals as bearers of a traditional sense of community and harmony. In *High Windows* several poems, like 'To the Sea' and 'Show Saturday', describe with loving care the communal rituals of such occasions as the annual seaside holiday and a rural agricultural show. They describe, in the same honest and unsentimental language of the description of the wedding parties in 'The Whitsun Weddings', the 'annual pleasure, half a rite' of family holidays and communal shows. The poet knows that such occasions cannot entirely overcome time's insidious attack upon individuals and societies but nevertheless they are to be welcomed and celebrated as

> something people do,
> Not noticing how time's rolling smithy-smoke
> Shadows much greater gestures; something they share
> That breaks ancestrally each year into
> Regenerate union. Let it always be there.

The unavoidable conclusion

In the end everyone must face the fate of time's embrace, the inevitable fact of old age and death. Throughout this poetry we have been made aware of that 'solving emptiness / That lies just under all we do' ('Ambulances'). It is a solving in two senses: it is death as the only certain solution to the riddle of the goal of life; and it is the awareness of the coming of death and man's 'costly aversion of the eyes from death' which *dissolves* any possibility of our dreams becoming the reality. Two poems from *High Windows* particularly express a middle-aged man's awareness of this inexorable decline towards oblivion.

'The Old Fools' is a desolating description of senile decay. It opens with a deliberately cruel portrayal of the breakdown in the behaviour of the old:

> Do they somehow suppose
> It's more grown-up when your mouth hangs open and drools,
> And you keep on pissing yourself, and can't remember
> Who called this morning?

The language is apparently callous, even flippant, but it in fact registers the poet's horror and astonishment. Disgust quickly merges with anger in this opening stanza, an anger directed not so much at these particular old people as at the common human condition that will lead us all eventually into such a state. By the end of the first stanza the poet asks, 'Why aren't they screaming?', to which the comfortless answer is that they do not realize what is happening to them. It is their ignorance of their own condition which most horrifies the poet. The gradual dissolution of identity and loss of self-awareness is acutely registered by a poet whose main concern has always been the sharpest kind of self-knowledge.

In the second stanza the poet realizes it is just this 'Not knowing how, not hearing who, the power / Of choosing gone' which signals the lack of control over their knowledge of themselves and their world and is the first unmistakable sign of that final state of complete unawareness: 'At death you break up: the bits that were you / Start speeding away from each other'. It is just this realization that the old are already in death's orbit which begins to bring the poet closer to them. From this point his horrified revulsion is increasingly tempered by a willingness to try to see what it must be like for the old. It is an attempt made all the more poignant because it is preceded by a brief lyrical image of life as 'a unique endeavour / To bring to bloom the million-petalled flower / Of being here'. The brevity of this image is itself all the more suggestive of life as a momentarily fragile flowering between oblivions. The question which ends the second stanza has a mixture of sadness and incredulity: 'How can they ignore it?'

The second half of the poem is a sustained attempt to understand their condition from the inside and is the beginning of the realization on the poet's part that he and they share a common destiny. This link is implied in the image of life as a shared landscape whose perspectives are seen very differently, depending upon the point reached in life's journey:

> . . . crouching below
> Extinction's alp, the old fools, never perceiving
> How near it is. This must be what helps keep them quiet:
> The peak that stays in view wherever we go
> For them is rising ground.

'The old fools', which was almost a term of abuse when first used, has by now become an expression of common compassion in its first declaration that we are all fooled by our lack of awareness of the approach of death. The poem culminates in a final single line, no longer a question expressing incredulity but a stark statement that draws attention to a shared fate. 'We' is used for the only time in the poem. It underlines the sudden horrified awareness that death is not to be avoided by anyone, not even with the power of self-awareness. The poem has moved as inexorably towards this chilling climax as life itself moves towards this final oblivion: 'We shall find out'.

'The Old Fools' is a devastating expression of the poet's feelings about the approach of age and death, its awfulness and strange otherness which will yet inevitably become the experience of us all. It enacts the middle-aged man's growing sense of time running out and his angry and bitter recognition that life can end in such a cruel and undignified way. The poet's proud determination not to be deceived here ends in a final awareness for which ignorance, in fact, could be the only palliative.

'The Building' reveals a more stoical acceptance of death. This poem sees the whole of life and death in terms of a busy hospital. All experiences flow together eventually in this place of life's beginning and end. The very form of the poem knits up all experience into a single strand by the way in which the carefully balanced seven-line stanzas rhyme across themselves (*abcbdcad*), overriding the stanzas' subjects, in eight-line verse paragraphs.

The realization that the opening description is of a hospital does not occur until the poem has been under way for several lines. At first the description would appear to be of any large public building where people are constantly moving in and out, waiting or looking for others – perhaps a hotel or airport lounge. Yet to the careful reader the selection of details not only gradually constructs a sense of the reality of the scene but also warns him of the true nature and function of the building: 'a *frightening* smell', people who '*tamely* sit' (having already resigned their lives to a control beyond themselves), 'the *ripped* magazines', the faces 'restless and resigned' (all italics mine). The variety of reactions of people faced with the seriousness of illness and death is already prefigured in these lines. There is an undercurrent of fear and confusion. All are 'caught / On ground curiously neutral' in which everyone has the same need of attention and all are equal in their suffering. The young, middle-aged and old are all represented here, and all arrive at the point at which all choice for them is ended and only 'the last of hope' remains. It is the point at which all illusions are finally stripped from people. They are not forced to be 'the less deceived' in this house of truth. They are all in hospital 'to confess that something has gone wrong'. This choice of 'confess' and the poem's insistence on the serious nature of the building's purpose and its connection with the truth of people's lives leads naturally to the hospital being regarded as performing some of the functions of a church in our secular age. We are reminded of the 'serious house on serious earth' of 'Church Going'. 'The Building' expresses the belief that our age has neglected to give social expression to our 'blent compulsions' except in the form of this clean, white, antiseptic building. 'The unseen congregations whose white rows / Lie set apart above' are a 'worship' to which we all respond because we recognize the truth of their condition. But the only cure we acknowledge today seems to be the bodily cure. The hospital is not equipped to cure souls, and yet this, the poem implies, may be as important in helping us cope with that 'coming dark'. Is this replacement of the church's role a final deception that man plays upon himself in a secular, rational age?

> This place accepts. All know they are going to die.
> Not yet, perhaps not here, but in the end,
> And somewhere like this. This is what it means,
> This clean-sliced cliff; a struggle to transcend
> The thought of dying, for unless its powers
> Outbuild cathedrals nothing contravenes
> The coming dark, though crowds each evening try
>
> With wasteful, weak, propitiatory flowers.

That last line captures all the doomed, but necessary attempts of man to appease his bleak knowledge of that final conclusion that none, not even the most self-aware poet, can evade.

'The Building' and 'The Old Fools' are chilly but honest poems which reflect the same strengths as most of Larkin's mature poems. They reveal a close observation of everyday life, they express a carefully controlled development of feeling and tone, they bear a clarity of language and immediacy of image, and, above all, they display the poet's determination not to flinch before the facts of man's frailty, failure and mortality.

Larkin's best poems are rooted in actual experiences and convey a sense of place and situation, people and events, which gives an authenticity to the thoughts that are then usually raised by the poet's observation of the scene. They frequently begin from situations we all may experience: travelling by train, watching crowds at the seaside or local show, observing mothers in a park or young people at a party, casually looking round an empty church, noticing the graffiti on a poster, speculating about the previous inhabitant of a rented room – all these give a solidity to the experiences of the poet and help the reader share in them because the mind of the poet is seen as rooted in an easily recognizable reality. The descriptions of people and events in, for example, 'Here', 'Show Saturday' and 'The Whitsun Weddings' capture a whole style of life in mid-twentieth-century British society.

Joined with this strength of careful social observation is a control over tone changes and the expression of developing feelings even within a single poem (for example, 'Church Going' or 'The Old Fools') which is a product of great craftsmanship. To these virtues must be added the fact that in all the poems there is a lucidity of language which invites understanding even when the ideas expressed are paradoxical or complex. Larkin commands a considerable breadth of idiom, a breadth that can span from the slangy to the stately within the space of a single poem. Similarly, the diction can partake of the crudely vernacular, the simple, plain speech of conversation, or the formally heightened vocabulary redolent of a more dignified age (as in the final lines of 'Church Going').

Despite the relative narrowness of his themes, Larkin writes with a wide range of tone and feeling. It is sometimes overlooked that the poet of 'Coming' or 'Solar' is also the poet of 'The Old Fools'. Although one's final impression of the poetry is certainly that the chief emphasis is placed on a life 'unspent' in the shadow of 'untruth', moments of beauty and affirmation are not entirely denied. It is the difficulty of experiencing such moments after one has become so aware of the numerous self-deceptions that man practices on himself to avoid the uncomfortable reality which lies at the heart of Larkin's poetic identity.

It is this consistent identity, recurring throughout the poems, that seems to divide critics in their final estimation of the poetry. All critics must acknowledge the subtle craftsmanship of the poetry, but those who consider Larkin's identity to be too negative come eventually to regard the poetry as suffering from limitations. They regard the identity as being too narrowly conceived and not capable of bearing the weight of universality which Larkin wishes to place upon it. There are other critics, however, who regard this identity as expressing the true spirit of mid-twentieth-century Britain.

This identity is most typically expressed as a middle-aged bachelor figure who believes we have little control over our fate and who sees us as duped by all manner of self-deceptions and wishful thinking. He seems to believe that the only honest response to life is to deny ourselves any dreams of fulfilment, and his resistance to being 'conned' by life leads him particularly to deny any possibility of lasting love. To him the role of a detached, if lonely, outsider is preferable to a false commitment in love or marriage. Honesty and awareness are his cardinal virtues. But he is no rebel: part of his recognition of man's illusions is that he sees acts of rebellion as empty romantic gestures, preferring to accept what he regards as the reality of everyday life. It is thus the identity of a disappointed man aware of life's defeats rather than the tragic identity of a man whose ideals have driven him to attempt to scale the peaks. This has divided readers and critics in their reactions to the poetry. To some such an identity speaks with the voice of experience and honesty, a voice to be valued above any frail dreams of possible fulfilment. But to others such honesty is a limited virtue which dulls the appetite for life and experience and which reneges on man's capacity to dream of ideals, to aspire to a life of larger ambitions.

Larkin himself feels uneasy under the criticism that he writes of only his own 'tenderly nursed sense of defeat', as Charles Tomlinson has called it:

> One thing I do feel a slight restiveness about is being typed as someone who has carved out for himself a uniquely dreary life, growing older, having to work, and not getting things he wants and so on — is this so different from everyone else?[15]

To this the answer must be 'perhaps not', and yet for many people this cannot be a balanced picture of life. The assumption of Larkin's poetry is that anyone who does not see reality under this light must be deluding himself. There are some critics (for example, Calvin Bedient) who see Larkin's poetic identity as the spirit of our age, a spirit of scepticism and disillusionment combined with the belief that the only ideal is to have no ideals to lose. But this is to make assumptions about our own age that may, in time, prove to have overlooked something. Larkin's poetry is a poetry of disappointment, of the destruction of romantic illusions, of man's defeat by time and his own inadequacies. It could be seen as the poetry of the impotent self, unable or unwilling to risk being wrong. Yet it is a consummately crafted verse and to be valued for its skill in creating a sense of our world that we all may recognize and for its honest adherence to one man's testing of experience. The reader may be grateful for this attempt to record things as they seem to the poet, and he may acknowledge that this is the way many of us at some time view our lives. But he might yet insist that this picture of a shrunken reality – what Bedient calls 'the withering of the ideal, of romance, of possibility'[16] – is not the total experience either of his own life or the life of our age. The great popularity of Larkin's poetry no doubt signals a delight in his craftsmanship, but it may also say as much about our age as about the poet's achievement.

We can agree with Timms[17] that part of Larkin's achievement is his refusal to compromise either the reality he personally perceives or the audience with whom he so earnestly desires to communicate. Yet it is open to the reader to feel that even such a considerable achievement as this unique body of verse none the less exemplifies the self-imprisoned limitations of an age that finds it impossible both to face reality and to retain its dreams.

2

Seeing and believing

The poetry of Charles Tomlinson

An independent

In April 1957 Charles Tomlinson published a vigorous attack on
the attitudes of The Movement poets whose work was popular at
that time and whose anthology, *New Lines*, he was reviewing.[1] It
is clear that this review gave Tomlinson an opportunity to define
his own conception of the poet's task. He did so by commenting
on what he considered were the most serious shortcomings of The
Movement poets. He believed these poets failed largely because
they did not 'see things anew', they lacked a sensuous apprehension and response to the universe around them, and they refused
to seek a 'a vital awareness of the continuum outside themselves,
of the mystery bodied over against them in the created universe.'
Tomlinson's own poetry has always been concerned to 'see things
anew' and to speak of the natural world, the world of man's
creation and the relationship between the two.

Tomlinson also disliked The Movement poets' apparent rejection of influences from Europe and the United States. He has
himself always been interested in modern movements in poetry
and painting on both these continents. He has recorded that he
knew French poetry earlier than he knew English,[2] and he has
always been an active translator of poetry from various European
countries. In an article published exactly twenty years after the
New Lines review, he wrote of his early interest in the poetry of
Americans such as Ezra Pound, Wallace Stevens, William Carlos
Williams and Marianne Moore.[3] What he appears to have
absorbed from the last two poets, in particular, is a certain kind of
stance towards his subjects and a freedom of rhythm (especially in

his adaptation of the Williams's triple line) rather than the adoption of their themes or tones of voice. This stance is one of keen and accurate observation, a detailed concentration on the subject that comes from a quiet, undominating perception of scenes, objects, places and people. In many of the poems of Williams and Moore (for example, 'The Term', Williams; 'A Jellyfish', Moore) we find a similar concern with the way places and objects *look* and with the way a careful act of observation reveals details of 'the fineness of relationships', as Tomlinson has put it.

The accurate presentation of a world outside the poet, whether of nature, place or people, demands a disciplining of the poet's ego so that he may record what is seen without drowning that world in his own feelings. Tomlinson has written:

> A poet's sense of objectivity . . . of that which is beyond himself, and his capacity to realize that objectivity within the artefact is the gauge of his artistry and the first prerequisite of all artistic genius.[4]

He does not deny the presence of deep feelings in poetry; he requires, after all, a *sensuous* apprehension of the subject. But the senses must be stimulated by an accurate perception of the object rather than by the mood of the poet. There is a sense in which it is correct to say that Tomlinson demands a quality of humility towards the poem's subject. This concentration on the subject and the search for a way of conveying its exact forms is partly a consequence of the fact that Tomlinson is also an accomplished painter, and his way of looking at the world around him reveals a painter's eye for shape, form and movement.

Tomlinson has so far published eight major collections of poetry since his early pamphlet *Relations and Contraries* (1951). In 1960 *Seeing is Believing* appeared in this country after first being published in America (where he found an appreciative audience long before becoming well known in this country), and it was followed by *A Peopled Landscape* (1963), *American Scenes* (1966), *The Way of a World* (1969), *Written on Water* (1972), *The Way In* (1974) and *The Shaft* (1978). Each volume has its share of interesting poems, and the overall output is a masterly achievement. Although new subjects and styles have been added during the years (for example, the addition of humorous social observation in *American Scenes* and *The Way In*), there has been an underlying continuity of theme and a gradual deepening of response to life rather than sudden spectacular jumps in totally new directions. The poems in *The Shaft* have similar concerns to those in the first two books. He returns again and again to his original belief in the importance of looking at our world, a perception so intense that it could see into the meaning of relationships. Such a meaning is to be discovered by watching the processes of change in an object or landscape as it undergoes the effects of altering light or the movement of clouds. The consequent awareness of change in a landscape led Tomlinson to be interested in place and in people's relationship with place. This, in turn, has entailed an increasing preoccupation with continuities and breakdowns of relationship between people and place and therefore an interest in history, moments of change and attitudes to time. In this chapter a number of Tomlinson's poems are examined in order to trace some of the characteristics of his act of perceiving nature, people and place and his struggle to express the relationship between people and their continuities with time and place.

A painter's eye

One of Tomlinson's most enduring concerns has been a search for precise means of expressing the act of perception itself. The details of the most delicately shifting shapes, colours, lights and textures of a scene or object, and the problem of re-creating these in words, is a continuous subject in his poems. In 'Distinctions' the problem of transmuting the act of looking into a work of art is made the subject of the poem. It asks if art can ever have the power to capture an actual moment of perceiving those fine gradations of colour, for instance, when we are looking at a seascape:

> The seascape shifts
>
> Between the minutest interstices of time
> Blue is blue.
>
> A pine-branch
> Tugs at the eye: the eye
> Returns to grey-blue, blue-black or indigo

> Or it returns, simply,
> To blue-after-the-pine-branch.

The poet struggles to render the exact changes of colour, but the difficulty of ever expressing them in words is indicated in the final clumsy compound of 'blue-after-the-pine-branch', a variation in hue that the eye may register but the vocabulary cannot. 'Art exists at a remove', as the poet notes. Yet Tomlinson is not concerned to render a scene by evoking the emotions it arouses in him so much as to let it speak for itself by finding in language the exact nature of the act of perception itself.

In 'Ponte Veneziano', for example, the poet's interest centres not on a description of the people (who remain only 'figures') but on the composition created by their presence, the line of their glance and the point of stillness they create in the centre of the scene with the bridge, the gondolier and the water. The light and shade, shape and stillness, are the true subject of this poem:

> A prow pinpoints them:
> They stare beyond it. The canopy
> Which shades a boat
> Flares from the line through which they gaze
> Orange against coolness.

The alliterated 'p' brings the figures and the boat's prow into conjunction, emphasizing the way the eye is caught by both at once; then the lines follow the line of vision of the figures (registering the fact of the canopy but hardly noting the purpose it serves as a shade-giver – that is the poet's explanatory aside and this is why it is dropped into a line of its own) and bring alive the colour of the canopy through the bright contrast it makes against the cool water. It is what the figures *see* that is crucial. This is made explicit in the later lines:

> Undistracted, their glance channels itself
> Ignoring the whiteness of a bridge
> To cross beneath, where,
> Closed by the vault,
> It broods on further light.

'Flares', 'channels', 'broods' create an active sense of the glance of the figures; their *looking* actually becomes ours as we read. The shock of contrasting light and shade, the mixture of warmth and cold sensed in the synaesthesia of 'orange against coolness' and their meditative dwelling upon the light under the bridge (suggested by 'broods') combine to make the reader experience the act of looking itself. Despite the fact that the poem's words re-create an experience in the reader which has already moved through the figures and been created anew in the poet's experience (that is, it is two removes from the original experience), it succeeds because Tomlinson describes the scene not by interposing his own feelings but by trying to grasp the meaning of the relationship between the constituent elements of the scene, particularly shapes and light, in the way that the figures originally tried to see it.

'Northern Spring' describes a landscape as the spring sun brings new life back to a cold land. The unique quality of the description arises from the manner in which light and shape are actually made active, as if the process of seasonal change were alive and moving before our very eyes.

> The sky flushes its blue, dyeing the grass
> In the promise of a more stable tone:
> Less swift however than the cloud is wide –
> Its shadow (already) quenching the verdure
> As its bulk muffles the sun – the blue drains
> And the assault renews in colourless ripples.

The diction expresses life and movement, constant change. It is a process that is enacted. This is why the lines can sustain an apparently archaic and sumptuous word like 'verdure' without becoming precious. The luscious colours of the grass under the new sun are caught in that word, as is the spreading richness of the new spring. The images move forward on a rhythm that flows and yet can check itself at a parenthesis without losing momentum. The perception of the scene gathered into these brief lines amounts to a momentary insight into the very process of nature. It is made possible only through the poet's intense concentration on the elements of the scene and the retreat of his personal emotions other than those directly created by the act of perception. 'The eye tactually commends' (a phrase from 'Chateau de Muzot') in a poem like this. That is, the poet is spectator more than participant

in the scene, and by trusting to his sensuous apprehension of the
subject he can give it body and life.

Tomlinson examines the relationship between this act of perception and the ability of the artist to re-create it in images in 'A
Meditation on John Constable'. The poem begins in clear,
unlaboured lines praising the painter for his realism and precision
of form in his handling of land and cloudscapes. 'The unman-
nered exactness of art' in his paintings is made possible through
his 'labour of observation'. The ease with which the final paintings create their subject is contrasted here with the prolonged
discipline and hard concentration ('labour') that went into the act
of looking which preceded the painting. The poem moves on in
lines 4–19 to re-create in words a sense of the liveliness and
movement of the paintings themselves. The lines are almost a
verbal replica of Constable's style of painting:

> Clouds
> Followed by others, temper the sun in passing
>   Over and off it. Massed darks
> Blotting it back, scattered and mellowed shafts
>   Break damply out of them, until the source
> Unmasks, floods its retreating bank
>   With raw fire. One perceives (though scarcely)
> The remnant clouds trailing across it
>   In rags, and thinned to a gauze.
> But the next will dam it. They loom past
>   And narrow its blaze. It shrinks to a crescent
> Crushed out, a still lengthening ooze
>   As the mass thickens, though cannot exclude
> Its silvered-yellow. The eclipse is sudden,
>   Seen first on the darkening grass, then complete
> In a covered sky.

This brilliantly re-creates both the original landscape and the very
texture of the paint on the canvas, particularly in the last five lines
where 'crushed out', 'ooze' and 'thickens' convey both the laying
on of paint and the sun's rays.

The second half of the poem is a reflection on the nature of
image-making in paint or words and its relationship to the facts of
a natural scene. It suggests that the power of a painter like

Constable lies in his capacity both to capture the nature of the subject, as it appears to be ('the plenitude of facts', as Tomlinson calls it elsewhere), and to comprehend the shape of the 'accidents' or chance surprises of feeling that the subject creates through the artist's sensuous awareness of it.

> Facts. And what are they?
> He admired accidents, because governed by laws,
>   Representing them (since the illusion was not his end)
> As governed by feeling. The end is our approval
>   Freely accorded, the illusion persuading us
> That it exists as a human image.

The paradox of true art is that it creates an illusion of the world which persuades us of the nature of reality. The artist represents reality by confining it in an artificial stasis (of paint or words), which allows him to create a detailed definition of the relationship of the elements of his subject by expressing as faithfully as possible the 'reality' he *feels* as he looks upon his subject. As he seeks to tell the truth about the reality he perceives, his creation of an illusion (art can never *be* that reality) will be honest to the subject and to his feelings in relation to the subject. Thus 'Art / Is complete when it is human' because the artist can be honest only when he expresses those 'accidents' of relationships which are 'governed by feeling' in that they are revealed by the artist's sensuous apprehension. Paradoxically, the artist's personality is kept from dominating his painting by his close attention to those 'accidents', the feelings that respond to the subject he paints, and keeping other feelings from an outside source under control. Constable may be called 'a descriptive painter' because he does not force his personality into the painting; yet his art convinces because his feelings for his subject are expressed in the exact form with which he chooses to represent his subject. The painting, then, is 'the index of a possible passion, / As the adequate gauge, both of the passion / And its object.'

By disciplining himself in attention to his subject, Constable (or any artist) defines his own being, 'for what he saw / Discovered what he was'. To know himself, the artist lets the world outside him govern his feelings through his close attention to the facts of the scene before him.

The poem ends on a definition whose meaning has been proved in the description of the paintings and the reflections on the painter's art:

> The artist lies
> For the improvement of truth. Believe him.

Art as an act of representation is an illusion – it cannot imitate reality – yet it creates a truth, a truth that speaks of the relationships perceived by an honest, unegoistic way of looking at the world. The truth emerges from the artist's capacity to see and our willingness to see through him (in both senses: to be made to see with his unique vision, but also to know the nature of his illusion). In this sense seeing is believing. The artist believes what he sees and we see when we believe him.

This poem partakes of the quintessence of Tomlinson's art in both its meaning and its form. It moves through a beautiful re-creation of its subject that not only gives a sense of 'the looped pigments' of the paint but actually creates the way that paint has been worked by the painter himself. This may be seen in Tomlinson's allusion to the very moment and texture of the paint as he describes the picture's display of light across cloud shadows:

> . . . a light, that strides down
> Over the quick stains of cloud-shadows
> Expunged now, by its conflagration of colour.

'Quick stains' and 'expunged' reflect the act of applying the paint as well as themselves mirroring the effect of the light. This poem has great beauty and strength, a complete interfusion of form and meaning.

The importance of the artist's self-discipline in his act of perception, his close observation of his subject, can be clearly seen in two particular poems, 'Object in a Setting' and 'Paring the Apple'. Both poems have very simple subjects which are treated without recourse to the presence of a human subject as the central focus of meaning. They are both made possible only by the poet's exact observation of apparently trivial objects.

'Object in a Setting' is a short poem which creates a sense of translucent light that is the image of the object being described. The poem springs from a combination of a winter's day of cold, sharp light and contrasting shadows and the poet happening to pick up and idly examine a piece of glass crystal. What exactly the crystal object is we are never told. The point of the poem lies not in the labelling of the crystal but in the apprehension of that glass in relation to its setting. The personality of the poet does not intrude, yet the feelings he experiences as he looks at the glass reflecting the light of the day *is* the real subject of the poem. The crystal, as perceived by the poet, transforms the outside scene into a clear, cool image of light, 'the marble city without trees'. The glass is 'Astral, clear: / To wish it a more human image / Is to mistake its purpose'. Tomlinson warns us not to intrude our purposes upon the object but simply to look and to see it in relation to its setting. In that setting it concentrates the whole winter's day into a single image of refracted music:

> The days turn to one their hard surfaces
> Over which a glacial music
> Pauses, renews, expands.

This music of the crystal image is also the music of the poem. It is a quiet, reticent poem, itself composed of hard surfaces and a glassy light. It is almost imagist in its reliance upon the conjunction of two different ideas (winter and the crystal) to be articulated in one description. The proper approach to this object is to relate it to its background; in so concentrating on this rather than ourselves, we may perceive a beauty, a delight and a meaning that would be denied were we to colour it with our concerns.

Similarly, in 'Paring the Apple' Tomlinson attends to the simple act of peeling an apple rather than to himself. In doing so he is making a comment on the difference between portrait and still-life paintings. The poem denies the usual assumption that portraits are inherently more interesting because of their human content. The poet insists that in a still-life there is a proper attention to objects, to the 'thingyness' of the world, which can give a knowledge and experience of the 'plenitude of facts'. In making this point the poem itself becomes a still-life, a description that freezes an action in order to draw forth its meaning, not by stressing it as a human act (this is why the choice of action described is relatively trivial) but by expressing the relationship of the movement, shape and colour of the apple:

Neither is less weighted
With a human gesture, than paring the apple
With a human stillness.

The cool blade
Severs between coolness, apple-rind
Compelling a recognition.

The human gesture is not more meaningful than the human stillness before an object. What gives meaning is the quality of attention to the object.

But this attention should not be construed as just being confined to the object. As his remarks on Constable have shown, Tomlinson sees the truth as a conjunction of careful attention to the object and the observer's expression of the feelings set in motion by what he sees, not his bringing of his prior emotions to cover the object. In the prose-poem 'Processes' he emphasizes the need to attend to process, to the minutest moments of change which will both prevent the object disappearing behind a cloud of the observer's emotions and stop the observer being overwhelmed by a static and untrue picture of reality:

One accords the process its reality, one does not deify it; inserted among it, one distinguishes and even transfigures, so that the quality of vision is never a prisoner of the thing seen.

The artist is more than a recording camera. The perceptive eye is also the creative eye. The poet projects upon the object his interpretative vision, but that interpretation must result from looking close and hard at the object, not just from the poet's inner world. The mind orders, clarifies and appropriates images to delight itself with re-creation, not just reflection.

This might be seen briefly in a poem about shadows on a thinly iced stream under a winter sun. It is called 'Reflections'.

Like liquid shadows. The ice is thin
    Whose mirror smears them as it intercepts
Withdrawing colours; and where the crust,
    As if a skin livid with tautening scars,
Whitens, cracks, it steals from these deformations
    A style too tenuous for the image.

53

The use of this image – suggesting that the shadows are being broken across by the cracks in the ice and that the cracks are like scars – reveals how the initial perception of the scene has been transfigured into a shaping vision by the observer's imagination. His vision is not just a mirror held up to nature; it is a new perception, but one anchored by its fidelity to the object. This poem goes on to reflect upon the way the human observer can direct his perception, 'free both to question this deployment / And to arrange it'. In making this point the poem itself enacts its own meaning.

Tomlinson regards the act of perception as an unravelling of the relationships between the elements of the scene, the perceiver and the object. His search for exact forms in which to express this relationship is carried out in terms of disciplined attention to the object which neither denies human feelings nor drowns the object in a flood of such feelings.

People and place

In Tomlinson's poetry the way of looking is a way of thinking about the world; there is a continuous interchange between seeing and believing. In those poems where the main concern is apparently to create an accurate image of a landscape or an object, a way of thinking about that landscape or object is inherent in the act of perception. The limits, beginnings and ends of what is perceived are ordered by the observer's mind as it gives a shape to the flux of movement, shape, light and colour. But this bringing of meaning out of a process of continual change is itself 'placed' by nature: 'as in a landscape, / All that is human . . . stands clarified / By all that accompanies and bounds' ('At Delft'). Nature, landscape and place are the boundaries of perception, and it is only in true relationship with these that a man may understand himself and his world. This understanding is explored by Tomlinson in terms of people and place. In the poems on this theme the importance of a non-egotistical relationship to nature is extended to become a comment on the way those people who are truly at home in their place in the world (in geographical, historical and spiritual terms) bring an unselfish appreciation to the natural world and the continuities of place.

Charles Tomlinson

'Winter Encounters' is very much concerned with this sense of
an appropriate relationship between a village and the valley in
which it nestles, between the community and its natural setting
and the sources of harmony in that community. This theme of
balance emerges not only from the meaning of the words but from
the very form and structure of the verse. It is constructed as a
sequence of linked lines whose two halves are frequently joined by
alliteration and balance on the silent pivot of a pause in the middle
of many lines. This can be seen most clearly at the beginning and
end of the poem:

> House and hollow; village and valley-side:
> The ceaseless pairings, the interchange
> In which the properties are constant . . .
>
> *   *
>
> . . . One feels behind
> Into the intensity that bodies through them
> Calmness within the wind, the warmth in cold.

The carefully balanced phrases suggest the connection between
nature and the human community (stressed in the choice of 'interchange', 'intersect', 'ties', 'exchange', 'met', etc., which occur
throughout the poem) and they create the verbal equivalent of a
scene where 'all moves / Towards encounter'. The way the community is part of its natural surroundings is suggested in the
description of one of the houses and the way it and its inhabitants
are 'meshed into neighbourhood' by their 'ties' with their surroundings:

> Lengthened shadows
> Intersecting, the fields seem parcelled smaller
> As if by hedgerow within hedgerow. Meshed
> Into neighbourhood by such shifting ties,
> The house reposes, squarely upon its acre
> Yet with softened angles, the responsive stone
> Changeful beneath the changing light. . . .

Here perception and belief are united. What the poet sees may be
just the scene, but his choice of words describes a relationship he
believes to exist between the village and the valley. The shadows

blur the outline of the fields, making them appear smaller and closer together, and the lattice of shadows thus formed ties house and hollow together to complete a natural encounter, one of 'the ceaseless pairings'. The 'meshed' metaphor works on two levels: it describes the network of light and shade which rounds the shape of the house, softens its sharp angles and merges it with the shadows on the fields; and it also suggests the interaction between man and nature.

This exchange between nature and man extends its harmonious affect to the lives of the villagers in the second half of the poem. These villagers have minds that 'lean at ease' in their talk of 'customary subjects', talk related to the life of the surrounding countryside. The continuities of village life are so deeply felt by the inhabitants that they have a sense of life at a level deeper than the gossip they exchange. Their right relationship with the continuities of place and time raises the ordinary day-to-day social intercourse to a more meaningful plane: 'one meets with more / Than the words can witness'. It is an unbroken continuity of life between nature and man which creates a warmth of community that can overcome the winter's cold. This poem is a celebration of the customary and the habitual in the lives of those who remain close to a sense of place; it is a meditation upon the possibility of encounter and exchange between members of a community whose harmony is a consequence of their right relationship with the non-human world.

A poem in a different tone but sharing a similar theme is 'On the Hall at Stowey'. This longer contemplative poem describes with beautiful clarity, through its slow, measured accumulation of detail, the house and farm the poet came across when he 'chose unwonted ground' when out for a walk. The ground is 'unwonted' because man has destroyed the kind of connection with the place that 'Winter Encounters' celebrates by abandoning this hall and allowing it to fall into decay. As the poet looks at it in its fallen grandeur he can still perceive the way 'the grange / That jutted beyond' the house must have tied itself to the fruitful earth and thus become part of the very landscape.

As in so many of these poems about places, Tomlinson creates a strong sense of the house, its history and its connection with the surrounding countryside. Even now, although the building is wrecked, it remains the bearer of a rich harvest. Where once the traditions of a whole way of life were garnered in the grange there is now only a harvest of overgrown weeds, and yet the description of their profusion, especially the accumulations of ivy, holds the house still as a symbol of the fruitfulness of man, place and nature.

> Out of the reddish dark still thrust up foison
> Through the browning-back of the exhausted year

These lines conjure up a rich harvest to keep life going through the year's exhaustion, even while reminding us of the hall's abandonment as a sign of man's neglect of his traditional and rightful relationship with nature.

On entering the house the poet is angered to discover that the last owner has gutted the inside, obliterating the traditional design of the house in a tasteless attempt to impose on it the ephemeral fashion of some contemporary interior decoration. Anger is not a common emotion in Tomlinson's work, but here it wells up as a denunciation of modern society's destruction of its continuities with the past – continuities that linked man with his natural environment: 'What we had not / Made ugly, we had laid waste'. He leaves the hall, unconsoled by the way in which nature may be seen rapidly reclaiming what man has neglected.

This poem implies the need for man to recognize, even in the structures he builds, the nature of what is outside himself. Stone 'cut, piled, mortared' can become 'patience's presence' and represents man's harmony with the non-human universe.

We can begin to see what Tomlinson meant when he attacked The Movement poets for not having any sense of 'the mystery bodied over against them in the created universe' and for not having any 'awareness of the continuum outside themselves'. The continuum between man and nature is that interchange he speaks of in 'Winter Encounters' and which he sees as being the tradition of a previous generation that built and lived in the hall at Stowey.

This right relationship between people and place is also explored in 'Return to Hinton' in which Tomlinson describes the contrast between a traditional village family life and the life of modern urban society – a contrast that overwhelms him when he returns to Hinton after travelling in America. The family in Hinton are described as having deep ties with the land that they farm.

The family has suffered a death since he last was with them, and it is their stoical acceptance of the loss and their continuation of their lives, made possible through the life-sustaining strength of their traditions, that the poet celebrates. The family's qualities

> are like the land
>   — inherited:
> but you
>   have earned
>   your right to them
>   have given
>   grief its due
>   and, on despair,
>   have closed your door
>   as the gravestones tell you to.

'You' is not only the family but all those who share their inheritance. Their qualities are inherited not only because they have been handed down through the family but also because they form part of a traditional relationship between a people and their land. This relationship is symbolized by the farmer's widow amid her 'tokens of an order' in the everyday activities in her kitchen. The old-fashioned kitchenware sits side by side with the new television set and both are contained harmoniously within a family life that is 'ballasted against the merely new, the tide / and shift of time'. While the son carries on the farm, the widow lives at the centre of a stable relationship with the land which gives her strength to cope with the vicissitudes of her life. She can mourn her loss (she does not try to outflank it by going on as if it had not happened), confident in the traditional rituals' power to assimilate it to life in such a way as to allow that life to move onward, saddened but not in despair. The bearer of such traditions cannot see time and death as enemies. The poet, himself outside such traditions, sees those who live in them as safer from death and the 'shift of time' than he or anyone who lives as part of a modern urban society. Yet, despite this, they are vulnerable to a 'surer death'. Their very traditions are threatened by 'progress', the lifeblood of modern man. This progress is represented in the poem by the American way of life, which the poet has just experienced, in that 'rich and nervous land' with its 'soft oppression of prosperity'. The sense of place, the rooted relationship to a locality and its traditions, must eventually fall victim to the spread of this modern prosperity. Such ties between a family and its land are 'mere grist / to build / the even bed / of roads.' These roads will lead to a common future which even the poet must admit is rational and secure but which will, nevertheless, be built only through the irrational destruction of such continuities with the land and the past from which this family draws its security. Tomlinson rejects such a future in favour of those 'farm-bred certainties' which – although narrow, as he admits, and from which he is already cut off himself – are nevertheless the right relationship for man to make with his environment. To the poet it seems that the only way to share that family's qualities is through his art, whose 'language is our land' which will not be squandered or sold out 'against a promised mess / of pottage that we may not taste'. The language of the poem is the poet's (and his readers') covenant with those traditions the family represents.

Tomlinson is aware that these traditions may be threatened in other ways too. In 'The Farmer's Wife' they are seen to be precarious because fewer and fewer people are still willing to carry them on. In this poem a woman proudly shows the poet round her old farm and its cider orchard. These are 'inheritances / to an eye / as pleased as yours'. Tomlinson dismisses any attempt to use them as cheap symbols, insisting that 'fact / has its proper plenitude' which the care and safe handling of generations has ensured. Those generations have not sentimentalized their existence; they have treated their world as fact, with a proper regard for its elements and a refusal to ignore its qualities by simply imposing on it their own will regardless of the needs of the orchard, its fruit and the seasons.

> A just geography
> completes itself
> with such relations, where
> beauty and stability can be
> each other's equal.

This 'just geography' is made possible by the same kind of self-discipline in the face of the land as that argued for in the poems on the act of looking. But in this poem the poet is acutely aware of the fact that the wife has no child to inherit the land, and at the poem's conclusion he is troubled by the thought that the 'rock of . . . ancestral certitude' will be smashed.

In his later poems, particularly in *The Way In* which includes several poems about his childhood landscape of Stoke-on-Trent, Tomlinson writes increasingly of the destruction of such continuities. In the poems he calls 'manscapes' he describes the breakdown of such continuities in the landscape that accompanied his own growing up or in the city in which he now works. He stresses man's vulnerability to change once he disturbs his sense of place.

'The Way In' is about the 'dismantling of a neighbourhood' through with the poet regularly drives:

> The needle-point's swaying reminder
>   Teeters at thirty, and the flexed foot
> Keeps it there. Kerb-side signs
>   For demolitions and new detours,
> A propped up pub, a corner lopped, all
>   Bridle the pressures that guide the needle.

Any control over this destruction is as precariously balanced as the foot on the pedal (as 'swaying', 'teeters', 'flexed' suggest). He is driving through what has become a common enough sight in modern cities: the chaos of the face of change and something the planners label 'progress'.

What is being destroyed is not merely buildings but a whole way of life. To the poet the old face of the city may have been 'a little worn' but it was 'homely' and its aged features could nevertheless express a 'grace' and style, a civility that the new landscape of 'mannerless high risers' cannot. The new buildings are rising behind the heat from the demolition fires which burn 'a century's lath and rafters'. Behind the flames the flats appear to 'tilt and wobble': they do not rise on the solid foundations of a traditional sense of place. The poet speculates whether their occupants will see the place differently from him – will they 'eye it all differently, the city spread / In unforeseen configurations, and living with this, / Will find that civility I can only miss'?

'Civility' is a key concept in Tomlinson's poetry. In the early poem 'Antecedents' he used it to express his rejection of the self-enclosed, egotistical world of the symbolist poets. In that poem 'a civil country' was one which was 'natural and profuse', a country where the individual seeks relationship with others and has a humility before the facts of nature and the environment he inhabits: it is 'neighboured, having earned relation / with all that is other'. In 'Return to Hinton' and 'The Farmer's Wife' the people had learnt to live in a giving of themselves to their land and to that nature outside themselves. It is the same unegotistic attitude as the attitude of Constable to his painting's subject. As Michael Kirkham has written, 'Civility is to live willingly within the boundaries of the possible and from a human–social centre, but not timidly.'⁵ In 'Las Trampas: USA', as Kirkham points out, the poet celebrates the ceremony in the behaviour of Mexican villagers who directed him to a church – a slight but significant sign of a civil relationship that embodies both a respect for others and a just relationship with the place they inhabit. Tomlinson himself has talked about his style as an attempt to make 'a civil language',⁶ a language bred from acknowledging the resistance of its subject-matter and not just 'playing with words as if they were plasticine'. All this stems from the desire for genuine relationships which requires a submission of the self's concerns to the realities of others and the 'plenitude of facts' beyond oneself (what he calls 'a shriven self' in 'Antecedents):

> And part of this undertaking . . . lies in a distrust of fixities of the self – its determination to have things on its own terms. If one can elude such demands, as one can in any genuine relationship, for example; if one can respond to the given and avoid merely secreting one's precious essence over everything one encounters, there occurs the chance of deepenings and renewals.⁷

The chances of such deepenings Tomlinson sees as destroyed when modern man brings down the old styles of living as represented by the hall at Stowey, the lives of the rural families at Hinton and even in the old Bristol and Stoke landscapes. In 'The Way In' the planners believe they will encourage a civility of living by their carefully designed landscaping and talk of 'community', but 'It will need more than talk and trees / To coax a style from these disparities'.

In 'The Way In' two tramps are seen gleaning a life from the remnants of the old buildings. They could be seen as Adam and Eve dispossessed of Eden but for the fact that the old man and woman have been failed as much by the old place as they will by the new. The flats are still not for them to live in. The way in to the future will not help them. Nothing can, other than for them to be repossessed by place and neighbourhood – a new civility which every mile driven down the new road seems to make less and less possible. Neither the tramps' patience nor the poet's anger overcomes the 'daily discontent' of the way in to an uncivil future.

What Tomlinson most dislikes in this changing landscape is what he calls a lack of style, which seems to mean a lack of any means of unifying man to his landscape and his traditions. It is a lack of real 'intention' in the haphazard redevelopment of the city which destroys true deepening and renewal. It is the same (as stanza 7 suggests) as the replacement of craftsmanship by an automated mass-production which severs the individual from his purpose and intention – he is literally not in touch with the process of creation.

This lack of a style that is the outward sign of civility is bemoaned in other poems in *The Way In* which record the poet's reactions to the 'manscape' of his birthplace. Thus in 'Night Ride' the poet is again driving through city streets, this time at night, when he is struck by the way the sodium lights have ousted the stars. 'Ousted' is a key word in a poem which measures the way modern urban life has dispossessed us of our traditional relationship with the natural world. Modern life lacks the space and time to create a style of life which has civility. Individual houses are parts of large impersonal estates, natural landscapes are irrelevant interruptions ('pastoral parentheses') and not central to the lives that are 'cramped in beside / This swathe of roadway'. The 'grip of this city' prevents the construction of meaningful structures to life.

In 'Etruria Vale' he remembers the landscape of his childhood, Josiah Wedgwood's 'factory and model cottages' now blackened into a muddled and depressing city landscape that betrays 'the clear wine of his intention'. What was his country seat has become a 'sooted house' through the smoke of his factory and the blackening of time. Tomlinson points out that the original fathers of the

Industrial Revolution never intended this desecration of life and landscape, but the haphazard, unplanned nature of change has destroyed the relationship of man to his environment as well as having betrayed the aims of those such as the Wedgwoods. When the poet lived in this landscape before the war, for all its depressing qualities, it contained life and a sense of community; but since then 'progress' has moved so fast that 'the biggest gasometer in England' now takes on 'the air of an antique'.

'Dates: Penkhull New Road' suggests that the end of the Second World War was this country's 1917 revolution. It marked the beginning of a new era, an age of planning and rebuilding that has cut us off for ever from our deepest continuities with the past. It may have been a necessary revolution that freed us from the old hierarchies (a world of beautiful architecture and gracious living only for the few) but it has also lost us some of the strengths of previous ages. The architecture of the Victorian industrial revolution had a style of permanence ('gravely neat: / Alleyways between the houses, doors / That opened onto a still car-less street. / Doorsteps were once a civil place.') It was a society in which a sense of community and relationship was possible, even if its hierarchical nature prevented certain justices and freedoms. Even in the poet's childhood, when a factory dominated the backs of the houses, the community could still see this factory as a warm, comforting brick beast. It is not industry as such that is to blame for the modern ugliness and loss of community. The styleless desecration of the landscape is particularly modern. 'Something had bitten a gap / Out of the stretch we lived in', and that 'something' suggests the impersonal and haphazard nature of urban renewal which Tomlinson abhors. The hill is supposedly rebuilt according to a plan, but it is one that has scrapped 'the architectural calendar' of an organized growth in a traditionally ordered life. Now the plans are 'dreamed up by the insuranceman', that is, they are determined by rather petty, penny-pinching bureaucrats. The result is that disparity of styles and lack of civility already pointed out in 'The Way In'. The poem ends confessing it is not simply that a lack of beauty is being bemoaned but that a place and its community should be so easily destroyed and left to live on only in the lines of a poem: 'Absurd / A place should be more fragile than a book.'

In 'Gladstone Street' the same destruction is recorded as the price to be paid for increasing prosperity and social change. In all these poems concerned with the 'ravaged counties' of the Midlands we see Tomlinson's attempt 'to rescue / What is no longer there.' Clearly the loss of what he regards as traditional 'civilities' angers him, and these poems are elegant commentaries on that loss. However, they seem to be almost entirely negative in their attitude to contemporary life and there is a conspicuous absence of any consideration of the gains to some sections of society in these social changes. Significantly these poems lack the presence of people as individuals rather than the ghosts of past communities, something in which they differ from those earlier poems celebrating the positive side of traditional communities. This rather abstract and general consideration of change in the relationship between people and place may leave the reader less convinced than the poet that he does care for something more than beauty.

Time and history

A concern for history and the passage of time has always been present in Tomlinson's poetry. In the poems about people and place he is a witness to certain losses brought about by the passage of time, but in some of the poems in *The Way of a World* and *The Shaft* Tomlinson looks directly at history and considers man's negotiations with time. The same concern with continuity and change, tradition and revolution, emerges in these poems.

'Against Extremity' is a brief poem revealing Tomlinson's attitude to these matters. He declares 'The time is in love with endings.' He sees our age as ignoring the continuities of tradition and denying the consequences that time must bring to every human act. Ours is an age that loves extremes and this is reflected in an art that is frequently apocalyptic. This poem is, in part, a comment on the famous assertion by A. Alvarez that contemporary poets can do justice to our time only if their poetry expresses the violent disorder and breakdown within our society.[8] It is because Alvarez sees Sylvia Plath as trying to do just this in her poetry that he has been a great advocate of her work. Her poetry (see Chapter 5) has little time for the idea of 'the shriven self' that

Tomlinson regards as the necessary identity for the artist, and it is therefore not surprising that 'Against Extremity' should make a reference to Sylvia Plath's art in negative terms:

> That girl who took
> Her life almost, then wrote a book
> To exorcise and exhibit the sin. . . .

She is seen as one of

> The time's
> Spoiled children [who] threaten what they will do,
> And those they cannot shake by petulance
> They'll bribe out of their wits by show.

But the poem is not a personal attack; it is about the response of any artist who is besotted by visions of a reality conjured up in the minds of those at the end of their tether. It seems to Tomlinson that these are unnatural responses for a human being, who is naturally a creature of time and cannot simply either give in to time or deny its consequences. Man is tied to his past and through the consequences of his acts is bound to the future. An apocalyptic vision is untrue in that it attempts to make a clean sweep of the past. Man must live with the continuities of time, and any meaning he draws from life can have significance only in so far as it stands the test of time:

> Against extremity, let there be
> Such treaties as only time itself
> Can ratify, a bond and test
> Of sequential days. . . .

That which lasts in time rather than tries to deny it is what will build a bridge to 'a given good / Or a good gained', both of which extremity will hate. Art and all man's endeavours are the productions of time. Man and his works must be given to history 'like the full / Moon slowly given to the night, / A possession that is not possessed.' Behind this poem lies the same insistence on man's humility and unselfish relationship with the outer reality as occurred in the poems concerned with the act of perception. The extremists in art and life improperly deny that continuum beyond ourselves.

'Prometheus' begins by placing man against that continuum in its description of the poet listening to a radio performance of Scriabin's 'Prometheus' during a summer storm.

> Summer thunder darkens, and its climbing
>   Cumulae, disowning our scale in the zenith,
> Electrify this music: the evening is falling apart.
> Castles-in-air; on earth: green, livid fire.
> The radio simmers with static to the strains
>   Of this mock last-day of nature and of art.

Nature seems to be in tune with the apocalyptic strains of Scriabin's visionary music. But the placing comment on such visions (whether artistic or political) which the poem is to become is prefigured in this opening. Nature outweighs human existence, 'disowning our scale in the zenith' ('scale' links the storm and the music). The music counterfeits its apocalypse (it is 'mock'), and the insubstantial vision of an idealized reality, suggested in the music, is hinted at in the phrase 'castles-in-air'; while the solidity of nature's power is implied in the way the static from the real storm can interfere with the strains of the music. 'Strains' itself suggests the tension between nature and art, and the break-up of any true sense of visionary ideal which should be rooted in reality.

The Russian composer's music reminds the poet of the other great Russian attempt to pursue an apocalyptic vision: the political revolution of 1917. The remainder of the poem is a passionate rejection of extremist solutions in history. Scriabin shared a common twentieth-century artistic and political belief that man can accomplish a radical transformation of his world by revolutionary action. But, to Tomlinson, these men of extremes neglect the true consequences of their Promethean myth of fire.

> Trombones for the transformation
> That arrived by train at the Finland Station,
>   To bury its hatchet after thirty years in the brain
> Of Trotsky.

Although they begin with a faith in their ability to control events, history has shown that revolutionaries end either as tyrants who change nothing but the name of the tyranny or who themselves are toppled from their zenith. The power of this poem lies in the way this point is made while at the same time enacting the 'cymballed firesweeps' of the music, the 'chromatic Prometheus'. The continuities of the notes are lost to the poet who cannot hear 'such music for its consequence'. Does revolutionary art succour extremist policies?

> Scriabin, Blok, men of extremes,
> History treads out the music of your dreams
> Through blood, and cannot close like this
> In the perfection of anabasis.

History will not stop, like the music, in the harmony of a controlled finale. The consequences of a political revolution are written in the blood of millions. The purity of the visionary ideal is sullied by historical necessity, the contingencies of reality.

As the music ends, the listener returns his glance to the scene outside. The storm here, too, has stopped. But its consequence is a true harmony, a life-sustaining continuity:

> The trees
> Continue raining though the rain has ceased
> In a cooled world of incessant codas. . . .

He sees the houses and scene around him which 'refuses to burn' with the ardour of the music. The only music is the tawdry jingle of an ice cream van touring the estate. This is the real world. Its music goes on for ever, including the ugliness which is the 'city's / Stale new frontier', and no revolutionary ideal will come to terms with it. Finally, if reluctantly, the poet recognizes that even the unidealistic ugly realities of our modern urban world are truer to man's history than are the idealistic fantasies of apocalyptic artists and politicians. Reality is a mercy in its consequences as compared with the bloody pursuit of apocalyptic fantasies, even though the ugliness which rules reality makes for a 'cruel mercy of solidities'.

This is a deeply conservative poem, but it springs partly from Tomlinson's continuing desire to achieve an honesty to the realities beyond the private dreams of the individual. That which is outside man must be given its due as a limit to the power man has to transform his reality. When he abuses that power, whether by destroying a traditional neighbourhood or by a more violent political solution to society's evils, man becomes a victim of his 'fixities of self' – a dogmatism of dream or ideal that denies true realities.

A revolutionary leader in the grip of the power of such dogmatic dreams of an ideal society was Danton, the French revolutionary. In 'For Danton', one of Tomlinson's most recent poems, he pursues the connections of man, extremist politics and the nature of time.

Danton is imagined leaning over a bridge peering at a stream during a brief visit to his birthplace in a moment of peace before his return to Paris and his eventual downfall. As he watches the water he 'thinks that he and not the river advances'. He is a man accustomed to considering himself at the centre of action, a man controlling the tide of events. He is also, whether aware of it or not, a man inexorably advancing towards his death. For the moment he seems oblivious of time slipping away from him – he who has held time in his control. 'Water is time' but he does not 'hear the links of consequence / Chiming his life away' in the water below. All he hears is 'Not yet, not yet'. He hears not the true chime of time but only his own song in the music of the stream:

> Its music deafens him
> To other sounds, to past and future wrong.
> The beat is regular beneath that song.
> He hears in it a pulse that is his own;
> He hears the years autumnal and complete.
> November waits for him who has not done
>
> With seeings, savourings.

But the context gives these lines a steady irony. In their regular rhythm and balance of phrase and line, they give a sense of completeness to Danton's interpretation of his life's work. He believes he has accomplished a great act – that time itself has been ruled by him. This same river that he watches had carried him as a child to see the king whom later he brought down and superseded. To him it is the confident maker of his progress and success. But its steady rhythm is also the beat of time's connections of events, and in this rising flood of time Danton will be carried off, not the master of events but mastered by them, his vision eventually dimmed by the flood of Robespierre's Terror.

Yet his return to his native town awakens a realization in Danton that although he is 'secure / In the possession of perfect power' nevertheless he walks in the fields and knows 'what power he had lost'. It is the power of truly seeing and savouring – seeing the beauty of the outer reality, beyond his idealist's dreams; seeing the natural world and not the world of the metropolis of political power. He has only a brief glimpse of the 'contrary perfection' of nature and natural relationships between man and time before he has to plunge back into the artificial perfections of his political visions. The final irony is that his search for perfection – his attempt to control time by deposing a king in the name of an idealized political future – will rebound upon himself. In the poem water is time and its chime rings the note of his own death, a note he does not properly hear:

> Before he catches in the waterchime
> The measure and the chain a death began,
> And fate that loves the symmetry of rhyme
> Will spring the trap whose teeth must have a man.

To the end Danton does not fully understand the power he has forfeited. It is the power of seeing to the heart of things, of understanding that there are necessary connections and consequences for every action. No man can defeat time except in his own deluded dreams.

In his poems concerned with history Tomlinson demands the same humility before the facts of time, a realization of the consequences of all our acts, that he called for in considering man's relationship with place. Both demands are consequent upon his belief in the need to accept the realities of what is outside man and to try to capture their exact forms without covering them with the secretion of our own precious essence.

The pure surprise of seeing

What exactly is this relationship between self and reality which lies at the heart of Tomlinson's act of looking, his concept of civility and his idea of man's attitudes to place and history?

'Four Kantian Lyrics' reveals something of an answer. The first lyric begins 'I stared, but not to seize / the point of things'. It is clear that the relationship does not mean binding the world to ourselves, not forcing reality into the shapes of our own thought, but rather a patient submission to the forms of the world, an acceptance and giving of ourselves to that world. The act of looking which represents that relationship is thus an act of love. By the final lines of the last lyric we come to realize that this is not simply a denial of self. On the contrary, the self must be at the tip of its senses, in close contact with the world of the not-self. Only in this way is a wholeness of relationship derived from the total act of seeing which carries us into a true continuity with the world:

> There are two
> ways to marry with a land –
> first, this bland and blind
> submergence of the self, an act
> of kind and questionless. The other
> is the thing I meant, a whole
> event, a happening, the sound
> that brings all space in
> for its bound, when self is clear
> as what we keenest see and hear:
> no absolute of eye can tell
> the utmost, but the glance
> goes shafted from us like a well.

The importance of 'shafted' is clearer since the publication of Tomlinson's latest book in which 'The Shaft', the title poem, describes an abandoned mine-shaft which looks 'like a place of sacrifice'. It 'opened beneath . . . all its levels / Lost in a hundred feet of water'. This shaft plunges deep down 'through centuries' and connects layer upon layer of history. It is a dark tunnel to the centre of things just as, in the image quoted above, the proper act of looking sees deep into the heart of reality.

In 'The Hill' the poet watches a girl climbing a steep slope, and the poem sees in her an image of the right relationship between self and reality and enacts in its own structure the very act of looking just described. As the unnamed girl climbs, watched every

70

step of the way by the attentive eye of the poet, her whole being is concentrated into action. Her thoughts and movements are a single 'thrust and rise'. She moulds her effort to accommodate the resistance of nature and by thus appearing to subdue her will to it she does in fact overcome its resistance:

> She inclines
> against the current of its resistance,
> (as simple as walking, this)
> and her bridge-leaner's stance
> subdues it with (almost) a willessness.

The parentheses comment on the girl climbing, making the exact quality of the effort clear, but they are asides because the poem's focus is the girl-and-the-hill. The real meaning of the act is carried in a submerged metaphor hinted at in 'current' and 'bridge-leaner's stance': her stooping forward suggests a stance of looking over a bridge at water, which is the slope flowing beneath her feet. That is, she *bridges* or connects nature's resistance to her will. The hill, or nature, or life itself appears hard, impenetrable and uncompliant to man:

> Nature is hard. Neither the mind
> nor the touch can penetrate
> to a defenceless part;
> but, held on the giant palm, one may negotiate
> and she, rising athwart it, is showing the art.

Nature cannot be subdued by intellect or by action; its stiff resistance can be overcome only by submitting our will to it. By such a submission the woman negotiates between self and not-self and gains a balance of relationship which the poem itself re-creates in its scrupulous observation of the act. Both the woman's action and the poet's re-creation of it are creative in the way they bestow a meaning through the relationship between 'the barrenly fertile sweep' of nature and the 'very fact' of existence.

In 'A Given Grace' not nature but the existence of simple, everyday objects is what is accepted as worthy of this same creative act of consciousness. In this case it is the act of looking itself which must submit to fact. Two cups become 'a given grace' when they are fully attended to, in and for themselves. 'They

71

unclench / the mind, filling it / with themselves', an act re-created
in less than a dozen words. The cups are

> afloat and white
> on the mahogany pool
> of table.

In this apparently unremarkable image we are presented with a
simple, commonly shared observation which yet attests to an
acutely sensuous apprehension and the poet's willingness to
attend to the everyday world without seeking to overload it with a
spurious significance derived from his own emotional obsessions.
The grace of being and meaning is bestowed only on the self that
concentrates on what is beyond itself.

The dependence of this 'given grace' of meaning on an unegotis-
tical attention to the world is seen clearly in two particularly beautiful poems, 'Idyll' and 'Swimming Chenango Lake'. 'Idyll' tells of
the poet's experience of watching an Italian-style San Francisco
square and its occupants. The square, however run down it may
actually be, is a haven of peace and rest from the 'constant
ground-bass' of the traffic and city noise. The poet is observing it
as the winter sunlight draws a shadow over its church whose
portico is decorated with a quotation from Dante's *Paradiso*. A
Chinese youth is sitting quietly reading between two old men who
sit 'in mingled odour / of cheroot and garlic spitting'.

The form of the poem consists of fairly short lines broken, as it
were, into three steps – a device that is used to produce a slow,
rather hesitant movement with the occasional line stopped short
after a key word, so that a surprise of meaning or a sudden change
of tone is emphasized. This controls the reader's perception of
events, isolating each observation, laying them out separately so
that the very act of seeing is itself accentuated. It is a common
device in Tomlinson. For example, in the following lines from
'Idyll' we follow the poet's glance across the square and feel his
very perception of light and form as he takes in the verse above the
church door as it is shadowed by the low winter sun:

> Cool
>   the January sun
>   that with an intensity
>   the presence of the sea

makes more exact,
chisels the verse with shade
and lays
on the grass
a deep and even
Californian green
while a brilliance
throughout the square
flatters the meanness of its architecture.

The lines of the verse are themselves syntactically chiselled, as it were, so as to render more sharply the contrast of light and shade, colour and meanness.

The eye is led leisurely round the square until finally focusing on the reading youth. His book is *SUCCESS in Spelling*. The poet asks how such a youth who is barely able to cope with the basics of his own language can possibly be led to appreciate the language, culture and tradition that produces a *Paradiso*. But the square itself reveals the answer. It is not necessarily a matter of reading Dante. The recognition of the *Paradiso* is contained in a moment of purely secular grace, a moment of living in the square which is preserved in 'Idyll'. It is that moment, possible for anyone to enter, when the act of looking rises to a sudden awareness of the essence of what is observed, a moment of the perception of being itself. The life of that square, at that moment when the poet, youth, old men, church and Dante are all related, transcends the poverty and squalor of the surroundings by creating a new beauty which bestows upon the participants in the event a grace of continuity and true relationship:

this poised quiescence, pause
and possibility in which
the music of the generations
binds into its skein
the flowing instant,
while the winter sun
pursues the shadow
before a church
whose decoration
is a quotation from *Paradiso*.

73

It is the achievement of this poem that the 'poise' and 'pause', the feeling of possibility, balance and momentary grace, are enacted in the rhythm and syntax of the lines themselves.

'Swimming Chenango Lake' creates a symbol of the right relationship between self and the world. The swimmer reads the water's 'wealth of ways', a water which 'is a consistency, the grain of pulsating flow'. The poem begins with an image of the light and movement on the surface of the lake and the reflection of clouds on it, likening the water to crumpled silk. That image is added to in the suggestion that the patterning on the surface is similar to the grain in wood. Thus the opacity of the element (its resistance) and its constant movement are both highlighted. The swimmer 'scissors the waterscape apart / And sways it to tatters' ('waterscape' both calls attention to the wide expanse of the lake and implies that the crumpled silk surface is cut to tatters). The swimmer understands his element, is at home in it and yet respects the 'coldness / Holding him to itself'. He must 'grant' the cold its grasp:

> For to swim is to take hold
> On water's meaning, to move in its embrace
> And to be, between grasp and grasping, free.

It is a freedom only maintained by balancing both the will's desire and the recalcitrant, hostile nature of the water: 'a possession to be relinquished / Willingly at each stroke'.

Alone in the lake the swimmer is born anew, his solitary action a rebirth of himself in relation to the elements, and he is seen by the poet as learning 'a lost language'. It is the language spoken by the Hinton family and the builders of the hall at Stowey. It is the language of the artist who is fully aware of the continuum of the universe outside himself and whose naming of the world is a bringing to birth of new being (see 'Adam'). The swimmer's submission to the 'densities' and 'derisions' of the elements is not a subservience but a respectful act of will. He cannot completely immerse himself,

> Human, he fronts it and, human, he draws back
> From the interior cold, the mercilessness
> That yet shows a kind of mercy in sustaining him.

He returns this 'kind of mercy' in his perception which is 'incessantly shaping' the waters whose nature he has come fully to know. In this perfectly realized poem, image and metaphor combine with rhythm (which in its deliberately uneven checking and hesitancy reveals the process of the poet's reflecting mind) both to present a scene and to articulate its significance. It becomes the perfect symbol of Tomlinson's concept of 'relations and contraries' between self and the world.

Tomlinson's poetic gift is the transmuting of what he sees into an act of thought so that seeing and believing become one in the poem. His constant search has been for that act of perception which, through its fidelity to the object perceived, will create a moment of perfection which, although remaining an illusion, is still part of a greater truth. Perfection can be experienced only as an image but the source of that image must be in reality. An image requires a mind that imagines 'guiding the glance the way perfection is'. Art can create that image by attending on that moment – whether in nature or in history – which can never itself be permanent except in the artist's re-creation of it. In 'The Perfection' (one of his most recent poems) Tomlinson says a moment's perfection, of a sunset, for instance, may never be known

> until it has been
> for the moment it is
> and the next has brought in
>
> a lost pitch,
> a lack-lustre pause
> in the going glow
> where the perfection was.

Throughout his poetry Tomlinson insists on the discipline of seeing as being a creative act. What is seen is the object in the form of an image that is filled with meaning by the perceiver's unself-centred attention to his world. Such seeing can truly be a revelation in which perception overcomes – or, rather, co-operates with – nature, time and history to create its own instant of perfection,

> . . . the moment itself, abrupt
> With the pure surprise of seeing,
> Will outlast all after-knowledge and its map –
> ('The Gap')

In his prose-poem 'The Insistence of Things', Tomlinson writes:

> At the edge of conversations, uncompleting all acts of thought, looms the insistence of things which, waiting on our recognition, face us with our own death, for they are so completely what we are not.

Yet the labour must go on to recognize and name our habitations – 'the simple recognitions that can be lured to inhabit a paragraph, a phrase, a snatch of words – and thus speak to us.' Tomlinson's poetry is a record of that labour to name our habitations and for them to speak to us through 'the insistence of things'. It is this which gives his work its characteristic self-control and sanity.

There are some critics who have interpreted this control as too cold and cerebral. While this can hardly be said to be an accurate description of his work if the argument of this chapter is conceded, nevertheless his sobriety, his 'touch of austerity', as John Press has called it,[9] will always meet resistance from those who enjoy the intoxication of words or believe that poetry today must be an art of extremism and breakdown.

At the heart of Tomlinson's attitude to poetry and to life is a unique combination of 'very acute senses with a habit of self denial'.[10] In their exact apprehension of our world and in their sense of our identity being involved with a right relationship between seeing, believing and responding, these poems of Charles Tomlinson give us the strength to recognize and live with that strange world of otherness in 'the continuum outside ourselves'.

> To see, is to feel at your back this domain of a circle whose power consists in evading and refusing to be completed by you.
>
> It is infinity sustains you on its immeasurable palm.
>
> ('Tout Entouré de Mon Regard')

3

'A courier after identity'

The poetry of Thom Gunn

Fighting terms

Thom Gunn's first book of poems, *Fighting Terms*, was published in 1954. In those early days he was seen by many to be a poet with similar ambitions to The Movement poets (see p. 3). In fact he was a contributor to the *New Lines* anthology which presented these poets to the public. This identification was made on the strength, particularly, of his attitude to form in poetry. He shared the belief of The Movement poets that poetry should be well made and craftsmanlike, utilizing traditional rhythms and rhyme schemes. Many of his early poems expressed fairly complex ideas within intricately extended metaphors, a style which helped earn him the label of 'a modern metaphysical poet', especially as these poems were often concerned with matters of love and passion, one of the traditional themes of the seventeenth-century metaphysical poets.

Now that he has published six volumes of poetry this view seems somewhat limited and cannot provide a full account of his strongly individualistic voice. He has said of himself:

> I think everything significant that happens to me, whether it's an event, or an idea or a dream, gets into my poetry eventually. Writing for me is a way of trying to understand what happens inside me and to me.[1]

Many of his poems, particularly his best ones, are linked closely to his life and experiences and especially to his exploration of his sense of himself and the possible attitudes and commitments he might embrace. There is a sense in which his poetry might be seen

77

as a continuously developing attempt to understand the intellectual's condition in modern life and to explore the divisions, conflicts, tensions and problems that he faces. His poems explore aspects of the rift between thinking man and acting man, between body and mind, self and others, self and the natural world.

In Iris Murdoch's novel *The Time of the Angels* there is a character called Pattie, a black servant who suddenly finds that after years of loneliness, grinding work and poverty, after the experience of an aching lack of companionship and affection, she is able, under the gentle touch of another's love, to let the bitterness and cold egocentrism of her earlier self melt into a new sense of identity. Her new self is able to respond to others. It is described at the moment of rebirth in these words:

> What then had happened this morning? In the sunlight and the snow some madness had come, some sudden amazing freedom. The black years had dropped from her heart, and she had felt again that free impetuous movement towards another, that human gesture which makes each one of us wholly himself. And it was indeed as if a new self had come to her so that in her out-going towards Eugene she was complete and there was none of her that was elsewhere.

This 'sudden amazing freedom' and its accompanying sense of completeness in responding to another is a perfect description of the goal towards which the poetry of Thom Gunn moves through his six volumes and which this chapter will seek to outline.

It is hardly a characteristic most easily perceived at first glance and particularly not if the reader concentrates only on the early, better-known poems. In these, Gunn's famous concern with the world of the leather-jacketed ton-up boys, and his apparent mistrust of love which almost amounts to scorn, prevents the deep groundswell of this theme being seen at a superficial glance.

Fighting Terms (1954, revised 1962), as its title suggests, promotes a tough, hardened stance towards the world and personal relationships. In the various situations and *personae* of these poems the individual, even when he is in love, is seen to occupy an embattled position. Poems like 'Lofty in the Palais de Dance' or 'The Beachhead' adopt an aggressive pose. They are not immediately personal poems, even when dealing with personal emotions. Gunn wears a series of masks and looks at a number of situations, writing as if from within a different character. There is a unity of metaphor and a similarity in the dominant attitude to the subject matter. This is seen at its most obvious in the poems about love. These are frequently built upon the structure of an extended metaphor which equates love and passion with battle and war and lovers' embraces with the tactics and stratagems of generals. Together with the frequent extreme self-awareness and self-consciousness of action and motive, these characteristics give the book an overwhelming image of man as being cut off from complete absorption in his experience and relationships by his fight to assert his individual identity. These features can be seen most clearly in 'To His Cynical Mistress' and 'Carnal Knowledge'.

In the space of two six-line stanzas Gunn reveals in 'To His Cynical Mistress' an accomplishment of form and announces his characteristic attitude to the idea of love. Love is a fight, a struggle between two independent nations with a climax that is no more than a compromise of uncertain peace which the poet affects to despise:

> And love is then no more than a compromise?
> An impermanent treaty waiting to be signed
>   By the two enemies?
> While the calculating Cupid feigning impartial-blind
> Drafts it, promising peace, both leaders wise
> To his antics sign but secretly double their spies.
>
> On each side is the ignorant animal nation,
> Jostling friendly in streets, enjoying in good faith
>   This celebration
> Forgetting their enmity with cheers and drunken breath;
> But for them there has not yet been amalgamation:
> The leaders calmly plot assassination.

Beginning with two questions, which are not hesitant but rather assertive and dismiss any sense of lastingness about the quality of love, the poem goes on to answer them with a resounding attack suggesting that the great god Cupid is a master tactician who merely poses as impartial in order to bring the lovers together apparently against their better judgement. In the fourth line we see a complex metaphor handled with fluency: 'while a calculating Cupid feigning impartial-blind'. This hangs together partly by means of the alliteration and partly by the steady flow of rhythm. It creates an image of love as something stronger than the individuals but less to be trusted than they are. In the second stanza the permanent peace is prematurely celebrated by the instinctual, animal selves who are drunk with desire and on the verge of a consummation which may join them now but will also sow the seeds of division.

Even while preparing for this consummative act the lovers keep a wary eye on each other's weaknesses, ready to exploit or destroy. This poem is clever, witty, carefully constructed, somewhat mannered after the style of the metaphysical poets. It generalizes its subject and is a poem of an idea rather than an evocation or realization of the passion of love.

In the original Fantasy Press edition of *Fighting Terms* the opening poem was 'Carnal Knowledge'. Beginning 'Even in bed I pose . . .', it introduced one of the dominant themes of the volume. From the outset Gunn saw the most intimate and deepest of human relationships as a matter of deliberately adopting a mask or pose. From first to last this particular poem shows a speaker self-conscious about his every move. In it the intellect is divorced from the body's act and stands aside to comment on that act.

Although early on there seems to be hope that 'desire may grow more circumstantial and less circumspect' (i.e. that the mind should become one with the body's desire) there is no real belief that it will. The punctuation of the first stanza, with its syntax controlled by commas, makes the poem not so much hesitant as full of qualifications:

> . . . desire may grow
> More circumstantial and less circumspect
> Each night, but an acute girl would suspect
> My thoughts might not be, like my body, bare.

The alliteration and equality of stress as between 'circumstantial' and 'circumspect' and 'would suspect', together with the rhyme, tie the words to one another to express a carefully controlled, qualified look at the situation. 'More' and 'less' introduce phrases which are balanced on the pivot of the conjunction which helps create the sense of the speaker weighing up the slender possibility of their desire growing into genuine love. By the end of that first stanza we know that the speaker queries not just his own motive but also the motive of his lover, and the daringly repetitive last line ('You know I know you know I know you know'), which teeters on the brink of absurdity, is nevertheless pulled back by the completion of the rhyme which has been carried over from the very first line of the poem, catching us up and taking us back to the connection of desire with pose.

This last line recurs with slight variations throughout the poem until in the final line it is cut off halfway at another moment when the connection between pose and knowledge is being implied, leaving us in no doubt that we are intended to regard even the apparently honest dismissal of the lover as just another sham. The awareness of the speaker of his inauthentic motives is seen both as damaging and as itself damaged. 'I am not what I seem,' says the speaker. He is a 'forked creature' both because he is devilish, a fraud, and because he lies, speaking with 'a forked tongue'. But the most damaging attack in the second stanza is aimed at the woman who is described as 'flaccid' and is seen as 'complicit' in the false act because she wants only 'a competent poseur'. As in the previous poem, love is seen as a 'seeming' rather than a reality. In the third stanza the physical act of love is seen as no more than an absurd, faintly ridiculous act and part of an inevitably tragic game. In the following stanza the body of the lover is described in terms of a lack of feeling, care or concern. As the poem develops it is clear that the speaker himself feels he is trapped in a relationship not of love but of contempt.

Although the penultimate stanza carries the idea of the speaker's dreams of genuine love, the nature of the image itself with its suggestion of death ('Then lifting from my lids night's penny weights') destroys even that hope, leaving a feeling not of love but of knowledge that 'lack of love contaminates'. The speaker's inauthenticity is caught by his lover. In the last line of the poem the knife is further twisted when it is admitted that even the speaker's self-knowledge, which has been his only saving grace, is revealed as itself a false pose.

This is a strong poem in which love is seen only through the mind. It is also savage in its view of love cankered from the outset and it leaves us with a feeling that even this willed combative posture of the speaker cannot satisfy for long because it can provide only the spurious freedom of a callous strength permitting him to cut loose and survive at the cost of denying the hurt done to both lovers.

Other poems in this book describe love in terms of a combat (for example, 'Lofty in the Palais de Dance' where the protagonist actually is a soldier) and are as savagely denigrating of the possibility of true relationship. Some explanation of how the poet comes to adopt this stance is to be found in 'A Mirror for Poets' which foreshadows later poems that are concerned with violent energy.

It celebrates the Elizabethan age largely because that was a time of great energy and vitality. In an implicit contrast with the 1950s and the Welfare State, Gunn emphasizes that the poets of Elizabethan England did not create images of imagined pain but actually wrote of real dangers. Gunn seems to be suggesting that in a society where everyday life is dangerous the artist will more easily gain a sense of the ultimate meaning of his life:

> In this society the boundaries met
> Of life and life, at danger; with no space
> Being left between, except where might be set
> That mathematical point whose time and place
> Could not exist. Yet at this point they found
> Arcadia, a fruitful permanent land.

It is a dangerous notion if it is intended to be taken literally and does much to explain why the young Gunn had a reputation for being a poet in love with violence.

In the last poem of the book, 'Incident on a Journey', the journey is to be seen as a metaphor for life. The poet imagines himself sleeping in a cave on his long trek through a harsh landscape, and he employs a Yeatsian refrain ('I regret nothing') and its variations to describe a man in whom action is a close and immediate response to strong feeling. This produces a wisdom that cannot be divorced from the action. Here the poet is making the first attempt to heal the split between mind and body by submerging the mind in the body's actions. The man gains strength and increases his sense of his own identity from action and, even when 'netted in a brawl' and beaten, he can still claim that although his body lies in the dust and he is isolated and lonely yet he remains free and regrets nothing. Only in the last verse, which shows him revelling in the 'uncaked blood in all its channels flowing', is there revealed any sense of his vitality and strength being a matter of *will* rather than experience. This is tellingly shown in the quiet change of the refrain from the earlier assertive 'I regret nothing' to the less certain but more hopeful 'I would regret nothing'.

Fighting Terms shows admiration for the man of action who seeks out his enemy and uses him as a spur to the protagonist's sense of identity. These poems have a strict structure (frequently a six-line stanza based on an iambic rhythm) with carefully developed imagery and fastidious rhymes which emphasize the intellectual control and sharp consciousness shared by the protagonists of the poem who try to overcome their detached nature by burying themselves in action.

A life of action and a life of pose

The Sense of Movement (1957) takes this theme further and uses a theory of pose as its vehicle. Gunn developed this theory while a student at Cambridge. He maintained that, since everybody seemed to behave quite differently with different people and in different circumstances, it would be best to be fully aware of this and to control such roles consciously. A poet, particularly, might use such a theory to write from outside his own personal experience. We can see this conscious adoption of different poses in both the first two books, but it is in the second that the theory is used to explore facets of contemporary life.

Many of the poems both employ the theory and at the same time hint at its limitations. The pose particularly pursued is that of the Hell's Angels motorbike gang member (these poems were written in the period of the James-Dean-style tough-guy rebellion). Its best presentation is the most heavily anthologized of Gunn's poems, 'On the Move'.

This poem describes a gang of ton-up toughs, 'the Boys', who race their motorcycles across the landscape, tearing noisily from one barely noticed town to another without any clear sense of direction. Around this central description Gunn weaves a series of ideas that convert the motorcyclists into a symbol for a particular response to life.

In the first line the natural world is presented as part of a process of movement that is built on instinct and has an equipoise that man cannot achieve: 'The blue jay scuffling in the bushes follows / Some hidden purpose'. Yet is it the attempt to emulate nature that lies at the heart of the motorcyclists' apparently unnatural disturbance of the landscape? This is the question posed by Gunn.

The entry of 'the Boys' in the second stanza has been brilliantly prepared for in the first stanza by this very description of nature's movement. The birds 'scuffling in the bushes', 'gust' in flocks and 'wheel' and 'spurt' about the sky. These images of energy and action prefigure the violent entry of the bikes, an entry which is given superb physical presence in the next stanza. They appear not as individuals but as the anonymous condition of man, embodied in their machinery. 'Small, black, as flies hanging in heat', they roar up the road. Images of noise, power and urgency predominate, rising to a crescendo of thunderous force in mid-stanza.

It is the recurrence of the word 'thunder' which takes us back to the last lines of the first stanza:

> One moves with an uncertain violence
> Under the dust thrown by a baffled sense
> Or the dull thunder of approximate words.

These lines appear puzzling at first until we realize they are connected to the Boys and that the use of the impersonal 'one' indicates we are to see them as representative of an aspect of the human condition. Human nature is being contrasted with nature itself. Any sense of purpose man may have is reduced to mere action which is produced in response to doubt about his meaning, or is a response to the rhetoric of language which is an instrument of propaganda that is too imprecise to convey the truth, yet powerful enough to persuade us to action. The action of the motorcycle gang is thus seen as their loud attempt to simulate some sense of purpose.

They achieve this sense by creating an image for themselves ('In goggles, donned impersonality') which is intended to cure all doubts but which turns out to be inadequate:

> In gleaming jackets trophied with the dust,
> They strap in doubt – by hiding it, robust –
> And almost hear a meaning in their noise.

The poet points to this doubt, and the rest of the poem examines this possible solution to a sense of meaninglessness.

> One joins the movement in a valueless world,
> Choosing it, till both hurler and the hurled,
> One moves as well, always toward, toward.

The solution of the Boys is generalized again into an image of modern man who, it is claimed, is born amid movement and who cannot properly control this very movement he is committed to because he has no sense of final goal. All he can do is commit himself to the ongoing action.

> At worst, one is in motion; and at best,
> Reaching no absolute, in which to rest,
> One is always nearer by not keeping still.

In a world where traditional values (the absolutes of religion, for instance) are no longer viable options it seems the only answer is to commit oneself to action, the outcome of which cannot be predicted.

Each stanza (except the first where the description is of the natural world) begins with a picture of the motorcyclists but ends in abstract commentary. At first the poem appears to extol the Boys' solution, but a closer reading reveals a hint of the limitations of this – 'It is a part solution, after all.' The positive stance of the Boys 'astride the created will', assertive and self-willed, is the answer neither of instinct nor of goodness ('home for neither bird nor holiness'). The strength of the Boys is more doubtful than it at first appears and though 'Much that is natural, to the will must yield', we begin to wonder what strength it can be that is built upon a toughness that is so forced and directionless.

In 'On the Move' Gunn successfully employs images from contemporary culture, but only in part to help him explore the motives for the behaviour of the rebellious youths that anonymously populate many of his poems. His real concern is to make them symbolize not just their own generation but a whole way of possible confrontation with our modern world. Whether the motorcyclists could actually see themselves in the way Gunn sees them is beside the point. What matters is the articulation of the poet's possible stance towards his world – a world which he sees in this poem as giving no sense of absolute value to man. 'Some hidden purpose', a crying out for meaning, is the expectation that is assumed by the poet, but the poem's valiant attempt to show this need reveals only a partial satisfaction in the posited solution of the creation of a self-willed image. This aggressive pose still leaves the reader feeling the sense of that need more sharply than its solution: 'It is part solution, after all.' We experience in this poem, as in many of the early poems, more a sense of the poet's vital energy than a conviction in his moralizing.

There are other poems in this volume (for example, 'The Unsettled Motorcyclist's Vision of his Death', 'Elvis Presley', 'Market at Turk') which explore similar ideas through contemporary images. But it is 'On the Move' that, more readily than any other, combines successfully the examination of an idea with the creation of the physical presence of its subject. It is in such poems that Gunn laid the groundwork on which his early critics erected an image of him as the 'tough-guy intellectual'. Yet this label neglects the fact that he has been a self-conscious writer from the very beginning, always aware of his limitations. 'On the Move' contains its own distancing comment on the posture it describes. This sense of the limits of the pose becomes increasingly explicit in the next book; meanwhile the remaining poems in the 1957 volume create a sense of modern man 'condemned to be an individual' in that he must explore the limitations of thought and of the world in which he lives, a world in which he can no longer wrestle a meaning from the historically meaningful traditions but must instead test all values through his own sense of the possibility of man. This idea is most clearly presented in the poem 'Human Condition', where modern man is seen as unable to clothe himself with traditional values. He must create his own values out of an authentic wrestle with his own life. Behind this and all the poems in this volume there lies a sense of man as 'a useless passion',[2] full of energy and potential in a world that cannot give him a sense of significance he has not created for himself.

'A Plan of Self-Subjection' explores the need for willpower and self-discipline to create the kind of authentic self that the poet believes can give a lasting sense of identity to the individual in his valueless world. But to the reader it seems that more often it is the energy of that will which predominates over any identity, as if the willing itself has become the end (there seems to be a suggestion of this in 'On the Move'), and one of the last poems in the book, 'Merlin in the Cave', faces this and reads like a summary of many of the earlier concerns.

Gunn adopts the mask of Merlin, legendary necromancer, wizard and wise man, who in the poem is an old man still searching for the key to his life. His life has been spent in desperate contemplation of an enigmatic universe: 'I peer at what I do not understand, / The movement.' The natural energy of the animate world is what has most perplexed him, and he admits, like the ton-up boys earlier, that man is denied any such animal instincts: 'I lost their instinct. It was late. To me / The bird is only meat for augury.' That last line embraces a pun in which 'meat' suggests the bird is reduced to food for man and at the same time retains its use as part of a ceremony of divination (the earliest meaning of 'augury') which is an aspect of Merlin's role as prophet ('meat' meaning also 'suitable for' when spelt 'meet'). Even in old age Merlin makes a last-minute attempt to regain the vigour of youth and test himself against the deepest passions of love,

> With aphrodisiac
> I brought back vigour; oiled and curled my hair;
> Reduced my huge obesity. . . .
>
> Love was a test: I was all-powerful,
> So failed, because I let no fault intrude.

In his studied perfection he was a *poseur* who consciously calculated his every move. This reminds us of the lovers of *Fighting Terms*. At last, however, Merlin is reduced to his bare, lonely cave and in his solitude dedicates himself to the pursuit of knowledge, coming at last to an apprehension of the world as it is and being glad to understand through the senses of sight and touch without

the misleading intervention of the calculating mind. He is condemned to ceaseless struggle, the ever-renewed attempt to seek
the synthesis of whatever his nature is in order to understand his
identity. The poem ends in a comment which itself relates back to
'On the Move' (particularly as the two poems share the same
stanza form):

> Knowing the end to movement, I will shrink
> From movement not for its own wilful sake.

Man must act because that is his nature – he is a purposive
creature – but the end is in the grasping of that action, or rather
'This is an end, and yet another start.'

The images that predominate in this volume are of toughness,
hardness and self-discipline. Their connotations suggest a view of
man imprisoned within his individual self, unable to know himself through any inherited value system and unable to lay hold of
authentic life except by self-control and conscious exploration of
his sense of apartness from nature and his fellow human beings.
This exploration can be achieved only through action and commitment in which the action is the greater part of the meaning. It is
not an achieved philosophy in which a man could rest for long,
and Gunn himself was unable to rest in it, as we shall see. In these
first books he laid bare, as it were, the assumptions from which
anything more satisfactory must be examined. It is as if in this
volume, as Frederick Grubb points out,[3] Gunn accepts the idea of
limitation as a challenge against which he pits his individual will.
In a poem like 'To Yvor Winters', however, this is qualified by the
suggestion of the need for a balance between 'rule and energy'.
This is the classical ordering of one's life by demanding the
control of the forces of passion by commitment. Gunn sees this as
having been achieved in the life and work of his one-time teacher,
the literary critic and poet, Yvor Winters. Yet in 'Allegory of a
Wolf Boy' he implies that the intuitive nature of man which brings
him closest to the world of nature must not be ignored or rejected
because that would dangerously imbalance man. This is implied
rather than fully stated in the poem. Thus it becomes clear to
someone reading all the poems of these first two books that what
were 'fighting terms' are slowly becoming seen as a onesided
answer from which we must count the losses as well as appreciate

the gains. There is a price to be paid by those who try to will desire
and control energy and action by disciplined order. In 'The Beat-
ers' there is a suggestion of the dangers involved. The enemy is
seen as necessary in order to provoke the required discipline, and
the implication is that life can be lived only by continually pro-
moting its own adversary. This is a dangerous stance which leads
inevitably to a split between people and a division within the
individual.

The divided self

My Sad Captains (1961) takes the examination of this danger
further and consciously elaborates it in the first half of the book,
while in the second half the first suggestions of a different direction begin to emerge.

In the first part there are still poems on motorcycle gangs
('Black Jackets') and tough heroes ('The Byrnies'), but these are
somewhat forced compared with earlier ones. For instance, it is
hard to believe fully in the gang in 'Black Jackets' because the
description is superficial, slick and reaches too pat a conclusion:

> For on his shoulders they had put tattoos:
>   The group's name on the left, The Knights,
> And on the right the slogan Born to Lose.

There is no real exploration of the theme, and the treatment does
not take us further than did the earlier poems. They are shown
growing into their own tough image of themselves by wearing the
insignia of outsiders, surrounding themselves with raw 'pop'
music and their violent initiation rites. Thus they are 'Concocting
selves for their impervious kit'. Perhaps there is a faint suggestion
here of the price to be paid for this self-created courage, this
aggressive assertion of self hardened by will. For a much more
impressive presentation of the strengths and weaknesses of this
pose of the isolated individual creating his own morality by force
of will and self-discipline, we must turn to 'Claus von Stauffenberg' and 'Innocence'.

'Claus von Stauffenberg' concerns the Second World War
German army officer, a maimed veteran of many successful cam-
paigns who became a member of Hitler's staff and who was part

of an unsuccessful conspiracy to assassinate the Führer. He is thought to be the man who planted the bomb which, in fact, led to his own death and not the death of Hitler. The poem suggests that, although the act is a failure in terms of its own goal, it succeeds in another way; for the act and man lodge in our memories, in history itself, as an image of the courageous individual action of a man who kept firm hold of his sense of morality while those about him who were most powerful were systematically deranging humanistic values. The poem creates a sense of Nazi Germany in brief but effective images of the country's bleak, snow-covered landscape (the winter of the spirit). It is a place made a landscape of despair by Hitler's thug politics and the lack of real leadership. The landscape is described as divorced from its real history, unable to give meaning to its traditional symbols. Von Stauffenberg and his co-conspirators are the only people left with a sense of morality sufficient to deny Hitler, the few that still 'have the vigour to deny / Fear is a natural state'. Ironically, von Stauffenberg, though maimed in body, is described as pure in spirit, capable of the necessary unbent will '. . . who can calculate / On two remaining fingers and a will' and who sees the position of modern Germany in the perspective of history. He is predestined to take the role of a modern Brutus. Gunn makes him the symbol of the rational man who gains honour and redeems history in the act of destruction which, although it fails, nevertheless allows him to emerge as the very image of vigour and valour. The snow of this bare landscape that von Stauffenberg falls into is also the snow that freezes and preserves his body at the moment of redemptive courage.

It is an effective poem binding together modern Germany, the historical roots of morality and the would-be assassin and redeemer of his country through the metaphorical description of the snow-laden landscape at the beginning and end of the poem. It is written in a cool, spare language with a traditional four-line stanza in iambic rhythm and rhyming *abab*.

This form is shared with 'Innocence', a poem that explores the other, darker side of the self-disciplined will. Again the subject concerns Nazi Germany, this time describing how a young boy grows through his Nazi youth to become a soldier on the Russian front killing partisans.

In the opening verse the young boy growing into manhood is emphasized in terms of healthy and bodily vigour, gaining a valuable sense of his capacities but also locked into 'the egotism of a healthy body'. In this there is already a hint of a narrowness of vision in the emphasis on the necessary discipline required to help him grow into physical fitness. The second verse begins with the phrase 'Ran into manhood', continuing the image of youthful vitality and the movement of unreflective action. He has no anchor of traditional values of knowledge or culture; what he possesses is potential. This is described as being rich 'like the bud's tipped rage' which gives a sense of natural growth limited by anger and resentment (conveyed by the pun on 'rage', indicating both anger and rage for life). This captures the ambiguous characteristic of the Nazi youth with its stress on courage, strength and loyalty and its neglect of compassion, pity and truth. To the man without a historical perspective these virtues seem sufficient morality. The poem describes this limitation as a confusion of 'morale' with 'morality'. The end of this third stanza leads on to the next without a break through the word 'until' which teeters over the end of the line and looks forward to 'The finitude of virtues . . .', thus linking the strength of the soldier's morality with the limiting and damning comments of that next verse. What, at first sight, appears to be innocence turns out to be ignorance of other people's feelings. When this ignorance is dressed up in a uniform that confers on its wearer a narrowly defined purpose (in which all doubts and sensitivities are denied – like the ton-up boys 'strapping in doubt' in their leather jackets), it becomes dangerous arrogance. This is seen as the inevitable development of 'The egotism of a healthy body'. The suggestion that this is the fault as much of the age as of the individual is now made clear. The outcome is described in the last two stanzas with sickening clarity: the lack of imagination which prevents the young soldier from penetrating the sufferings of others allows him to stand by and watch the partisan burn to death. His blindness to feeling reveals itself in the only complaint he makes which is directed at the stench the burning body makes. This is innocence turned through lack of awareness into sin. The reader registers the reality of the horrible scene and is shocked all the more because what he has followed in the poem is the development of unawareness and he is now left to feel the horror that the youth is unable to feel.

We have in this poem a strong image of the warped self. It uses a ballad-like stanza but does not so much tell a narrative as describe a sequence of conditions which are both commented on and placed at the same time. It reveals the limitations that result from the development of self through action that has no regard for any goal. The innocence is turned into a dangerous egotism that reduces man to his physical self and, paradoxically, blinds him to the bodily suffering of another. We are left asking if this is the inevitable price of courage and if this is what the Boys of 'On the Move' must eventually come to?

In these two poems we see the two separate selves of the poet as portrayed in the early books. In *My Sad Captains* it is as if Gunn has arrived at the point where he is able to see both the strengths and weaknesses of this divided self but is as yet unable to heal the rift. That is why the book ends with the title poem which is a valediction to these early heroes. However, a more hopeful change is seen developing in the poems of the second half of the collection which immediately precede this valediction. These show the influence of Gunn's decision to live in California, several of them being about his life there. They also show a move towards looser rhythms and forms. Many are written not in traditional forms but in syllabics. These are composed of lines of equal numbers of syllables (usually six, seven or nine) and with a rhythm of two main stresses and two subsidiary stresses to each line, the stresses occurring in irregular sequences. It is a rhythm more American than English (it has been perfected by William Carlos Williams and Marianne Moore, although W. H. Auden has made good occasional use of it). Its freedom shadows the freer themes of the poems.

In the first half of the book is a poem called 'The Annihilation of Nothing'. Here the poet contemplates a universe in which matter has no purpose and can give no meaning to man. It ends by asserting a nihilistic position in which the individual must accept meaninglessness:

> Only an infinite finitude I see
> In those peculiar lovely variations.

It is despair that nothing cannot be
Flares in the mind and leaves a smoky mark
Of dread.

Look upward. Neither firm nor free,
Purposeless matter hovers in the dark.

The poem is entirely successful in realizing a completely abstract, philosophical concept (related to existentialist philosophy and particularly the ideas of Jean-Paul Sartre) and it is achieved in an abstract language which is yet translucent and resonant. This negative poem seems to demand the more positive rejoinder of the poems of the second half of the book which tentatively explore a different kind of relationship to the matter of inanimate nature.

These poems are frequently about the Californian landscape with its eucalyptus and giant redwood firs and, especially, the peculiar clarity of light which typifies California. There seems here to be the beginning of an openness towards a new sense of delight and awe in the presence of nature which has not previously appeared in the poetry of someone who earlier celebrated city scenes because they are 'extreme, material and the work of man' ('In Praise of Cities'). For instance, in 'Waking in a Newly Built House':

It wakes me, and my eyes rest on it,
sharpening, and seeking merely all
of what can be seen, the substantial,
where the things themselves are adequate.

So I observe them, able to see
them as they are, the neutral sections
of trunk, spare, solid, lacking at once
disconnectedness and unity.

Or, as the poet flies over California, he becomes conscious of 'a cold hard light without break / that reveals merely what is – no more / and no less'. This is a light which appears to be all the more revealing of nature as it is (as opposed to what we wish it to be) precisely because it is a light that gives a candid recognition of limits, 'that accuracy of the beaches' seen below, which is an integral part 'of the ultimate richness'.

Again in 'Lights Among Redwood' it is the light 'in quick
diffusing patterns' that attracts the poet to look upwards towards
the tops of these huge trees and in so doing stand

> and stare – mindless, diminished –
> at their rosy immanence.

We have here in the simplest terms a sense of the immediate
presence of nature. This is a quiet poem that does not force itself
on the reader and yet which convincingly points out the tone,
shade and light of these Californian natural wonders. In that brief
suggestion of the loss of self in this experience, we begin to sense
Gunn's moving away from the old attitudes, from the egotism of
those whose only answer to living in a meaningless universe is to
'renew the wasteful force they / spent with each hot convulsion'
('My Sad Captains').

In 'My Sad Captains' Gunn takes leave of his tough-guy pose.
Whatever meaning he once found in it he now recognizes as
significant only for the individual who experiences it – it contains
no power to relate that individual either to nature or to others.
The old heroes are stars that 'turn with disinterested / hard
energy', shining with a light which, however brightly it appears
in the firmament, cannot cast any real illumination across the
dark universe.

Touching

It is in the 1967 volume that, as the title *Touch* suggests, we see the
poet exploring how contact can be made with nature and with
other people. The centre of the book is the long poem sequence
'Misanthropos', arguably one of Gunn's most effective poems. In
it he imagines a solitary man in a bare landscape, apparently the
sole survivor of a holocaust. In some poems he is described from
outside by an observer–narrator, in others he speaks with his own
voice. We accompany him through the landscape as he learns to
move in it and survive by becoming part of the natural world; we
follow his thoughts as he remembers his previous social life, and
we watch him as he makes his first, surprised contact with other
survivors. It is a poem of varying forms and stanza structures, as
well as changing rhythms. It is composed of seventeen individual

poems which are grouped into three parts: 'The last man', 'Memoirs of the world' and 'The first man'.

In the beginning the protagonist has 'the entire world to choose from' because, he believes, no other human beings remain. His sense of exploration and dominance over nature that was a part of his previous social personality are gradually stripped from him and his assertive character is submerged in his desire and ability to merge into nature. As part of the landscape, dependent upon it for his life like the birds and animals, he becomes 'self-contained' and learning

> . . . like them to keep movement
> on the undipped wing of the present.

This cannot entirely prevent him remembering the holocaust at first and this in its turn prevents the purification of the hatred and anger which still runs in his veins. But eventually he becomes no more than a cipher of physical life,

> . . . clothed in dirt. He lacks motive.
> He is wholly representative.

In the second poem a clever use of rhyme beautifully mimics the echo of the man, and it is the echo which gives the man a spurious feeling of contact with the outside world. He moves in a false dialogue from the positive

> . . . are you near,
> Man whom I cannot see but can hear?
> > Here

to the stripped self of

> What have I left, who stood among mankind,
> When the firm base is undermined?
> > A mind.

and finally, to the negative

> Is there no feeling, then, that I can trust,
> In spite of what we have discussed?
> > Disgust.

The essence he is stripped to is hardly yet perfection.

It becomes clear in the third poem that the isolated man must drop all his poses, 'Now that, alone, / He cannot seek himself as messenger', and wearing the skin of animals he comes to realize that now his only uniform is poverty (spiritual as well as material), thus leaving him with but a single task: the pursuit of his real self. He is no longer in the regard of others and yet there remains a deep need to know himself. He is a messenger running after some news of his self:

> A courier after identity, and sees
> A pattern grow among the disarray.

In the following poem he reflects that 'the ancient rhythms' of the natural world almost comfort him. Yet there still remains a lack because he cannot escape his consciousness which prevents him from ever completely merging into nature. His consciousness is indissolubly linked to life itself ('linked catastrophes' he calls them). The possibility of escape from the pain of awareness by committing suicide is set aside for 'He must use / The heaviness, the flaw, he always bore'. Consciousness may seem his disaster now for it detaches him from his experiences, and yet it is also the only instrument by which he may conduct his search for the meaning which lies in that experience. He is trapped into being human.

He begins the search by recalling his life before the holocaust. He realizes now that it was a life not fully lived but instead a kind of enormous procrastination in which he always avoided the present. Now the calls of the birds around him seem to mock him with this realization: 'Not now, not now,' they seem to call. Living among others he wore a variety of disguises including the masks that Gunn has written of in earlier poems (those roles of suspicion and distrust – the spy, the spied-on, master and servant):

> I was presence without full
> being; but from the corner,
> in the mere fact of movement,
> was I entering the role
> of spy or spied on, master
> or the world's abject servant?

His past cannot give him the identity he seeks. Only a memory of someone else can begin to stand for what he seeks, an authentic existence. It is the memory of one man, Anton Schmidt, a German who during the war risked his life to help Jews escape the Nazis. This man 'who burnt from sympathy alone' was perfectly free, free and yet with a sense of movement as direction – a goal of genuine sympathy for others. He is an image of man as most himself when involved with others.

This poem is followed by the section 'The first man' in which this survivor comes so close to his environment that he is no longer modern man but more like the primitive link between apes and *homo sapiens*. This is the man who is rudimentary, 'An unreflecting organ of perception', pure instinctual response that bypasses thought. This is perfectly realized in lines 15–23 of poem XIII. It is while he is in this state that he is amazed to observe forty men and women walking in twos and threes up the hill towards him. As he watches from his concealed position he sees the last man stumble, fall behind and lean against a rock. The observer notices the man is wounded. At first he is unmoved, merely watching until suddenly

> . . . he performs an action next
> So unconsidered that he is perplexed,
> Even in performing it, by what it means –

He steps forward, at first frightening the other man into falling, but he helps him to his feet again. For a moment he too has burnt from sympathy. He who has become unreflecting, whose consciousness has become perception only and who is thus linked intimately to his environment, is at last able to move outwards to bestow the touch of humanity on another. It is an act of feeling rather than will and, despite the evident nausea he feels from the repugnant smell of a strange man after all this time alone, he persists in making his act of recognition.

In the final poem of the sequence the touch reminds and binds them in their two moralities. The poem leaves us with the two looking at each other and meeting in that look which is a recognition of shared life and death in which the mortality is made bearable by the sharing.

> The touched arm feels of dust, mixing with dust
>   On the hand that touches it.
>
> Turn out towards others, meeting their look at full,
>   Until you have completely stared
> On all there is to see. Immeasurable,
>   The dust yet to be shared.

This is a fine poem, full of variety but with strict control of the developing theme which traces a whole movement of possible thought and describes the incredibly difficult leap from 'the imprisoned self' (as Martin Dodsworth describes it[4]) through the mysterious and irrational, to the touch of human sympathy.

This book as a whole celebrates a growing awareness of the need for this touch and the spontaneity that can offer it. In other poems, such as 'Back to Life' or the title poem, we observe the tentative recognitions of the significance of human contact that

> . . . seeps
> from our touch in
> continuous creation, dark
> enclosing cocoon round
> ourselves alone, dark
> wide realm where we
> walk with everyone.

>   ('Touch')

In 'Back to Life', the last poem of the book, we discover an ending with this same realization: that there is no way in which man can completely merge with others – he is condemned to remain solitary – and yet this very recognition shared by all is the only redeeming possibility for communication. In the poems of this volume we see the protagonist experiencing his sense of touch, not just physically but also in the sense of 'getting in touch' with others, sympathizing with and understanding someone beyond ourself. Although the sense of the other is vague and shadowy in many of the poems, it does nevertheless provide the first experience at the feeling level of the protagonist's responses in his fumbling search for genuine communication.

Widening sympathies

Moly (1971) is the collection in which Gunn wrote of his experiences with the drug LSD. Moly is the ancient name for a hal-
lucinogenic drug, referred to in the *Odyssey* where it is given to
Ulysses as the antidote to restore his sailors to human shape after
Circe had transformed them into pigs. This legend is recalled in
the preface. In an interview[5] Gunn remarked that his poems are
explorations of meaning for him and that anything important in
his life will eventually find its way into a poem. This is true of his
first 'acid trips' taken at the age of thirty-five and of which he has
said, 'LSD shakes complacencies, it opens doors on other worlds.
I learnt about my own nature that I had concealed from myself.'[6]

In their form these poems return to carefully developed structures and frequently employ traditional metre and rhyme
schemes. This reflects Gunn's feeling that careful ordering is
necessary to balance the content: 'A trip is a loose structured
experience and this is a way, perhaps, of filtering it through the
finite and of keeping control over the material.'[7] Clearly the book
suggests that a new freedom – even revelation – has been obtained
through the drug, but it is not advocating its wholesale use.
LSD/Moly signifies the need for an openness to experience and
the need to articulate a new vision.

The nature of this vision can begin to be seen when we realize
that many of the poems are concerned with transformation (many
poems in Gunn's books describe changes in a person). Some of the
central poems are to do with half-men, half-beast creatures
('Moly' and 'Tom-Dobbin'), and others concern the transformation of vision ('The Colour-Machine', 'Three').

In the title poem we find a poetic counterpart to the preface's
quotation from the *Odyssey*. It describes the sailors changed into
swine, 'a nightmare of beasthood', and it is seen through the eyes
of a single character who is one of the sailor-animals. He wakes
from the drugged sleep under the spell of Circe to find himself an
animal, although at first he cannot tell of what kind. From his
skin, his tough hide, his hoofed feet and his great, grey ears, he
realizes he has been turned into a pig. The only remaining connection with his human personality and appearance is his long
eyelashes:

I am the snouted creature
That bites through anything, root, wire, or can.
If I was not afraid I'd eat a man.

But a man's flesh is in him and the mingling of the two is clearly stated. The reader is surprised by the following couplet which shows man-swine greedy to search out the root of the plant that brings changes that 'are all holy'. The acceptance of man's swinishness and animality is what makes possible that search, and the ending implies that the beast in man needs the drug to hold him within (not to overcome it but to give man's animal self its rightful place):

I push my big grey wet snout through the green
Dreaming the flower I have never seen.

There is an ambiguity here which suggests either that the magic root has yet to be discovered and therefore that which is a vision has yet to become a reality, or that the drug is required to produce that vision. The light, brisk couplet suggests a lucidity that is not so easily discovered in the meaning.

In the 'Tom-Dobbin' sequence the man-beast creature is used to symbolize a sense of the old division between animal instincts and the conscious, deliberating self of the mind. The mind is that part of the self that looks on uninvolved as the other part indulges in the sexual act. The two are joined briefly only at the moment of ejaculation. The third poem in the sequence suggests that it is only in that orgy when the senses overwhelm the reflective self that the world can be related to as part of the self. The poem as a whole is summarized by the final poem of the sequence, a single six-line stanza in which Tom-Dobbin is in a state of being which does not know which sense of identity belongs to which half ('which is me, which him'). Joined in the one body the only unity *is* that body, 'Selves floating in the one flesh we are of'.

In 'The Colour-Machine' we are actually present at an LSD trip and experience it from within. We are made to feel the difficulty with which the poem's speaker, under the influence of the drug, still has to wrestle with himself to continue to reach out to someone else, especially as he remembers the experience of a friend who so gave himself to a trip that he never returned to reality. The speaker wants to give himself completely to the experience, wondering if, in doing that, 'the moment of giving [might make] the fact of ... disintegration something of negligible importance.' He hangs back, lacking the courage and impulsiveness to throw himself wholeheartedly into the experience and, although this ensures his sanity, he cannot help but speculate as to whether he might not have also sacrificed some ultimate richness of meaning that is to be found only in the complete surrender of self.

The final poems of the book are about the attempt to merge with surroundings in a meaningful unity through the effect of the drug. 'The Garden of the Gods' creates a mythic sense of divinity, a magical nature which is a rich profusion of delights and the source of fecundity in man. It is a beautiful description of an Eden-like garden in which 'It was sufficient, there, to be', an existence in which meaning-as-explanation was superseded by meaning-as-simply-experience. The conscious mind becomes perception within a fully living body.

> This was the garden's place of birth:
> And rooted in the death-rich earth.

An equally effective poem, but one impossible to do justice to in paraphrase or commentary, is 'Sunlight'. This last poem in the volume enacts a sense of unity of desire and knowledge, expressed in the common sight of sunlight flashing upon rails, but which is turned into an extraordinary transcendental illumination of the sun as the

> Great seedbed, yellow centre of the flower,
> Flower on its own, without a root or stem,
> Giving all colour and all shape their power,
> Still recreating in defining them,

and ends with the wish for it to

> Enable us, altering like you, to enter
> Your passionless love, impartial but intense,
> And kindle in acceptance round your centre,
> Petals of light lost in your innocence.

Where *Touch* used the sense of feeling as a central trope, this book employs light and the sense of sight as its central motif to reveal a moving out towards the natural world.

In *Jack Straw's Castle* (1976), Gunn continues the theme of the previous book in poems written after the LSD experience which, benefiting from the liberation which that experience wrought, attempt to translate it into the events of ordinary reality. There are poems suggesting how life may be lived with an intimate sense of relation to our world, but they are realistic in measuring the possibility of failure to do this and the consequences flowing from it. The kind of success that can be achieved, and the recognition of the inner self's properties which must be given their full weight if that success is to be gained, are dealt with in the two long poems on which the book is centred.

'Geysers' adopts an irregular, fragmented line which represents the *experience* of the subject matter, rather than commenting on it from outside. The subject is an account of camping out in the hills above a group of warm water geysers in Sonoma County, California. As the campers move among one another, they go down to join strangers in a primitive communal bathhouse, taking part in what becomes a drugged, bisexual orgy. In this experience their conscious wills are subordinated to their feelings and desires. The latter part of the poem describes the break-up of the poet's individual self through a loose-limbed form of broken, trailing line that mirrors the breaking up and reshaping of consciousness. It ends with the sense of becoming

> torn from the self
> > in which I breathed and trod
> I am
> > I am raw meat
> > > I am a god

There is a merging of divinity with the body, and the poem fuses the drug and the natural commingling of the campers into a kind of sacred and profane love machine. In this poem the divided self which has formed the staple image of so much of Gunn's poetry, even when the attempt to touch was made, becomes at last a unity. The experience that is evoked is impossible to describe and can only be *felt* as read. It is possible that the weight and effect of the

poem as Gunn might wish a reader to experience it can be brought
out only for someone who has been prepared by reading all the
previous poems. But it remains the one poem of his that has come
closest, not to describing, but to *enacting* the desired experience.
In many ways it is the freest of all his poems.

In the title poem of the volume Gunn uses looser forms again,
although they are not as free as in 'Geysers'. He takes up the
children's rhyme and employs it to symbolize the poet's mind (his
conscious, subconscious and unconscious selves) in describing the
rooms of the house/castle in which he lives. Much of the poem is
concerned with a nightmare that turns the rooms into hellish
horrors with images of the demonic murderer Charles Manson
bobbing up wherever the poet looks. In these horrors, drawn from
real life, Gunn seems to be suggesting a recognition of feelings,
desires and responses that he possesses deep down in his normally
buried self which, when brought to the surface, reveal us all as
implicated to some degree in the pain and suffering that a man like
Manson creates. Perhaps it is not far-fetched to regard the Manson figure as related to some of the self-willed tough-guys of the
early poems, and to consider that in this poem Gunn recognizes
and controls them. The control is far from easy, being formed
rather by faith than by the will. It is a new faith in others which
cannot exist without the realization that

I am the man on the rack.
I am the man who puts the man on the rack.
I am the man who watches the man who puts the man on the
rack.

This multiple awareness appeared in Gunn's early work, as early
as 'Carnal Knowledge', but here the knowingness is fleshed out
and there is a complete admission that the man who suffers, the
man who creates the suffering and the man who permits it to go
on are one and the same. In the final part the speaker wakes from
the nightmare to reality and sits in the house while a storm rages
outside. He experiences difficulty in feeling this castle as his home
any more. He is no longer snug inside his self and he has a moment
of panic: 'I'm loose, I rattle in its hollow core.' He hopes the
nightmare has ended but continues to give it its due (as the
dungeon room of the unconscious):

> I hope I'm through with that. I flick the light.
> And though the dungeon will be there for good
> (What laid those stones?) at least I found I could,
> Throw down, escape by learning what to learn;
> And hold it that held me.
> 　　　　　　　　　Till I return.

The rhyme which returns at this point after a long absence becomes more insistent than before and underscores the renewed balance and control. But the form does not allow us to forget the possibility of the nightmare returning. The positive assurance of 'And hold it that held me' drops momentarily as the line and voice themselves drop to the last three words.

Not action but self-knowledge has provided the strength to control the worst manifestations of the self in this poem. In so doing he redeems the isolated self and claims an identity for him which is no longer the body detached from action and feeling. In the last lines the protagonist goes to bed where he finds himself experiencing the feel of sharing his bed with another. They lie back to back, just touching, and he dare not turn round to check if his companion is real. He cannot be sure that he is not still dreaming. In the brilliant metaphor of the hinge, Gunn creates a sense of connection between the two that is firm and yet does not deny their separate movement:

> And that mere contact is sufficient touch,
> A hinge, it separates but not too much.

Touch and separateness; contact but not the loss of individuality – this is a long way towards the goal of the quest established at the outset of Gunn's writing. The essential capacity to achieve this has come, as 'Jack Straw's Castle' indicates, from the realization at last that

> The beauty's in what is, not what may seem.
> I turn. And even if he were a dream
> – Thick sweating flesh against which I lie curled –
> With dreams like this, Jack's ready for the world.

The quest has shown Gunn moving from the hardened separate self who took his stance from his opposition to the world in the early books, through the releasing visions of unity induced by his LSD experiences, to the point in this last book where he can accept his solitariness and define his identity in relation to others by faith instead of seizing and controlling by the will. Self and reality become related.

'Jack Straw's Castle' ends on a positive note, like many others in this collection. It is an acceptance that our sense of identity is given significance precisely through the existence of others and that by trusting in their reality and their goodness we may achieve our own power of touch. In this book a new freedom has been acquired. The divided self may not be entirely healed, but at least that part of the self which is conscious, detached and willed is finally able to merge with experience and become 'as if' something beyond its own boundaries. A striking example of this is the poem 'Yoko' – a *tour de force* in which Gunn writes as if he was a dog speaking of his love for his master and his joy-in-the-world that he experiences when out walking with his master. It is virtually the only complete poem of Gunn's entire output in which he writes as if from inside the skin of a subject totally different from himself. The nearest poem to it is 'Considering the Snail' but there the snail is commented on, not just re-created. In 'Yoko' the poet *is* the dog. It is not a pose or a disguise, but rather a true creation of another world that is felt, not willed.

In two other poems we see Gunn leaning out of himself, as it were, keen to grasp experience and not just comment on it. In 'Thomas Bewick' he writes of a new kind of hero, far removed from the earlier ones. This quiet man who wrote the superb *The History of British Birds* is praised for his capacity to emerge from his conscious self and achieve knowledge by identifying with the birds he studies, '. . . not yet / separate from what it sees'. And in 'Breaking Ground' Gunn writes about his mother's death. At first horrified by the realization that all her characteristics of gesture, word and act which made her so dear are now utterly lost, he goes on to remember her before her death. He imagines her in her garden as he listens to a singer at a concert on the other side of the Atlantic and suddenly realizes that his mother is not lost but is dispersed among the listening crowd, some of whom have her touch, some her eyes, some her voice. The individual is preserved in the merging of all and the poem ends with a beautiful quotation:

Shee
is gone, Shee is lost,
Shee is found, shee
is ever faire.

Gunn's poetry is the account of an existential quest, a pursuit of a sense of personal identity and meaning in a world where the traditional supports for life's meaning are being questioned. It is a quest that may not yet be finished: a resolution that so far has been perhaps more often stated than enacted would imply this. Nevertheless it is a quest which in its manner of proceeding has produced some fine poems that articulate the genuine response of a late twentieth-century man to the possibility of identity. Slowly he has moved towards a position where he is beginning to be able to convert those forces ranged against the individual, even death, into something positive. Taken as a whole the poems of Thom Gunn repudiate the criticism of someone like Alan Brownjohn who has said that Gunn idealizes 'the brutal, the irrational and the wilful'. In so far as some early poems may appear to do this, these may be regarded as the few failures of Gunn's work. But if the poems are taken together, in support of one another, the reader can discern a deliberate moving away from the early fantasies and false poses towards a more hopeful, more realistic acceptance of self and the world in which the whole is always greater than its parts.

4

Elemental energy

The poetry of Ted Hughes

Since the publication of his first volume of poetry, *The Hawk in the Rain* (1957), Ted Hughes has had many admirers. Today he is often spoken of as one of our best poets, frequently regarded along with Philip Larkin as representative of that poetry of the last two decades which is considered most likely to endure. However, it is not always the same readers who admire the work of each of these poets, for they have distinctly different voices, attitudes and powers.

As we saw in Chapter 1, Philip Larkin first became well known as a poet when The Movement poets were at the height of their reputation, and when the taste in poetry seemed to be for strongly formal, quietly detached and ironic verse. From the outset of his career Ted Hughes set his face against this kind of poetry and pursued his own, highly independent way. The nature of this independence can begin to be appreciated by briefly contrasting his work with that of Philip Larkin.

They differ most markedly in their choice of subject matter, in their handling of forms and styles, in their characteristic tones and in their attitude to the role of the poet. Larkin's subjects include incidents, moods and moments of everyday life particularly in the hopes, fears and disappointments of contemporary suburban man. His themes focus on time, memory and the prospect of a future that can lead only to old age and death. He is concerned with the various ways in which man picks up 'bad habits of expectancy', and with the shadow that falls between desire and reality, and he often expresses images of the restorative power of certain traditional social rituals. Hughes, on the other hand, writes frequently of animal life, of nature and the elemental forces of non-human life and the inner turbulence of modern man who is seen as cut off from the instinctual sources of his power. His themes express the powerful, often violent energies of nature as well as the relationship between these energies and the divided nature of modern man. Larkin usually writes in traditional forms, prefers a relatively colloquial idiom and works frequently with formal rhythm and rhyme patterns. Hughes has written poems that share these characteristics but more commonly he makes use of freer forms, relies less on strict metrical rhythms and rhyme schemes and is more inclined towards a hyperbole of diction and image. The two poets differ most sharply in their characteristic tones of voice. Larkin has the scepticism and deflating irony of a humane, rational and rather conservative observer of human affairs who refuses to be under any illusions about the life of the society around him or his relationship with that society. Hughes, in contrast, runs the risk of appearing to speak almost in an arrogant tone at times when he struggles to express the intense energy and physical presence that his subjects create, and he rejects the note of the coolly detached observer, preferring instead to express the life of these subjects (whether human or non-human) as if from within. He makes frequent use of imagery and symbols to create a sense of living power which, even at his most nihilistic, produces a tone of urgency and command that would be alien to Larkin's more cautious, less excitable voice. This reflects a further distinction between these two in the way they view the role of the poet. Larkin regards poetry as an attempt to preserve what he has seen, thought and felt. His muse is memory; his imagination is kept strictly under control by his rationality and keenly deflating irony. Hughes works within the tradition of the poet as inspired visionary or shaman (a poet whose function is to employ language to conjure up the gods that control our being). His imagination reaches out and into his subjects to re-create their presence from within and his rational intellect is kept subservient to the supra-rational powers of image, symbol and myth.

These differences serve to emphasize the contrasting perspectives of the two poets' work. They also explain why, even when both are admired by many readers, there is frequent disagreement over the value of their achievements. In this chapter an attempt will be made to explain the developing ideas of Hughes's poetry in relation to his major collections of poems.

Hughes has so far published eight major collections (as well as several limited editions published by small presses) in just over two decades. He has also written poetry and prose for children, plays for radio and stage, short stories, and some very fine critical essays. In *Poetry in the Making* (1967) he has also published one of the most exciting and useful accounts of poetry for younger readers. This is a very full range of work and represents a great variety of forms and intentions. Within the eight major volumes of poetry there is also a great variety of subject and treatment. This is a fact sometimes overlooked by readers unduly influenced by the label of 'animal poet' or 'nature poet' that was attached to Hughes in the early sixties. Too great an attention to this early aspect of his poetry has led to misunderstanding and even dislike of Hughes's later work.

In *The Hawk in the Rain* and *Lupercal* it is certainly the poems about animals and nature that make the greatest impact. His creation of hawks, jaguars, pikes and thrushes are vivid, vibrantly energetic exercises in taking the reader into the very feelings and actions of the animals, and these poems must rank as the best of their kind since *Birds, Beasts and Flowers* by D. H. Lawrence (with whom Hughes shares some preoccupations). But Hughes's total output encompasses far more subjects than animals and far more moods, feelings and ideas than are contained in these intense, strenuously active descriptions. He is also capable of writing with tenderness, or with quiet, lyrical grace, or with a sense of play and humour. However, it is true that the dominating impression that his poems leave with a reader is a sense of the vigour and frequently violent energies of both the non-human world and the inner world of man's own emotions.

In fact it is not his especial concern for animals that seems to have drawn Hughes to write about them so frequently in his poetry. It is rather that he sees in them the most clear manifestation of a life-force that is distinctly non-human or, rather, is non-rational in its source of power. Hughes observes in modern man a reluctance to acknowledge the deepest, instinctual sources of energy in his own being, an energy that is related to the 'elemental power circuit' of the universe and to which animals are closer than man. Hughes's concern, therefore, has always been wider than the simplistic labelling of him as 'animal poet' implies. It is true that he began in the first two books by exploring the primal energies of the animal and natural world that stressed the absolute otherness of that world. Since then he has moved on to express a sense of sterility and nihilism in modern man's response to life, a response which he connects with the dominance of man's rational, objective intellect at the expense of the life of the emotions and imagination. In *Crow* he created a mythical story to express this nihilistic universe and to show that beneath the feelings of complete despair there was still an active voice of unyielding energy and survival – the voice of the Crow. In *Gaudete*, he has gone on to explore in symbolic terms the divided nature of modern man's soul and the need to reconcile the inner and outer lives of man if his sense of pain and evil is not to become self-destructive.

The argument of the following exploration of Hughes's poetry is that it is possible to perceive a developing task in his work. Briefly, that task is to explore and express what he has called 'the war between vitality and death'.[1] It is a war he sees most clearly waged in the natural world where no consciousness of self intervenes to manipulate an animal's response to his condition. Man, as a result of the power of his consciousness (his intellect and imagination), is able to stand back from the situation that confronts him and not just respond instinctually. His capacity to do so is both a strength and a weakness. Hughes seems to be suggesting that in modern man it has become a serious weakness because he has allowed too large a gap to develop between his consciousness and his instinctual reaction to his condition. He has cultivated his rational, cognitive powers too exclusively, neglecting his inner world of feelings, imagination and instinct, and has therefore divided his own nature, cutting himself off from the natural energies of the universe. In 'Myth and Education',[2] a key essay for an understanding of his attitudes, he writes of the way in which modern man has narrowed his vision until he is looking only at the outer world. He regards this as a consequence of the rise of the scientific ideal of objective intelligence but sees our too exclusive concern with such intelligence as producing a rigid and suicidal stupidity.

It is a scientific ideal. And it is a powerful ideal, it has created the modern world. And without it, the modern world would fall to pieces: infinite misery would result. The disaster is, that it is heading straight towards infinite misery, because it has persuaded human beings to identify themselves with what is no more than a narrow mode of perception. . . .

Scientific objectivity . . . has its own morality, which has nothing to do with human morality. . . . And this is the prevailing morality of our time. It is a morality utterly devoid of any awareness of the requirements of the inner world. It is contemptuous of the 'human element'.

This inner world of our bodies, of our 'archaic energies of instinct and feeling', is rapidly being lost to us. The traditional means of embracing and humanizing these energies was religion. Without religion these powers have become dehumanized and our inner life 'a place of demons'. Cut off from those powers, 'All we register is the vast absence, the emptiness, the sterility, the meaninglessness, the loneliness.' Having depicted this situation, Hughes has gone on to seek a means of reconciliation with those inner powers. The traditional means of such a reconciliation has been the use of the imagination, which has been called 'creative' and 'divine' because it has the power to help us negotiate between the inner and outer worlds. The traditional language of this negotiation has been religion, myth and symbol. In his later poetry, Hughes seems to be making increasing use of myth and symbol to explore man's divided nature and to express some kind of resolution. This is not to suggest that he is moving towards some religious stance (in the Christian sense). It appears he looks back beyond Christian sources towards myths which have their beginnings in the experience of seasonal and natural cycles, and which express an almost fatalistic acceptance of suffering while celebrating the sheer power and energy of the life process itself. The tool to re-create an understanding of these sources is the imagination and the artist is its guardian. The artist and his work are thus the key to the resolution of these conflicts:

The character of great works is exactly this: that in them the full presence of the inner world combines with and is reconciled to the full presence of the outer world. And in them we see that the laws of these two worlds are not contradictory at all; they are one all-inclusive system. . . . They are the laws, simply, of human nature.[3]

The question is not how far these ideas of Hughes may be true – at least not at this stage – but, rather, how his poetry reflects them and what kinds of artistic success the poet achieves in following his task. If this is the task that Hughes has undertaken, it is a difficult one for an artist living in a civilization that prefers to think no longer in terms of myth – that appears, indeed, even to pride itself on its demythologizing fervour. The immensity of the task and the belief in the artist as a last guardian of essential truths can lead to a poetry with an aim that may sometimes elude its grasp, and may, in fact, lead to the inconsistencies of voice and tone that some critics point to in the poetry. Hughes himself has spoken of writing from 'three separate characteristic states of mind, which are fairly different',[4] and these states of mind may reflect different possibilities of expression as well as different experiences. The voice of nihilism in many *Crow* poems, the voice of confused search in 'Wodwo' and the voice of divided man in *Gaudete* are only some of the voices of a poet who seeks to express our modern sense of ourselves as varied and contradictory.

'Things present': the physicality of the early poetry

The Hawk in the Rain (1957) and *Lupercal* (1960) share sufficiently similar concerns to make it worthwhile to consider them together. Both are particularly powerful in expressing the physical presence of the animal world, the relationship of man to nature and Hughes's sense of the reality of natural energies. This theme may be seen in the opening poem of the first book, from which the volume takes its title. 'Hawk Roosting' from *Lupercal* has a similar subject and offers a useful comparison with the first poem.

'The Hawk in the Rain' opens with an assured, rather assertive description of the poet crossing a ploughed field in the rain.

I drown in the drumming ploughland, I drag up
Heel after heel from the swallowing of the earth's mouth,
From clay that clutches my each step to the ankle
With the habit of the dogged grave. . . .

The conflict between vitality and death is announced in the first line. The earth is an active, cruel force and the man's strength is painfully tested. The image of drowning in the rain and the image of the earth as a beast that swallows its human victims combine to represent nature as a violent and active enemy. The earth is an open grave that 'dogs' our life, following us at every step. There is a suggestion that this is not just a walk across a field but a lifelong condition. The obtrusive alliteration and the heavy stress taken by the participles and verbs (the words describing movement) together create a vigorous conflict between man and the elements. Yet no sooner is this established than the stanza moves on to the contrasting situation of the hawk. We are prepared for the contrast by the pause and 'but', and left at the end of the stanza with a keen expectancy, resulting from the way the description of the hawk hangs over the line and stanza break and then falls strongly on the key word 'effortlessly':

> . . . but the hawk
> Effortlessly at height hangs his still eye.

The unusual word order insists that the line be read slowly, giving each word careful enunciation to prevent them running into one another, and this serves to emphasize further the hawk's mastery of the air and his cool, superior calm. The bird is above the struggle that the man is engaged in; he is detached and seemingly weightless in his riding of the air. Man's desperate and uncertain struggle for life against forces of nature looks limited, pitiful and doomed against the hawk's masterful composure. In that first stanza we experience the weight and bodily limitations of the man which contrasts dramatically with the 'weightless quiet' of the hawk, his steady balance on the wind and his commanding view embracing 'all creation'. The hawk's freedom from the struggle with the elements becomes a matter of admiration to the man and provides him with a sense of something to emulate. He sees the hawk's achievement as 'the diamond point of will', a willpower which pivots on 'the master- / Fulcrum of violence where the hawk hangs still.' This still centre is at the heart of the warring forces of nature and will.

But even the hawk's mastery cannot last for ever. In the final stanza he meets the weather 'Coming the wrong way' and is hurled to the ground, his blood finally mixing with the same 'mire of the land' which claims the man in the opening lines. The bird's mastery of the destructive forces is an illusion, the realization of which casts light back on the reference in the second stanza to the hawk being 'Steady as a hallucination in the streaming air.' The difference between hawk and man is not that the hawk can escape eventual destruction but that it can accommodate itself to those forces that threaten its survival. It is a creature of instinct whose will is in accord with nature and not pitted against it. The importance of the phrase 'suffers the air' in the last stanza is that it describes the hawk's relationship with nature. 'Suffer' is used both in the sense of undergoing the pain of death and in the sense of permitting it to happen. The hawk is a part of the elements in a way that man cannot be.

The companion poem, 'Hawk Roosting' from *Lupercal*, reveals an extension and maturing of Hughes's handling of language, tone and theme. This poem also uses the hawk to comment on an aspect of man's nature but accomplishes it by more subtle means. It relies more on statement than on metaphor to present its theme, and the alliteration and sounds of words are kept under control so that they do not become obtrusive.

This time the bird is not described from the outside. It is not its behaviour that is observed. We are plunged into the hawk's head, and it is its state of mind that is imagined and re-created. It is this state of mind which gives the poem its forceful, confident, even arrogant tone. This poem also emphasizes the strength and power of the bird but does so with a greater insistence on the isolation of the bird and on its brutish strength which has no room for feelings of compassion. The hawk sees himself as the apotheosis of power:

> It took the whole of Creation
> To produce my foot, my each feather:
> Now I hold Creation in my foot.

Unlike man, the hawk has 'no sophistry in my body', he has no doubts, no delicate and weakening scruples that prevent him from accomplishing his will, his nature. 'My manners are tearing off heads / The allotment of death.' In the final lines the hawk refuses to countenance any change. He makes himself the arbiter of his world:

> Nothing has changed since I began.
> My eye has permitted no change.
> I am going to keep things like this.

There is an unmistakable tone of menace in these short, sharp statements.

This menace lies in the hawk's assumption of godlike powers and his utterly amoral, inhuman attitude. According to the poet, 'what I had in mind was that in this hawk Nature is thinking'.[5] It is a nature that has nothing to do with morality, compassion or justice.

When it was first published this poem led some readers to charge Hughes with deliberately taking pleasure from, even extolling, violence. He is doing nothing of the sort; there is no admiration involved. The poem simply describes an amoral nature and imagines the awful power of non-human life, contrasting it with the limitations of the power of human nature.

It is clear from these two examples that the animal poems in these volumes are not mere descriptions of creatures but are intended as comments on aspects of human life, particularly in man's relationship with nature. Nevertheless, Hughes's ability to re-create the physical presence of the natural world is one of the first qualities that the reader responds to in these volumes.

Hughes can capture the essence of an animal's appearance and behaviour in a simple simile, as in this description of parrots in a zoo:

> The parrots shriek as if they were on fire, or strut
> Like cheap tarts to attract the stroller with the nut.
>
> ('The Jaguar')

His power to reveal the very consciousness of an animal is expressed in these lines from the same poem which describe the concentrated vigour in the jaguar's stare and the suppressed rage in his pacing:

> . . . a jaguar hurrying enraged
> Through prison darkness after the drills of his eyes

On a short fierce fuse. Not in boredom –
The eye satisfied to be blind in fire,
By the bang of blood in the brain deaf the ear –
He spins from the bars, but there's no cage to him

More than to the visionary his cell. . .

The intense stare of the second line is carried through to the image
of the visionary's prophesying of new freedoms in the last line.
The active, energetic verbs ('hurrying', 'spins', etc.) combine with
the use of contrasts of light/dark, action/containment, and the use
of rhythm and alliteration to register the sensation of a throbbing
pulse, and together they express the barely suppressed rage of the
jaguar.

'The Thought-Fox' is a poem about the mind's creation of an
imaginary fox which is also used to symbolize the creative faculty
of the artist. Here, too, the presence of the animal with its 'sudden
sharp hot stink of fox' is captured lightly and yet perfectly,
even down to the adroit mimicry of a fox's cautious movements:

Cold, delicately as the dark snow,
A fox's nose touches twig, leaf;
Two eyes serve a movement, that now
And again now, and now, and now

Sets neat prints into the snow
Between trees. . . .

Reading these lines aloud reveals the effect of the punctuation. It
enforces a sequence of pauses which, in combination with the
subtly varying degrees of stress (for example, in the fourth line of
the quotation), create a nervous, hesitant movement in the lines
which is a verbal counterpart of the careful movements of an
actual fox.

In 'The Bull Moses' an old prize bull is described as 'In the
locked black of his powers', a phrase immediately suggesting the
bull's hidden, dangerous force. In the last line of 'View of a Pig'
Hughes captures in one startling simile the whole meaning of the
poem, the shocking contrast between the once squealing, running
liveliness of the pig and its now absolute lifelessness after slaugh-

ter: 'They were going to scald it, / Scald it and scour it like a doorstep.'

The two most obvious impressions these poems leave with the reader are, on the one hand, the tremendous sense of the animals' vital and potent energies and, on the other, the complete otherness of animal life. The impression of the strenuous activity and swagger of life with which these animals are invested is often created by concentrating on their movement:

> Wanders, cries;
> Gallops along land he no longer belongs to;
> Re-enters the water by melting.

> ('An Otter')

> Terrifying are the attent sleek thrushes on the lawn,
> More coiled steel than living – a poised
> Dark deadly eye, those delicate legs
> Triggering to stirrings beyond sense – with a start, a
>   bounce, a stab
> Overtake the instant and drag out some writing
>   thing.

> ('Thrushes')

Even a description of two pikes killed by each other as they tried to eat one another leaves a sense of violent movement and miraculous strength that is not even lost in death:

> One jammed past its gills down the other's gullet:
> The outside eye stared: as a vice locks –
> The same iron in this eye
> Though its film shrank in death.

> ('Pike')

These examples also show the other impression made on the reader, the complete otherness of non-human life. Hughes resolutely refuses to sentimentalize his descriptions. He never clutches his animal subjects in a humanizing embrace, and the ones he chooses to describe are those least likely to be befriended by man (jaguar, pike, otter, bullfrog). It is their rich, instinctual life of feeling and action that most fascinates the poet. His most frequent response to the life of nature seems to be a mixture of awe and

117

fear. The details most often selected for comment, as in the example above from 'Pike', are those with the least human qualities. It is as if the very vitality of animal life is what makes them least like human beings. Unlike man, animals live by instinct and achieve a unity of feeling and action that fascinates Hughes.

Even in inanimate nature Hughes still discovers great life and energy. His descriptions of landscapes are not less active than those of animals. In 'Pennines in April' the 'hills [heave] / Out of the east, mass behind mass' and 'come rolling westward through the locked land.' In 'Wind' the element and the landscape become like animals themselves, 'The woods crashing through darkness, the booming hills, / Winds stampeding the fields under the window'. In 'October Dawn' the description of the first signs of winter frost proves Hughes's ability to create natural descriptions without obtrusively forceful language, rhythm or image. The fires of earth are damped down and frost will soon grip the land in its fist of cold. This is delicately suggested in the image of a wine glass left outside overnight after a party, which 'by dawn / Has dreamed a premonition / Of ice across its eye. . . .'

The human element

It would be quite wrong to gain the impression that Hughes writes only of animals and nature in these early volumes. In fact, there are many poems about people. These often suggest that man has become afraid of his instinctual life and treats strong emotions as something to be avoided. Yet, paradoxically, it is at the moments of extreme feeling that a man may be most alive. In the poems about men at war and those describing violent deaths, even pain is seen as capable of creating a sense of purpose and wholeness of response in the individual that in his day-to-day life seems beyond his grasp.

In 'Famous Poet' and 'Secretary' Hughes deplores examples of ways of life in which the life-giving energies have been denied, lives in which passion has been avoided or in which the true sources of feeling have been rejected. The famous poet is a 'monstrosity', a pygmy, and not the great writer his public acclaim makes him out to be. He has died as an artist not so much from the drink or the sex which his bohemian life has permitted him (and which are popularly seen as the weaknesses which led to his downfall as a writer), but from listening too much to the flattery of his admirers. He fails because he tries to please his public by continuing to write in the same style that brought him his early success. It is the poet's refusal to develop as an artist and to stay true to his inner flame that Hughes exposes. This is an early poem, written in the mid-fifties, and may be Hughes's warning to those who admired his early animal poems that he did not intend to go on just writing that kind of poem and trying to live off his first success.

The secretary in the poem of that title is a person shut off from life. Although she moves among people all the time she remains withdrawn from their contact and would 'shriek' and 'weep' at any physical touch. She 'scuttles down the gauntlet of lust / Like a clockwork mouse.' Both these poems, as well as 'Macaw and Little Miss', chide those people who restrain their deepest feelings or allow them to be killed off. It is as if they were written in the light of Blake's proverbs: 'Prudence is a rich ugly old maid courted by Incapacity' and 'He who desires but acts not, breeds pestilence'.

Man (and especially woman, it seems from the evidence of 'Soliloquy of a Misanthrope') must acknowledge 'the commitments of flesh'. Such commitments imply allowing love to enter our lives. This is the theme of 'The Dove Breeder' in which love appears as a hawk striking into the dovecote and destroying the pure but effete pedigree pigeons. The breeder's first reaction is despair, but he comes eventually to admire and tame the hawk, so that 'Now he rides the morning mist / With a big-eyed hawk on his fist.' In this poem love is a passionate, disruptive and violent force which can be changed from a destructive to a creative energy. But this energy, the closest of man's emotions to those instinctual passions that characterize animal life, is double-edged. It can be creative but it may also destroy. This ambiguity is the theme of 'Incompatibilities', where the lovers are both consumed and separated by the love they feel for one another.

There is a hint in these early poems about love that life is more unified, purposeful and imbued with creative energy when the individual is in touch with his instinctual springs of feeling. This hint is supported by a group of poems concerned with war and violent death. Man is so far cut off from the springs of his instinctual life that only moments of the acutest pain remain to awaken him to the voice of feeling.

Hughes grew up hearing his father's stories of the horrors of the First World War and he spent part of his childhood in the middle of the Second World War.[6] In several poems he explores war and its effects on both combatants and those left to remember the war when it is over. In 'Bayonet Charge' the young soldier awakes from his dreams of patriotism that had brought him to fight only at the moment of charging the enemy. 'In bewilderment then he almost stopped' because he becomes aware for the first time of the inhuman, calculated and mechanical way in which nations had seized their youth and put them to death over causes whose origin the soldier neither knows nor cares about. Stripped of all emotions except a desperate will to survive, the soldier focuses only on the charge and in his yelling advance plunges past his own terror and goes on to endure. The killing happens not for reasons of 'King, honour, human dignity' but because the ordinary soldier can subdue his fears and his sense of futility only by forcing himself on into the centre of a climactic energy. In this poem Hughes not only exposes the falsity of patriotic sentiments about killing but also and, more important, suggests that only by being in touch with these moments of climactic energy (even when they serve a destructive purpose) does a man take charge of himself.

The actual confrontation with death is found not so much in the poems about war as in two poems that describe violent deaths. 'The Martyrdom of Bishop Farrar' concerns the burning at the stake of a Christian martyr and 'Casualty' is about the death of a flyer.

Bishop Farrar was burned at the stake by Bloody Mary's men as a heretic, but on being chained to the stake he uttered these words: 'If I flinch from the pain of the burning, believe not the doctrine that I have preached.' The poem re-creates the horrible event with a realism that is almost repellent in its force. That it finally does not repel is due to the fact that the power of the Bishop's final stoic endurance is equally well portrayed. He commits himself to the flames, becomes that unbelievably painful experience, without crying out, and thus secures the faith of his followers in defiance of his persecutor. He is committed to his flesh even at the cost of

enormous suffering, and the truth of his doctrine and the keeping
faith with his body are one together in his acceptance of pain.

In 'The Casualty' an airman falls 'out of the air alive' from his
burning plane. He falls to his certain death but does not die
immediately he hits the ground. For a moment he lies, 'his groans
and senses groping', his spine smashed. His rescuers are helpless
and can only stand and watch him die. Thus the man in his death
becomes the centre of experience. The onlookers' sympathy turns
into a kind of insolent curiosity in their eagerness to be part of this
climactic experience. It is they who seem the more dead, 'helpless
as ghosts', while the dying man 'Bulks closer greater flesh and
blood than their own'. The paradox at the centre of this poem and
'The Martyrdom of Bishop Farrar' and 'Bayonet Charge' is that
the moment of ultimate danger or suffering is the moment which
most defines a man's meaning and experience.

In 'The Casualty' the human reaction to the dying man is
contrasted with the reaction of the animal life that has been
disturbed by the man falling among them. The animals are as
frightened by the casualty as are the humans and are even less
capable of anything like sympathy. Yet their reactions seem more
positive, more involved in the action than those of the helpless
spectators:

> In the stubble a pheasant
> Is craning every way in astonishment.
> The hare that hops up, quizzical, hesitant,
> Flattens ears and tears madly away and the wren warns.

The animals react not to the man's suffering but to his falling into
their midst – that is, to the action. They follow their instincts but
their behaviour unites feeling and action in a way that ensures
their survival. The onlookers' sympathy may 'fasten to the blood
like flies' yet they cannot connect feeling and action and are
helpless either to prevent the pain or to experience it fully for
themselves. Sagar suggests that 'the central impulse of "The
Casualty" is . . . to lay open the reader to a wider, deeper reality
than he is normally aware of.'[7] In these last three poems Hughes
appears to imply that man is cut off from his instinctual energies
and cannot unite act and feeling, and that this is a grave loss.

If these poems suggest that it is only in moments of extreme pain and suffering that man can regain some contact with his lost inner world of feeling, then the implications might be thought to be dangerous. It certainly seems that there are moments in that 'war between vitality and death' which Hughes has said he explores where the sources of both factions are seen as identical. But Hughes's apparent concern with violence is not an admiration for a life of violence; it is part of that exploration of the battlefield of man's experience of the war between life and death. In his descriptions of non-human life he reveals nature as independent of man, beyond good and evil, and a source of creative energy. This source has strength *and* violence (even the animals can be destroyed: the hawk dies, the pikes consume each other) and for man to be cut off from these sources is to run great risks of the instinctual energies being perverted into destructive paths. As the later poems will show, to lose touch with these energies is to divide, diminish and finally destroy man.

This is the theme of 'Lupercalia', which symbolizes man's sterility and his need for the restoration of those vital energies. The Lupercalia were Roman rituals celebrated to restore fertility to barren women. Animals were sacrificed, their blood mixed with milk and spread on the bodies of athletes who ran through the streets hitting the women with whips as they passed. The rites are described as an invocation to the 'maker of the world' to visit this barrren earth and unfreeze the cold wombs of the unconceiving:

> Maker of the world,
> Hurrying the lit ghost of man
> Age to age while the body hold,
> Touch this frozen one.

Significantly it is the sacrifice of animals that is the necessary rite with which to reclaim the woman 'from death's touch'. The condition of man, it seems, is a death-in-life without the revivifying power of the instinctual feelings. 'The lit ghost' that is man reminds us of the onlookers in 'The Casualty', 'helpless as ghosts'. Man cannot unify thought, act and feeling until he is made whole and is living in contact with the elemental energies of the natural universe.

To Hughes, as to William Blake before him, 'energy is eternal delight'; energy is creative, and its source lies in the continuum which relates man to animal and to the whole natural universe. In his first two books Hughes has only begun to express and explore the forces of the natural universe and to question man's relationship with it. The burden of consciousness prevents man from obeying his instincts and, in divorcing his intellect from his deepest feelings, that consciousness runs the risk of diverting the deeper energies into their destructive paths. In poems like 'Dick Straightup', 'November' and 'Acrobats' Hughes briefly sketches figures who suggest it may still be possible for man to acknowledge these energies without his being destroyed by them. The eighty-year-old Dick Straightup is still a man of enormous strength, 'strong as earth':

> Age has stiffened him, but not dazed or bent,
> The blue eye has come clear of time:
> At a single pint, now, his memory sips slowly,
> His belly strong as a tree bole.

Drunk, he falls into the gutter and sleeps there through a frosty night and 'Grew to the road with welts of ice. He was chipped out at dawn / Warm as a pie and snoring.' Hughes commemorates him as a man who lived close to nature all his life and who knew and trusted himself to it. It is this same trust which keeps the tramp in 'November' safe from the foulest weathers. And it is trust in their willpower and skill that allows the acrobats to 'hurtle and arc' and flash

> Above earth's ancient inertia,
> Faltering of the will,
> And the dullness of flesh –

Seeming to defy the elements the acrobats, in fact, understand the relationship between man, his body and the natural laws. They achieve 'the dream's orbit', the condition of right relationship of mind, body, feeling and will, which the spectators can only wonder at with a mixture of fear and awe.

Wodwo: who am I and how do I endure?

From *Wodwo* (1967) onwards Hughes is increasingly preoccupied with describing the divided nature of man and his relationship to the non-human powers of the universe. The animal poems in *Wodwo* are more sharply symbolic than those in the previous books, but do not sacrifice the accuracy and carefully observed details which bring the animals to life. These poems and some of the short stories (for example, 'The Rain Horse') convey the force of those non-human powers and their effect on man.

'Ghost Crabs' reveals the power of Hughes's symbolic use of animals as well as the dark exuberance of his imagination. It creates a weird phantasmagoria, opening with an ominously quiet description of nightfall on a beach and the cold, inhuman pallor of moonlight on half-submerged rocks among the withdrawing surf. But these are not rocks at all. There is no reliable solidity or stability in this moonlit world.

> Gradually the labouring of the tide
> Falls back from its productions,
> Its power slips back from glistening nacelles, and they are crabs.

'Power' and 'glistening nacelles' suggest the enormously frightening power of a jet engine (it is an image arising from the way the light of the moon turns the smooth curve of a crab's shell or claw into a glistening, grey metallic sheen). It is clear from this beginning that these are no ordinary crabs. And so it is that they emerge as giant crabs, gaining in bulk as they move forward on to land and becoming increasingly menacing as they stalk through each line of the poem 'under flat skulls, staring inland / Like a packed trench of helmets.' 'They emerge' – and these two words, isolated in a line by themselves, emphasize the danger from the crabs and their slow, powerful, imperturbable advance. They invade the land, moving towards the sleeping town. Nothing holds them back. In their 'slow mineral fury' they eventually enter our bodies. They fasten on all our lives, dominating our thoughts and creating our nightmares. They hunt, fight and breed in our minds. They are the forces of that continuum that connects man with the non-human world and which he prefers to deny. In their rejection these forces turn against us. They terrify as they

> Press through our nothingness where we sprawl on our beds,
> Or sit in our rooms. Our dreams are ruffled maybe.
> Or we jerk awake to the world of our possessions

With a gasp, in a sweat burst, brains jamming blind
Into the bulb light.

These forces are beyond our control. 'They are the moil of history'
and 'God's only toys'. This last comment implies that these relentless, destructive forces are the deliberate amusement of this
world's creator, but the point is not elaborated here.

This poem appears early in the book and establishes a sense
of the world for man as a nightmare in which powerful forces
beyond his control rule him and reduce him to a state of nihilistic
terror. *Wodwo* appeared some time after the poet had undergone
some cruel personal tragedies and there is an almost unbearable
burden of awareness of the uncontrollable forces of destruction
present throughout the volume.

'Pibroch' expresses this hard centre of experience with which
the book as a whole seems to be trying to come to terms. It is a
description of land and seascape in which the sea, the stones, the
wind and the tree (life pared down to its minimal shape) are given
a spare existence in five five-line stanzas with a chillingly bare
diction. The sea cries with a meaningless voice, the stone is
'Created for black sleep', the wind is 'Able to mingle with nothing'
and

> Minute after minute, aeon after aeon,
> Nothing lets up or develops.

The world is here described in human terms, but terms of boredom, lack of purpose and devoid of feeling. Nor is it going to
improve or be a test of fortitude preparing man for a paradise
elsewhere ('this is neither a bad variant nor a tryout'). Yet the tree
drinks the sea and eats the rock in a continual struggle to make its
leaves. It is the only life in this sterile world and its struggle seems
almost doomed to failure. Yet to endure is all: the fight back in the
face of this meaningless existence is all that remains. The anthro-
pomorphizing of the scene makes it clear that this poem is an
expression of the human condition.

From beginning to end this volume expresses the tension between the experience of life in an apparently meaningless and
frequently hostile universe and the refusal of man to give up or
withdraw. Man himself is the battleground between vitality and

death. From the first poem, 'Thistles', in which these unregarded and demeaned weeds stand their ground and fight off the attacks of cows and men to achieve their annual 'revengeful burst / Of resurrection', to the last poem, 'Wodwo', which expresses a proto-human creature's determined search for his identity, these poems give life to an aggressive determination to endure.

The reader experiences this endurance not only in the meaning of the poems but also in the very vigour of the language and rhythm which carry those meanings. It is a vitality enhanced by Hughes's continuing genius for detailed observation of natural life and the originality of image in the expression of those observations. Thus in 'Thistles', for example, he transposes the pointed leaves and white beard of the weed, together with its persistent presence on the slightest scrap of unattended ground, into an image of the weapons of Viking soldiers (themselves representative of potent, fighting powers). The thistles are

> a grasped fistful
> Of splintered weapons and Icelandic frost thrust up
> From the underground stain of a decayed Viking.

In 'Still Life' the small and unnoticed harebell 'trembles, as under threats of death', but nevertheless continues to survive. The fragility of such survival is perfectly rendered in the lines, 'filling veins / Any known name of blue would bruise / Out of existence', where the paleness of the flower's colour is also suggested. The almost unseen suffusion of colour, however, hides an energy that is 'The maker of the sea' (the same blue is the base colour of both), and this delicate flower may even outlast the rock with which it is contrasted in this poem. Despite its apparent solidity the rock will crumble and be replaced by another before this same species of harebell has been extinguished.

In 'Cadenza' the music of a violin is actually re-created in the dazzling imagery of the poem. The network of surreal images and the patterned sonorities of sounds suggest the swelling climax of power and energy that the music creates ('The husk of a grasshopper / Sucks a remote cyclone and rises'). It is expressive of the survival of beauty amid the flow of deadening experiences. At the end of the poem the sudden plummet of the violin's sound ('the whole sky dives shut like a burned land back to its spark') and the suggested regrouping and intensifying of its energies create a remarkable image of the soloist mustering his small forces in the face of the overwhelming odds of the orchestra as it prepares to play once more:

> Blue with sweat, the violinist
> Crashes into the orchestra, which explodes.

This poem successfully transmutes the experience of listening to music into a verbal pattern that mimics the musical sound of the original experience. It is a highly unusual performance.

'Skylarks' is one of the finest animal poems in this volume. Reading it we understand exactly what Alvarez meant when he said that Hughes has the ability to present animals 'as though from the inside in their fierceness, animality and solitariness'. Although the skylark is hardly a fierce creature, Hughes does present it as having an indomitable fierceness of spirit, and the bird becomes yet another symbol of a fight to endure in a hostile universe.

Unlike Shelley's skylarks, which were more spirit than bird, Hughes's skylarks are closely connected to the earth, and when they lift away from the ground towards the sky they rise with the sense of carrying a burden. Their flight is described as an escape and they go up 'Like a warning / As if the globe were uneasy'. The similes which describe the appearance and behaviour of the birds all carry overtones of strength, fortitude and adaptation to a hard existence – they are 'Barrel-chested for heights, / Like an Indian of the high Andes' and have 'A whippet head, barbed like a hunting arrow'. The birds are like a bullet shot as a warning signal and then become (in exploiting the full associations of the word 'shot') 'leaden / For ballast / In the rocketing storms of the breath.' The whole flight of the bird and its song are conceived as a struggle in which the bird supplants 'Life from its centre'; a struggle against the pull of the 'Earth's centre'.

The bird is created through vivid metaphors as a small but solid creature, full of strength of muscle and sinew, battling its brave heart out to clear the earth and deliver its song. It is a battle to overcome gravity and escape its natural habitat. The lark is 'shot through the crested head / With the command, Not die. . . .' Its famous song is not a matter of beauty without pain (as Shelley's rapturous bird suggested) but is 'incomprehensibly both ways', both a paean of exultation and a cry of pain. The first four parts of the poem build up this double feeling by the language and rhythm which alternately describe the pull of the earth and the desperate climb of the bird:

Up through the nothing
Its feathers thrash, its heart must be drumming like a motor,
As if it were too late, too late

But it is in the astonishing fifth part of the poem that the language and rhythm most perfectly combine to re-create the bird's return to earth. The curve of image and rhythm, reinforced by lineation, is an exact mimesis of the lark's sweep down to earth which both creates the sense of freedom which is part of the theme of the poem and gives an accurately observed picture of a real lark's behaviour:

And maybe the whole agony was for this

The plummeting dead drop

With long cutting screams buckling like razors

But just before they plunge into the earth

They flare and glide off low over grass, then up
To land on a wall-top, crest up,

Weightless,
Paid-up,
Alert,

Conscience perfect.

The bird does not supplant life's centre (which would kill it) but its conscience is clear because it has followed its inner nature, at whatever cost of pain, against the odds 'In a nightmare difficulty / Up through the nothing'. It is an image of man whose experience of life's agonies bludgeons him into believing there is no meaning in life but who yet resists and rises again and again simply to express his existence even when there is no guarantee that existence is purposeful.

To take this description of the bird also as an image of man may seem strained on the evidence of the poem as printed in *Wodwo*; but that it is not too fanciful is made clear in the revised version of the poem in the later edition of *Selected Poems 1957–1967* (1972), where two further parts are added. These relate the birds to the Cuchulain figure of Celtic mythology. Cuchulain defies death by his prodigious strength even though he is aware that ultimately he cannot succeed. But whereas Cuchulain cannot overcome the universe's dark forces, and is wrong to believe he can, the larks are seen as sacrifices whose song tells the hero he is still doomed. The larks are obedient to these forces and in their 'blind song' warn the hero that he will be trapped and killed by a 'sorry little wight more feeble and misguided than thyself'. In this addition to the poem Hughes reveals less faith than previously in the power to endure. As Sagar points out in his useful discussion of the later version,[8] these additions are written in the spirit of *Crow* and change the nature of the original poem in a way that makes it less convincing. But there is no doubt of the original poem's masterful re-creation of the skylark's actions and the successful symbolizing of man's inner state through the image of the bird.

A similarly successful use of an animal to embody a state of mind of a man occurs in the short story called 'The Rain Horse'. In this story a man is walking the fields when he is caught in a violent rain storm and is pursued and attacked by a strange horse. But such a simple summary conveys nothing of the power of the description of the terrified man's flight from this threatening horse which seems to appear by magic at every twist and turn of his escape. The rain, the horse, the man's mounting terror as he realizes the horse is deliberately pursuing him, are all described with great realism and force. The story may simply be enjoyed as a remarkable description of a perfectly possible situation. Yet the reader soon begins to wonder how far this horse is real and how far it is a manifestation of the man's haunted imagination. It is perhaps a visitant from his deeper, submerged self (a creature like the ghost crabs). The question of the exact nature of this horse has to be resolved by the reader, but in the context of the poems it seems right to assume the story is an expression of events within the man's psyche. The story is powerful and convincing precisely because subject and symbol are one; there is no sacrifice of realism to the psychological events. Nevertheless the horse is a symbol of those non-human powers which stalk through the rest of *Wodwo*.

This is the first of five stories and a radio play that occupy the centre of this volume and which are intended to support the poems. They share thematic links. The stories are written with much the same energy as the poems and express experiences close to those explored in 'Ghost Crabs'. The natural world is in the foreground and the forces that emanate from it are threatening to the people in the stories. There is a confrontation between man and these forces in most of them (we have seen this in 'The Rain Horse', but it also occurs in 'Sunday' between Billy and the rat, in 'Snow' between the survivor of an air crash and the hostile elements, and in 'Harvesting' when the man shooting hares is knocked unconscious by the recoil of his own gun and in his half-conscious state becomes himself a hare harassed by the harvesting machine). In all these prose-pieces (including the radio play) a man experiences a nightmare-like loss of his hold on rational life and is temporarily in touch with the forces of another reality. In 'The Rain Horse' the man does not escape from the horse's attack until he gives up trying to circumvent it and becomes so furious that he drives it off by attacking it with stones. In the end he escapes, but he does so by denying that reality which the horse represents; and that this reality is a part of man's deepest identity becomes clear from the final paragraph:

> The ordeal with the horse had already sunk from reality. It hung under the surface of his mind, an obscure confusion of fright and shame, as after a narrowly-escaped street accident. . . . Piece by piece he began to take off his clothes, wringing the grey water out of them, but soon he stopped that and just sat staring at the ground, as if some important part had been cut out of his brain.

The 'superior guidance' that led him to think of attacking the horse may be the guidance of the intellect, but we are left wondering if the escape is only temporary and if the inner forces which the horse represents must eventually be acknowledged and understood before they are changed through denial and neglect into totally destructive powers.

Wodwo has a greater range of style than has perhaps yet been indicated. It includes the naturalistic realism of 'Her Husband', the expressionism of 'Cadenza', the symbolism of 'Thistles' and the beautifully delicate lyricism of 'Full Moon and Little Frieda'. In 'Gnat-Psalm' there is an almost perfect synthesis of description and vision, and in 'Reveille', 'Logos' and 'Gog' there is the beginning of the creation of a mythic story which anticipates *Crow* and *Gaudete*. But for all this range of style there is a close unity of theme. In different ways there emerges from the stories and poems a sense of an indifferent or even hostile universe which man faces with his refusal simply to give in. There are hints that man must acknowledge some connection with such forces if he is to endure. Such an acknowledgement might redeem the destructiveness of those forces in himself which have been perverted by denial.

In 'Logos', 'Reveille' and 'Wodwo' the identity of man and the nature of creation and man's understanding of it are explored in what amounts to a prefiguration of the *Crow* poems. They are the beginnings of Hughes's revaluation of the Christian myth, particularly in the Genesis story. 'Logos' employs the pre-Christian myth that Robert Graves describes in *The White Goddess* (a book which has profoundly influenced Hughes). In this book Graves claims that 'Logos' is the name of the god prior to his creation of the world. It represents Universal Mind, and man has made of it a god who is above nature as the source of truth. This conception of a pure god (who in *The White Goddess* is divorced from the female will and is therefore a divided god) is a desperate misconception on the part of man. It fails to fit the facts of evil and suffering in the universe. The poem 'Logos' is about this god of 'perfect strength' whose power is a pentagram that blinds the frail body of man. Man cannot grasp truth or everlasting life. 'Creation convulses in nightmare', a primordial chaos which cannot dispel nightmare simply by giving birth to the conception of a perfect god. The first birth which begins everything is the birth of this nightmare in the form of the god of the material universe. Sagar interprets this obscure poem in this way:

> As soon as 'ancient law' and all the 'truths' of the well-meaning God of the Logos descend into matter, they are broken down by the still more ancient powers of nature which are inimical to all laws and truths and whose highest purpose is to streamline its

killers so as to destroy the more efficiently everything it creates
– creates, apparently, for the purpose of destroying.

    'God is a good fellow, but his Mother's against him.'

    God has the best of intentions, but he is at odds with a
goddess older and still stronger than himself.[9]

This difficult poem makes little sense without some such commentary from *The White Goddess* source and therefore cannot be
regarded as a total success. But it is important in showing the
direction of Hughes's thinking. He regards the Christian myth as
a half-truth. The logos (the god of pure goodness, of logic) is not
the true creator. There exists a creator prior to him who is the
White Goddess. Man's enthroning of the logos leads to a dualism
of mind and body, intellect and feeling, and divides man's nature.

    'Reveille' concerns the realization on the part of Adam and Eve
that sexuality and death are part of their world. Again it is an
awakening to nightmare. The serpent is not created by the logos
but is the representative of that primordial nightmare which
bypasses the god of pure goodness and awakens man with his bite.
In a simple yet magnificent image, the whole crushing weight of
this nightmare force which is experienced as sexuality and death is
described as the serpent's body whose 'coils / Had crushed all
Eden's orchards',

    And out beyond Eden

    The black, thickening river of his body
    Glittered in giant loops
    Around desert mountains and away
    Over the ashes of the future.

This death-in-life force extends over the whole universe and cannot be overcome by god as logos. In 'Theology' it has spread
throughout man to become 'the dark intestine', and God is powerless to deliver us.

    The title poem of the volume also concerns the relationship
between man and creation and is easier to understand than the
previous poems. 'Wodwo' is a dramatic monologue expressing
the thoughts of a creature half-man, half-beast. (Wodwo =
wuduwasa in Old English, the early Briton who hid in the woods
to escape the Romans. In the medieval romance, *Sir Gawayne and*

the Green Knight, 'wodwo' is a wild man of the woods.) This creature is on the verge of self-consciousness and seeks knowledge of his identity. The poem is written without punctuation (apart from interrogatives) and the words and ideas run together in a stream-of-consciousness that suggests the half-rational, confused state of mind of this proto-human creature. He inspects the frog's 'most secret interior' and makes it his own. His curiosity is insatiable because he mysteriously feels himself to be somehow at the centre of things, and he is searching for the roots of his identity:

> . . . I suppose I am the exact centre
> but there's all this what is it roots
> roots roots roots and here's the water
> again very queer but I'll go on looking

The poem has begun with 'What am I?' and is a record of a search for an explanation of self, an attempt to discover a pattern of meaning in the universe. Wodwo is without a god to guide him. He finds himself apparently casually dumped into life with a terrifying freedom, and his only uncertainty is that he will go on looking for some explanation and understanding:

> I've no threads
> fastening me to anything I can go anywhere
> I seem to have been given the freedom
> of this place what am I then?

Only half connected to the natural world, without the instinct or poise of the animal, with no clear sense of purpose, confused by powerful feelings he cannot understand and faced with a universe whose secrets he cannot grasp, Wodwo is modern man desperate in his desire to know himself.

In this poem and the group of poems concerned with creation, Hughes is articulating what he takes to be modern man's experience of living in a universe that surrounds him with chaos and which seems to offer no obvious purpose. Wodwo asks, as man has asked, is this universe the product of a creator who is good? It seems he cannot accept this possible explanation. What if God himself cannot control the creation? Man remains a wodwo: facing a confusing existence with only his desperate need to know pushing him on to endure.

Wodwo as a volume goes beyond the simple re-creation of the elemental energies which dominated the first two books. It expresses man as overwhelmed by the experience of a universe he cannot understand, a pain he must face up to without any redeeming grace. But like the skylark he is 'shot through . . . with the command, Not die' and knows he must endure. Just how great is the strength of both that endurance and of the forces it must encounter can be seen in *Crow*.

Crow

It becomes increasingly clear, as we read the volumes of poetry in the order that Hughes wrote them, that he has come to concern himself more and more with a subjective exploration of the inner realities of man:

> Though [the inner world] is the closest thing to us – though it is, indeed, us – we live in it as on an unexplored planet in space. It is not so much a place, either, as a region of events. And the first thing we have to confess is that it cannot be seen objectively.[10]

In *Crow* Hughes sets about expressing his sense of modern man's inner world. But the exploration of such subjective experience lacks a language in which to express it. The epoch of the scientific ideal has either driven expressions of that inner reality into realms of fantasy or reduced them to psychoanalytical jargon. The traditional language of this 'larger drama of moods and energies which it is hard to name – psychic, spiritual, cosmic' is the language of myth and religion. It is this language that Hughes speaks in *Crow*. What he speaks is the experience of that inner world which has been stripped of any mediating language between itself and the universe.

The outer world has become the dominant existence in man's cosmology as a result of the rise of science. The dispassionate eye of objectivism has destroyed the last myth that helped relate man to his inner and outer worlds – the myth of Christianity. This and all religions can no longer perform their task of humanizing the cosmic drama and giving a form and shape to the instinctual energies. The cause of much of modern man's feeling of alienation from those deep powers both within himself and within the outer world is the destruction of this humanizing language. *Crow* is the only language remaining and his songs sing of that alienation.

This is why it is inappropriate to do as some critics have done and charge Hughes with indulging himself in too black a vision. Hughes gives no approval to the dark, violent, death-ridden universe he describes in *Crow*. It is not a matter of approval or reproof. *Crow* embodies the inner experience of modern man who, lacking religious explanation in which he can believe, faces an apparently meaningless existence in which pain and evil frequently outweigh any redeeming possibilities.

Crow consists of the songs from a longer prose narrative which Hughes originally intended to write. The remaining poem is his own creation myth, a kind of black Genesis. It appears to have been the poet's original intention to write a story in the stark and simple style of traditional creation myths (for instance, the Eskimo legend of the black raven and white snow). It was to express the idea that even a life of great pain and suffering could still contain an irreducible force for survival. Among other things, Crow is the spirit of endurance, the basic grit of survival at the bottom of even the worst experiences.

Hughes has several times made brief statements about his conception of the epic folk-tale he originally intended and how the poems fit into this framework. Speaking at Loughborough University in 1977, he said this:

God tries to sleep but cannot because he is disturbed by a nightmare of a hand (which is also a voice) throttling him and picking him up and ploughing the earth with him and dragging him all round his creation. At last, not able to understand how something beyond him in his own creation can exist, God communicates with it. It turns out that this is at first a voice of mockery that taunts him, until at last God gives in and demands that this voice do better in creating the universe. So this voice descends into the heart of matter and creates from within it, and creates Crow. And Crow, to survive, must answer the examination [which he does in the third poem]. Then Crow travels into the womb and out of it into Eden and out and everywhere (for all time is present and all things exist simultaneously in this world). And the poems are the attempt of Crow to sing; the songs of all sorts of turns of experience.

Thus the language and forms of the songs are deliberately simple, repetitive and reminiscent of Old Testament verses, nursery-rhymes, old-charm rhymes and fairy stories. Hughes has said that 'the first idea of *Crow* was really an idea of style' and that he sought 'songs with no music whatsoever, in a super-simple and a super-ugly language'.[11] These songs work in a cumulative way, piling up example after example of the blackest experiences, often in a vernacular of bludgeoning force. The diction is suitable for the raucous squawk of a crow. Crow, fighting a bird-headed monster, 'smashes the egg-shell object to a blood rag, / A lumping sprawl, he tramples the bubbling mess.' In 'Crow and the Birds' 'Crow spraddled head-down in the beach-garbage, guzzling a dropped ice-cream.' 'Crow turned the words into bombs' and those bombs explode on every page. This diction and the simple but vividly ugly images create a violent and nihilistic world. As David Lodge has pointed out,[12] this technique is deliberately unsubtle with no room for nuances and tentative evocations. He suggests that the poem has surreal qualities and creates a kind of black caricature, making the same impact as does a cartoon character who always survives whatever awful suffering he is subjected to. The sense of an ever-present, indestructible force is as Hughes intended.

So these are the songs of a bird that cannot sing. It is the effort of life to express itself at the reduced level of sheer survival. But Crow is several aspects of experience in tension at once. He is not a simple cipher. In one poem after another he is the spirit undergoing trial, he is courage, he is the essence of ruthless willpower, he is amoral energy and he is the radical doubter of God's purpose and capacity. That is, Crow experiences modern man's struggle to survive in a world of relentless suffering and pointlessness and which is as much a test of his endurance as of his understanding.

The sequence begins with two brief prefatory poems, 'Two Legends', which relate the sequence to religious creation myths. They continuously return to the word 'black' like a bell tolling a death-knell rather than celebrating a birth. But it is a birth that the legends record, a birth into darkness (the scream of nightmare from 'Logos'):

> Black the blood in its loud tunnel
> Black the bowels packed in furnace . . .
> Black also the soul, the huge stammer
> Of the cry that, swelling, could not
> Pronounce its sun.

The primordial chaos — that nightmare over which God is supposed to cast his light — remains a darkness. In the second legend Crow is born into this darkness and flies over an emptiness, himself part of that emptiness. He is 'a black rainbow', a dark covenant, unable himself to lighten the blackness and unable to see God do so. Even at the creation, the world is in the stranglehold of death. The only positive note in the poem is the final word which describes Crow as 'flying'. His flight over this 'egg of blackness' is his 'command, Not die' (in the later version of 'Skylarks' it is Crow that leads the lark to Cuchulain). It is his indestructibility, his passionate and unremitting demand for life whatever the filth of the nest into which he has been born, which is celebrated in the following poem, 'Lineage'. This poem employs the incantatory biblical rhythms of the Old Testament 'begat' verses. The poem reverses the Christian tradition of the logos ('In the beginning was the Word'):

> In the beginning was Scream
> Who begat Blood
> Who begat Eye
> Who begat Fear. . . .

Creation begins in pain which is at the heart of all physical, bodily existence and, as the poem goes on to tell us, at the heart of non-human life, sense experience, music and beauty, work, man and the God who created man. The poem reverses the Christian teleology and suggests it is Adam who begat Mary who begat God and that man mistakenly made of this God a creator of goodness, of the Word and light because of his desire to believe only in perfect good and to reject pain and evil. But such a God begat Nothing. This Nothing begat Crow. God is not the greatest force and the Christian God is a man-made creation brought into being to relieve our sense of suffering. Hughes has written that Christianity is 'just another provisional myth of man's relationship with the creator'.[13] Once we lose this faith, we are abandoned to a sense of nihilism, to 'the horror of Creation' ('Crow Alights'), and Crow is what appears to outbid that nihilism. Crow flies 'the black flag of himself' over the abyss of our unbelief and incomprehension. This may not be the truth of the universe but it is as it frequently appears to late twentieth-century man. Crow is black selfhood, surviving everything but unable himself to create light.

The remaining poems expand facets of this Crow-experience. In 'Examination at the Womb Door' the rhythms of ritualistic catechisms are the underlying form of the poem producing a monotonous hammering at the door of birth. Crow is cross-examined:

> Who owns these scrawny little feet? *Death.*
> Who owns this bristly scorched-looking face? *Death.*
> Who owns these still-working lungs? *Death.*

Crow gives the same answer to each aspect of himself and finally is asked what is stronger than hope, will, love and even life itself. To all these questions he answers, *'Death'*. Finally he is asked who is stronger than death, and is allowed to pass when he answers, *'Me, evidently.'* This examination is modelled on *The Tibetan Book of the Dead*. In this book the desired outcome of the examination is that the soul should not pass into birth and thus into life again because, in the Buddhist religion, reincarnation into the material world of illusory desires means the soul is not yet ready to leave its attachment to life. Thus Crow fails by being born at all. His attachment to self prevents his success. Crow's birth occurs in a poem called 'A Kill' and when he is born 'everything went black'.

In 'A Childish Prank' Crow intervenes in God's problem of how to bring life to Adam and Eve. The problem is so great that God sleeps on it, and while he sleeps Crow, laughing, bites the worm in half and stuffs half into Adam and half into Eve. Ever afterwards the two are continually trying to come together for the two halves of the worm to join up:

He stuffed into man the tail half
With the wounded end hanging out.
He stuffed the head half headfirst into woman
And it crept in deeper and up
To peer out through her eyes
Calling its tail-half to join up quickly, quickly
Because O it was painful.

It is a sardonic view of sex. This is one of the most successful of the individual poems. It creates speedily and simply with force and black humour an alternative to the traditional biblical creation story.

In 'Crow's First Lesson' God attempts to teach Crow to express love. Crow tries hard. In a final show of strength he speaks no word but vomits the head of a man which is quickly followed by 'woman's vulva dropped over man's neck and tightened'. God ineffectually tries to separate them while 'Crow flew guiltily off'. It is not in Crow's nature to create anything good but he retains a consciousness of the hell he brings into being.

'Crow Tyrannosaurus' is a powerful poem expressing Crow's inability to transform the nature of this world – a world in which one creature can only exist at the expense of another. Crow is aware of the suffering but is powerless either to stop it or to absent himself from it. 'Even man he was a walking / Abbattoir / Of innocents'. The poem ends in a lamentation which combines through the carefully lineated phrases, the lack of punctuation and repetition of key words, the sound of compulsive killing amid a wailing universe.

And he heard
Weeping

Grubs   grubs   He stabbed   he stabbed
Weeping
Weeping

Weeping he walked and stabbed

Thus came the eye's
        roundness
           the ear's
              deafness.

Suffering and living are unavoidably intertwined.

Crow searches for the source of evil in 'The Black Beast' but fails to pinpoint it. In a series of poems at the centre of the sequence ('Crow's Account of St George', 'Crow's Theology', 'Oedipus Crow', 'A Horrible Religious Error') the fight against evil is seen as doomed because the fighter himself has the evil within him. In 'Oedipus Crow' Crow is disgusted by the indifference of his mother and the incompetence of his father. In 'Song for a Phallus' (a jarring, vulgar nursery-rhyme like song) Crow attempts to murder his parents (that is, the ineffectual god of logos and the primordial power of the universe) but fails. As the sequence moves towards its end the world is described as completely penetrated by evil ('everything goes to hell'). Yet Crow remains; even when the truth kills everyone, he hangs on. But, as 'Crow Blacker Than Ever' makes clear, this power to endure is all the talent he has. After the world has been burnt and the sun has 'raged and charred' against everything, Crow's eye-pupil remains 'in the tower of its scorched fort'. Finally in a poem with the imagery suggesting the crucifixion ('King of Carrion') Crow is left presiding over a silent, empty kingdom.

It is a bleak, black vision. There appear to be no consolations in this kingdom. *Crow* takes a look at the worst man must face. It is a song of darkness and one which has angered some critics. Homberger has accused Hughes of 'academic primitivism'[14] and Thwaite[15] talks of the abnegation from poetry and wisdom. But a large reading public (unusually large for contemporary poetry sales) has responded to it. It is not a question of 'liking' the poems' meaning. The poet may not like the world described in them. What he believes is that he expresses an authentic vein of experience.

That experience is negative and one in which the creative spirit cannot dwell for ever. Poems that are part of the Crow sequence have been published since the first appearance of the book. In some of these there is a suggestion of something more positive. In, for example, 'How Water Began to Play' and 'Song of Woe' there seems to be an implication that the recognition and living through of the experiences of Crow are the only ways in which man can break through to a new wholeness. In 'How Water Began to Play' the water 'having tried and failed both to live and die, weeps itself clear of both life and death', according to Sagar's interpretation.[16] 'Song of Woe' describes how the ego-state of ordinary, selfish existence must be destroyed so that our woe can struggle out and the 'howling transfigured double' thus created might be acknowledged and defeated. This double-image anticipates the situation of *Gaudete*. But paradoxically, if the meaning of the poems in *Crow* allows for no transcendence of the darkness, the omnipresent vigour and vitality of the very expressiveness of the poetry stands as a condemnation of any permanently nihilistic condition.

A glance in another direction: *Season Songs*

Season Songs (1976) is very different from *Crow* and is a return to the poetry built upon closely observed details of the natural world. It is composed of a series of lyrics on the turning seasons. Originally written for children, the publisher's blurb states that they are for younger readers. Nevertheless the volume contains poems that a reader of any age should not overlook. It also reminds us that Hughes has a lighter, gentler vision.

The strength of these poems stems from his longstanding gift for accurate description, as in 'A March Calf' where the innocent, expectant, nervous liveliness of a new-born calf is captured:

> He shivers for feel of the world licking his side
> He is like an ember – one glow
> Of lighting himself up
> With the fuel of himself, breathing and brightening.

In the marvellously visual 'March Morning Unlike Others' an early spring day emerging from the long winter gloom is expressed in the small movements of insects, flowers and birds:

> Blue haze. Bees hanging in air at the hive mouth.
> Crawling in prone stupor of sun
> On the hive-lip. Snowdrops. Two buzzards
> Still-wings, each
> Magnetised to the other
> Float orbits.

This poem carefully but simply organizes the rather obvious metaphor of 'earth invalid dropsied, bruised, wheeled / Out into

141

the sun' to create a feeling of gentle recovery and increasing strength until we are convinced 'She is not going to die'. In autumn a precise picture of the opposite season is caught in 'A Cranefly in September':

> She is struggling through grass-mesh – not flying,
> Her wide-winged, stiff, weightless basket-work of limbs
> Rocking, like an antique wain. . . .

The book is full of such lively, original and lightly sketched imagery. It employs rhyme quite frequently (fairly rare in Hughes), and it works with song-like rhythms and refrains, simple chains of metaphors and images.

'Swifts' is a minor masterpiece showing again Hughes's gift for perceptive observation and the power of expressing a living creature's being without sentimentalizing it. The swifts appear as if from nowhere with their characteristic sudden diving and wheeling flight caught in the opening lines.

> Fifteenth of May. Cherry blossom. The swifts
> Materialise at the tip of a long scream
> Of needle. 'Look! They're back! Look.' And they're gone
>
> On a steep
>
> Controlled scream of skid
> Round the house-end and away under the cherries. . . .

From 'Materialise' (suggesting a sudden, magical experience) through the synaesthesic blend of sound and sight in the image of the screaming needle (suggesting speed, urgency, excitement) to the use of a break between both line and stanza in 'On a steep / Controlled scream' (which imitates the dash and dive of flight), these lines create both an image of flight and the delighted response of the spectators.

A rush of images of movement ('erupting', 'jockeying', 'swat past', 'veer', 'frenzy', etc) flows throughout the poem and leaves a sensation of the speed, activity, feeding and breeding of these birds that do everything on the wing. Then the poem recalls each year's 'misfit', the inevitable young bird that falls from its nest and is doomed despite 'the fiery hospital hours / In a kitchen'. The poem ends by completing its own cycle with the child burying the

dead bird 'the charred scream / Folded in its huge power.' There is
no sentimentality, however, for we are left in no doubt of the
sudden bursts of power, the relentlessly hard, unfeeling progress
of nature with its indifference to weakness. Yet the world of
Season Songs is different enough from the world of *Crow* to have
room for a child's small act of mercy, even if it is ineffectual.

The progress of the seasons, the weather, animal life, birds and
insects dominate these poems in vividly realized images. In this
book the poet breathes in the pleasures of nature's teeming life,
and it radiates a bright energy that is very far from the blackness
of *Crow*. This is the other side of Hughes's poetic universe – and it
is not just a universe for children. Nature is observed not with a
naïve eye but with an eye that is innocent. Perhaps the adult with
his Crow-experiences cannot regain this kind of vision. Some
readers may regret that Hughes cannot combine both his visions
in one poetic universe. But Hughes continues to develop and he
may yet create a unified vision that does not deny the truth of
either experience. It is possible to read *Gaudete* as just such an
attempt to understand this double vision and to seek to bring
together the two halves of man's divided nature.

Gaudete: searching for a unity[17]

Hughes's most recent full-length publications are *Gaudete* (1977),
Cave Birds (1978), and *Remains of Elmet* (1979). Of these
Gaudete is the more interesting volume, a larger, wider-ranging
attempt than was *Crow* to create a story of mythic dimensions. It
is also written in a totally different style from that of the previous
book. It is by no means easy to understand, although it is easy to
read. The details of the individual poems (apart from the Epilogue)
are not obscure but the underlying intention of the poem as a whole
is. What follows is neither an assessment nor a commentary, but a
possible provisional approach to the poem that relates it to the
preceding account of Hughes's poetic task.

There is a sense in which *Gaudete* is a counterpart to *Crow*. In
the later book there is an exploration of man's divided nature and
a suggestion that the division may be healed and the Crow-
experience of life be overcome. *Gaudete* is about man's divorce
from his own inner life. It is a long narrative poem which operates

at a symbolic level to explore man's relationship with that inner world. It is an extended fantasy (that is, a creation of imaginative truth rather than a literal mimesis of reality), but it is not composed of unreal episodes; for each of the many individual scenes is realistic in its descriptive details. The progress of the narrative is episodic, the scenes being brief, in the present tense and made up of actions rather than commentary. These features may be the legacy of the poem's original conception as an idea for a film script. The action is crowded with detail and creates a vivid sense not so much of what happens externally to the characters (although this is clear) but of their emotional and mental states. In this example (from 'In Estridge's Lens'), Estridge, a retired sailor whose daughters are seduced by Lumb, is fond of scanning the horizon with his binoculars. In doing this one day he catches sight of Lumb entering a neighbour's house with the neighbour's wife:

> His hands gather up her skirts
> As his foot closes the door
> And Estridge's brain wrings
> To a needling pang, as if a wire might snap.
>
> His bulging eye
> Hammers the blunt limits of object and light.

In those lines we are presented with all the mixture of sharp, painful realization, fear, fascination and furious frustration of the observer. In another episode Mrs Westlake's state of acute anxiety as her mind churns over the possibilities of abandoning her husband, of finding the truth from Lumb, even of killing herself, is all caught in the description of her *physical* state ('Mrs Westlake'). Or, again, these lines which describe Mrs Holroyd sunbathing and show that the poem's re-creations of these physical and emotional states do not have to concentrate on moments of highly charged or violent emotions:

> She squirms her toes, feeling inside her shoes the faint
>   clammy cold of the dew, which will hide all day in the
>   dense grass.
> She turns her freckled face shallowly
> In the doubtful sun

And watches through her eyelashes a dewball jangling its
  colours, like an enormous ear-jewel, among the blades.
Closing her eyes
Concentrating on the sun's weight against her cheek,
She lets herself sink.

('Mrs Holroyd')

The idiom of the narrative is that of everyday speech, and the
episodes include prose as well as the loose-limbed, unrhymed free
verse which, at climactic moments, tightens up into a tense,
vibrant imagery. This form has an elasticity that adapts its pace
and rhythm to the shape of the narrative. The constant present
tense, the strongly visual imagery and the varying rhythms contri-
bute to an odd sense of timelessness (as if in a dream) which yet
still manages to create a sense of the inevitable acceleration of the
action towards its climax. This is further emphasized by the
constant cutting back and forth between short scenes and the
complete absence of dialogue. The reader is thus placed in a
position firmly outside the events, uninvolved, and yet registering
their full impact on the characters (as the language and visual
detail insist). It is as if we see through a glass clearly but that, as
with Estridge and his binoculars, although we may zoom in on the
action the glass wall between ourselves and what we observe will
never dissolve.

The comments so far made, however, apply predominantly to
the very long central narrative section of the poem. *Gaudete* is, in
fact, composed of three separate but related sections: a Prologue
(approximately 10 pages), the narrative (more than 140 pages)
and an Epilogue (27 pages). The Prologue introduces the protagonist, the Reverend Nicholas Lumb, an Anglican vicar, who
undergoes a strange nightmare in which he falls out of this world
into a kind of Hades where he is confronted by half-savage,
half-animal spectres who torture him and put him through a kind
of bloody initiation rite. At the end of the Prologue he is replaced
in this world by his double, and it is the adventures of this double
which occupy the main narrative. This *Doppelgänger* seduces the
women of his parish in a mysterious messianic cult which centres
on the local Women's Institute. Lumb has convinced the members
that a new Messiah is to be born to one of them. The climax of the

tale is the menfolk's discovery of what has been going on and their attack and revenge on Lumb who, along with his particular girlfriend who is sacrificially slaughtered in a cult ritual, is hunted and killed. In the Epilogue a strange man (apparently the original Lumb, now deeply changed) reappears in this world, in Ireland, and, after performing the miracle of conjuring up an otter from a lough to amaze some children and inspire an old priest, he departs, leaving behind some mysterious and obscure lyrical poems which form the matter of the Epilogue.

Paraphrased in this way the story must appear weird and absurd. It is clearly not intended to be a realistic tale. It is a tale with much violence, sex and general mayhem and the events it portrays may best be understood as the events taking place within the psyche of a representative of modern man's spiritual existence. These are the scenes of an inner world.

Before trying to understand these events, it is necessary to suggest that the scenes of violence should not be detached from their context and thus be overstressed in the way some of the critics of the poem have done. This leads to an inappropriate judgement of the poem as gratuitously nasty. It is not. The theme of the poem concerns the violent underworld of feelings inside man and the way these have been perverted into destructive emotions. It is true there is much violent action in the poem. Sex, suicide and murder are all depicted. Perhaps the most awful scene occurs in the Prologue when Lumb is forced by the strange people he meets to lie spreadeagled beneath a white bull that is swinging from a slaughterhouse roof. The bull is ripped open and its guts cascade on to him. But this seemingly gratuitous unpleasant description has a meaning in its context, as we shall see. In any case there are moments of peace and gentleness to contrast with the violent images, as in this beautiful description:

> The parkland unrolls, lush with the full ripeness of the last week in May, under the wet midmorning light. The newly plumped grass shivers and flees. Giant wheels of light ride into the chestnuts, and the poplars lift and pour like the tails of horses. Distance blues beyond distance.

There are numerous quickly sketched images of scene or event which describe and place the characters (although they are also intentionally stereotyped as retired army major, doctor's wife, barmaid, etc.) and which express the inner world of the main character. No scene or image or description should be torn from context and judged in isolation.

But what, then, is the meaning of the poem as a whole? Something of an answer to this question may be gleaned by attempting to unravel the symbolic nature of the work.

The poem is prefaced by two quotations and a brief prose Argument. The first quotation is from Heraclitus and identifies Hades and Dionysos as one, which suggests that the powers of the underworld and the non-rational powers in man are to be regarded as linked. The second quotation from *Parzival* suggests that the poem's main theme is the divided and warring nature of man which 'Contending here from loyalty of heart, one flesh, one blood, was doing itself much harm.' The Argument emphasizes the poem as an account of a learning experience – a learning by the real self, the whole self, from the wisdom of the powers of the inner self.

Some of the remarks that Hughes made in his article 'Myth and Education' help to orientate the reader in his approach to this poem. In that article he talks of how the ancient myths and the later religions served to preserve our knowledge of the inner world and provided a means of mediation between the outer, material existence of man and his inner, spiritual experiences. According to Hughes, the coming of science has led to such an insistence on truth as capable of being expressed only through objective, rationally assessable laws that not only has the credibility of religion been shaken but also man has destroyed the means of coming to terms with his inner life. We are utterly in thrall to an objective view of knowledge and regard only what is outside us as real. 'As the religion was stripped away, the defrocked inner world became a waif, an outcast, a tramp.' Without any means of mediation between the outer and inner worlds those 'archaic energies of instinct and feeling' which are within us are denied by us and their force is thus perverted into destructive paths. 'The small piloting consciousness of the bright-eyed objective intelligence has steered its body and soul into a hell.' This is the hell of the Prologue but because we 'lack the equipment to pick up [the signals of the inner world], we are not aware of it.' All that man feels is a desperate emptiness and meaninglessness, the experience of the universe as described in *Crow*.

Thus *Gaudete* (meaning the imperative: 'Rejoice!') concerns the need for man to learn once more to get in touch with that inner world, to listen to those old energies of instinct and feeling and, by embracing them, to restore the old unity of feeling, thought and action and to rejoice in a new unity of being. In the Prologue Lumb is given a chance by the powers of that inner world to relearn to communicate with them. The choice of Lumb, an Anglican clergyman, is made for this representative trial because he symbolizes the only modern man who has not killed God and therefore (however mistakenly in his interpretations) has kept open some sort of channel to this inner world (which the rest of mankind has 'defrocked'). Although Lumb 'has no idea where he is going. Or where he is' nevertheless he is 'searching in himself for control and decision.' 'He realises he is lost' and is aware of a task to be put upon him (the name Lumb associates him with the experience of numbness – 'Lumb stands, numbed' – but might also hint at the lamb of traditional Christian sacrifice). It is the powers of the inner world that abduct him, telling him he has been searched for everywhere. He is taken to face a mysterious 'woman tangled in the skins of wolves, on the rock floor, under the dome of rock'. She is half-animal and is watched over by an ancient man. Her significance is understood by referring to *The White Goddess* (Graves's morphology of myth and ritual). In it we are told that the wolf was sacred to the moon-goddess and the new moon is the White Goddess of birth and growth (that is, of inspiration and imagination). Lumb realizes he has been brought to the wolf-woman to save her from her sickness, to return her to life and energy. This is his task but he has no idea how to accomplish it. This is the tragedy of modern man who cannot bring back to potency the powers of his inner world, whose imagination has been allowed to die. Lumb fails at the moment of need and is set upon by the powers who looked to him for help. Rejected, they rebel against him, overwhelm him and flay him alive. Neglected, the energies of instinct and feeling are turned against ourselves. While 'Lumb chews earth and loses consciousness' he becomes two Lumbs. Thus man suffers the rejected forces and is divided against himself. It is at this point that he is forced to sacrifice a huge white bull and then to be baptized in its guts. In the Cuchulain saga two bulls, one brown and one white, represent the two halves of the hero's identity. The brown bull kills the white because it refuses to serve the goddess Maeve. Lumb is baptized in the blood of the white bull after he has proved unable to serve the wolf-woman who is related to the White Goddess, a female deity like Maeve and the source of the inner powers.

Lumb's self is divided and that part of him which has denied the inner forces returns to the outside world. In that world he attempts to re-create the inner experience, but he has not taken on the powers of that experience and is thus led into a false and doomed messianic vision which sees sex and the body as the instruments of the powers of redemption but without the support of the creative imagination. The other self remains in the inner world and is given the chance to undergo a genuine transformation by putting himself in touch with the White Goddess. It is this self who will reappear in the Epilogue. Meanwhile in the main narrative the self is misguided in his belief that he is in touch with the sources of his deepest being, and his attempts to regenerate the spirit through the body are futile, only capable of releasing the inner powers in a dangerous and self-destructive way. The climax occurs in the final abortive rites which lead Maud, his house-keeper, to play a witchlike role and where his genuine girlfriend, Felicity, becomes the innocent victim of Maud's perversion of Lumb's intentions. Lumb's ideas have got out of hand and are taken over by the evil powers that Maud symbolizes. These final rites take place in a drugged, Charles-Manson-like atmosphere – which may indicate a belief that the recent psychedelic drug cults are a misguided manifestation of a superficial awareness of the need to reopen a dialogue with our inner being. But that dialogue cannot take place through a systematic derangement of the mind. The only faculty that modern man must cultivate to begin such a dialogue is the imagination. As Blake held nearly 200 years ago, that faculty is divine and, as Hughes remarks in 'Myth and Education', 'that is the only way of saying that it is the faculty without which humanity cannot really exist'. The false Lumb destroys himself and all those in touch with him by his perversion of that faculty.

In the epilogue the other Lumb returns to this world in the west of Ireland (the home of the pre-Christian Celtic mythology which includes the Cuchulain story).[18] This Lumb has learnt to see with his imagination and to reconcile the outer and inner worlds. He is in harmony with the non-human forces of nature (as is demonstrated by his calling forth an otter from the lough) but he is under no illusion that this is an easily achieved or necessarily permanent condition. The cryptic poems he leaves behind him seem to show this. They appear to be addressed to the White Goddess and are very difficult to understand. Nevertheless, some are very beautiful. We might, perhaps, have expected that the climax of a narrative such as this would have raised a paean of praise to the beauty of this world as it would be revealed through the eyes of the newly transformed, unified self. But Hughes's myth is tougher than that. He knows the immense difficulties man must face in achieving his transformation. Thus the poems of the epilogue record the struggle and fitful realization of the possibilities of this new unity of being. There are no certainties of success: 'Am I killed? / Or am I searching?' The state of the new self is precarious and uncertain. The Crow-experiences are not so easily discarded. But he pursues his fight to pull off the mask of the false self. By the final poem it seems that the reader is to be given to understand that the fight is won. It expresses the possibility (a slight and fitful one) of catching our true self as it comes and goes; it cannot be forced to emerge. In achieving this, the darkness that was present at the birth of Crow, if not to be eternally annihilated, can, for the space of this life, be illuminated enough to merge light into darkness:

> Glare out of just crumpled grass –
> Blinded, I blink.
>
> Glare out of muddled clouds –
> I go in.
>
> Glare out of house-gloom –
> I close my eyes.
>
> And the darkness too is aflame.
>
> So you have come and gone again
> With my skin.

This is a personal reading of *Gaudete*. The poem has not been in existence long enough for us to have completely absorbed its meanings. But such an interpretation does make sense of much in this weird, rather mixed work with its obscurities, its intermittent power and beauty and its teeming liveliness. Here Hughes seems to be creating his own myth (or reinterpreting a forgotten one) and exploring a way of combating the Crow-experience.

Crow and *Gaudete* should be read together. The centre of their concerns and the task which Hughes has found himself involved in from the earlier volumes is voiced by another poet when he comments on the drama of Hughes's poems in a review written before either of the last two books was published:

> The frightening and insoluble paradox that man at his peril . . . denies his animal nature, but at the same time that very nature, when it gets out of hand, makes him bestial and hateful and can also kill him. By the same token, man's consciousness, while useful, is also dangerous, and when divorced from his deepest nature is feeble and useless.[19]

If Hughes's central concern is to dramatize this paradox, he has involved himself in a large task. He inevitably runs the danger of appearing to exaggerate the black and violent experiences of man. It has been part of the argument of this chapter to show that this violence is not gratuitous. If his expression of the unity of being that he desires is much less in evidence, it is because as a man and poet he writes from within our divided nature.

It is undeniable that Ted Hughes has large gifts of imagination and originality of expression. Whether he will achieve what increasingly appears to be his goal – the creation of a body of poetic myth that will stand for our unique late twentieth-century experience – remains to be seen. But the watching and waiting, if sometimes an uneven experience, nevertheless always provides an interesting and frequently a more rewarding experience than that provided by any other poet now writing in English.

5

'Dying is an art'

The poetry of Sylvia Plath

It is always difficult, if not impossible, to give a true estimate of contemporary literature. It is frequently a problem of distinguishing what is of permanent importance in a work from what is interesting to the reader merely by virtue of it being an assumption shared by the author and his reader living at the same period of history. This problem may be compounded if the author's behaviour and opinions have already brought him a notoriety in his lifetime that deflects interest from his work to his biography. Throughout its history poetry has had its martyrs, scandals and legends, and many a poet – from Rochester, through Byron and Shelley, to Dylan Thomas – has had his value as an artist obscured by his fame as a personality. The heady mixture of adulation and hostility which such poets have often aroused among their contemporaries has frequently led to the creation of a cult that has had little to do with the intrinsic merit of their poetry.

Since her death by suicide in 1963 there have been many who seem determined to turn the life and work of Sylvia Plath into a matter for literary myth and legend. The almost unprecedented commercial success of *Ariel*, her posthumous collection, which sold over 5000 copies in the first ten months, unfortunately may represent an interest that does not entirely result from literary appreciation. Over the last decade and a half there has been a steady stream of slim memoirs by early acquaintances of the poet who have claimed to know 'the real Sylvia', and there have been many critical articles and books which have made the poems documents in the speculative psychoanalysis of their author. The effect has been to make it very difficult to evaluate the poetry

without inflating its worth through our response to her short life
and tragic death, or without producing critical explications that
are biographical impertinences.

Even Ted Hughes, the poet's husband, may seem to encourage
an approach to the poetry that gives equal weight to her biography when he writes: 'She faced a task in herself and her poetry is
the record of her progress in the task. . . . The poems are chapters
in a mythology.' It is natural for a reader interested in a writer's
work to want to know something of his life and undoubtedly we
cannot completely avoid 'reading her poetry and brooding over
her life' when we approach the work of Sylvia Plath, as George
Stade has expressed it.[1] Attention to the life of a writer becomes
inappropriate only when we allow our response to its facts completely to overrun our evaluation of the work of art. This becomes
a distinct possibility in the work of artists who have made themselves the very centre of their art. Although, to some extent, all
artists have to do this, at least since the Romantics, English poetry
has had a strong tradition of poetry whose central subject has
been the poet's sense of his own identity.

The great Romantics, in placing their own identities in the
foreground of their poetry, always assumed that they could use
the sense of their unique experiences to comment upon more
generalizable emotions and thoughts. In speaking directly of their
own feelings, they were also creating what they believed to be the
shaping spirit of a universal imagination. As Rosenthal says,

> They found . . . cosmic equations and symbols, transcendental
> reconciliations with 'this lime-tree bower my prison', or titanic
> melancholia in the course of which, merging a sense of tragic
> fatality with the evocations of the nightingale's song, the poet
> lost his personal complaint in the music of universal forlorn-
> ness.[2]

With the influence of the French symbolists, particularly
Baudelaire, Rimbaud, Corbière and Laforgue, who 'used poetry
as a means of illuminating psychic regions in themselves that
would otherwise have been kept concealed',[3] the early poetry of
this century explored a decadence and breakdown of values in
both culture and individuals. At least this could be argued as a
central driving force in the Eliot of *The Waste Land and Other*

Poems, of Pound's *Cantos* and parts of Yeats. But in these poets there remains that assumption that they were writing not just of their own sense of a crisis of values but of that shared by a whole society, and they wrote from the position of a strong and authoritative, if at times ironical, sense of their own purposeful identity. More recently, particularly among American poets like John Berryman and Robert Lowell (the latter was highly regarded by Sylvia Plath), there has emerged a poetry which seems less concerned to generalize its explorations and expressions of the poet's own inner state. It is a kind of poetry which the American critic M. L. Rosenthal has called 'confessional', because it seeks to remove any mask and to make the speaker of a poem unequivocally the poet's literal self, the subject of the poem being that self at its most naked and vulnerable moments. Sylvia Plath's poetry is of this kind and it makes great demands upon the reader. The life and death of the poet stare out from almost every line, and the poetry as a whole creates an intense world out of the poet's own psychological state. The emotional landscape of the poems is one of deep personal crisis, and the existence of others or the nature of an outer reality is coloured entirely by the poet's sense of her own fragile identity.

The nature of this identity is seen in the novel *The Bell Jar* which makes a useful preface to Sylvia Plath's poetry. It is a compelling and moving fictionalized account of her breakdown and attempted suicide at the age of nineteen. Although there are many characters in the book, only one really emerges as real, and indeed reality is perceived only through her eyes. This is part of her own tragedy. Esther Greenwood is an academically and socially successful American girl who has won a journalist's prize which takes her to New York as guest editor for a month on a glossy woman's magazine. But, despite the trappings of success and the sophisticated delights of New York, Esther comes increasingly to feel herself alienated from the life around her. Even in moments of the most personal of experiences she feels dissociated not only from those around her but also from herself. She describes it as being like living beneath a bell jar, aware of everything about her but being cut off from it by an invisible barrier. She begins to feel cut off from her own life and the roots of her identity: she is reduced to a series of actions and events, and unable to give herself meaning, conscious of existing but not relating to herself or to the world. Overwhelmed by this feeling of nothingness, with no meaning at the heart of her concept of self, she tries to kill herself. But she is discovered before the act is completed and goes to hospital to recover. The novel ends with her apparent recovery and return to her former life. But the reader – and we suspect the author – is not confident of her future success. The emptiness of identity seems to remain. 'The vacuum of her own ego', as Esther describes it, has not been filled. The novel portrays a sensitive and highly intelligent girl's alienation from a promising life and career through her own acute sense of inner nothingness. Her family and friends, her hard work and talent, gain her this promise of success, but her honest vision reveals the hollow core of her self. It also reveals a similar core at the heart of the life she sees around her, the triviality beneath the charade of modish success; and the double awareness gives her no stand from which to fight back. She experiences no stability or solidity of self: 'The silence depressed me. It wasn't the silence of silence. It was my own silence.' And in a previous attempt to drown herself she admits: 'I thought I would swim out until I was too tired to swim back. As I paddled on, my heartbeat boomed like a dull motor in my ears. I am I am I am.' The insistent pull of life is a reminder of her own lack of being; she is reduced to a mere existence without meaning. At the end of the novel, returning home from hospital, she describes her heart as making that same 'brag' – 'I am I am I am' – and it remains the burdensome clang of mere existence rather than the genuine rhythm of being.

That particular 'brag' actually recurs in the poem 'Suicide Off Egg Rock', and many aspects of the novel may be found throughout the poetry. This poetry is also an expression of the struggle with this sense of a lack of meaningful identity, the tension between an acute experience of the world and a lack of a stable core of the self with which to come to grips with that world. This struggle at the heart of Sylvia Plath's poetry may be understood by looking at a selection of poems from *The Colossus* (1960), which was published three years before the novel, and *Ariel*, published in 1965, two years after her death. Two further collections of poems have been published: *Crossing the Water* and *Winter Trees* (both in 1971) and a selection of prose pieces, *Johnny Panic and the*

Bible of Dreams (1977). These later books contain many individual works of great power, but the first two volumes give a representative selection of the developing themes and style of her work.

A sense of threat

The Colossus is an impressive first collection. Although it does not have the terrible intensity and startling originality of the later poetry, it does contain a number of poems that combine a strongly individual vision with a sophisticated technical control which together give shape to unusually heightened imagination and pressure of feeling. Some individual poems, for instance, 'All the Dead Dears', 'Black Rook in Rainy Weather' and 'Suicide Off Egg Rock', are as powerful and original as any later poems.

The volume as a whole articulates a deep dread of experience: a dread felt in the hostility of the natural universe, a preoccupation with the more sinister and threatening forces of the inner life, and the absolute subservience of the poet to an unreclaimable past. The self that projects her emotions over the entire volume is expressed most intensely, if not most lucidly, in the final poem, 'Poem for a Birthday', in which the poet retains no clear sense of her identity and is unable to experience the significant, life-giving meaningfulness of love. Everywhere in this volume the sense of self is menaced by nothingness in a universe from which people have withdrawn leaving the world in the grip of dim, dangerous shadows – the Presences of 'The Disquieting Muses'. As Alvarez said in a review of *The Colossus*: 'It is this sense of threat, as though she were continually menaced by something she could see only out of the corners of her eyes, that gives the work its distinction.'[4] This vulnerability to hostile forces both within and without the poet's own personality is at the core of the poems. It occupies the imagery of a poem concerned with the indifference of the non-human world in 'Hardcastle Crags' as well as a poem like 'Poem for a Birthday' with its strange, strangled cries from deep within the poet's own psyche. Compared with the burning images of *Ariel*, however, this earlier volume has a cooler surface, a slower and more cautious approach to its themes. If Sylvia Plath is to be labelled as a 'confessional' poet, it is not because she merely indulges in self-exposure. There is always a great art, a crafts-man's skill of ordering and shaping, at work. In this first volume the controlled style has a persuasively rational tone but it nevertheless expresses a view of the world and the self which is moving swiftly towards a dark and negative vision. These poems have a lucidity compared with the later ones, their occasional obscurity stemming from a highly compressed and individual choice of metaphor. The intense emotional response expressed in the poems is created by the building up of a carefully controlled pattern of rationally presented images and metaphorical frames. Despite this, they leave an overriding impression, not of a description of a scene, situation or event which is the ostensible subject of the poems, but of the explosive inner response of the poet as she confronts her subject.

This effect may be clearly seen in 'All the Dead Dears'. This is one of the earliest poems in the volume, written when Sylvia Plath was a student at Cambridge. It begins with an exhibit of a fourth-century skeleton of a woman in the Cambridge museum. Beside the skeleton in her coffin are the skeletons of a mouse and shrew, and the ankle bone of the woman has clearly been gnawed. This bizarre subject is developed through six six-line stanzas which drag the reader further and further away from the museum and deep into the poet's mind. The skeleton of the woman quickly becomes the skeleton of the dead of the poet's family. What begins as an apparent *memento mori* meditation develops largely through the power of its metaphors into an expression of death as a devourer of life. It turns into a frightening expression and realization of the poet's inability to conceive of her destiny except in terms of being in thrall to those 'long gone darlings' of her family who riddle her life with their ghosts and determine her sense of herself. From the moment of her birth the past reigns, 'taking root as cradles rock'.

In the first stanza the skeletons are 'poker stiff' with a 'granite grin': the rigid attitudes of death are not to be denied. The animals which gnaw at the body come to the fore by the end of the stanza and provide the central metaphor of the poem which is to suggest that life is 'the gross eating game'. This peculiarly unpleasant image holds together several ideas at the centre of the poem. It suggests both that life is a nasty game in which the living compete to subdue and consume each other, and that death eats into life, swallowing us all in due time. In the final line of the stanza the image is extended by the reference to the 'stars grinding, crumb by crumb, / Our own grist down to its bony face.' Whatever is done by the living is grist to the mill of death which grinds us down to nothing. This second metaphor connects us with the first through the 'crumb' images, knitting together the idea of life as consuming and reducing man to a state of nihilistic competition with the notion of death as the consummation of the living. In this way a metaphorical reductionism serves to express a literal reductionism. It is an image which expresses the eating away of the individual's sense of meaning and purpose and is one that will be repeated in several later poems.

The awful and persistent presence of the dead is expressed in the following stanza in a series of metaphors that move from describing the dead as barnacles stuck fast to the living body, to the idea of them as being leech-like parasites sucking the lifeblood out of those bodies. This image also extends the central 'gross eating game' metaphor in its suggestion of death picking at the bones. The total effect of this sequence in the first half of the poem is to produce an overwhelming presence of death – and death not as a passive end to life but as an active agent continually robbing life of any significant or positive meaning.

In the second half of the poem a mirror image is introduced. This will recur with great frequency in later poems. It is related to the theme of a search for a sense of identity, a pursuit of a reflection of meaning. It displays the poet's increasing preoccupation with her sense of self. In this poem the mirror is also a pool reflecting the poet's past and her family forebears who 'Reach hag hands to haul [her] in'. The dead grapple with the living through images of scenes from childhood, memories of her grandmother and her father. These deal violently with her and show no pity as they seize her and pull her under the surface of the mirror-pond. There could be no more powerful image of the past attacking the present.

The final two stanzas are cooler and more detached in tone as the poet seems to step back and contemplate her seizure. Now the experience is generalized beyond her personal predicament. She argues that we all receive a 'touch, taste, tang' of the dead in the

Sylvia Plath

everyday rituals of birth, marriage and funerals and in a dozen ordinary family celebrations. Even in the silences between the ticks of a clock we dwell for a moment in the midst of our own dead and the shadow of meaninglessness they throw across the living. In a final image the individual is revealed as a death-ridden explorer tied down by the swarm of the dead (each of us a 'skulled-and-crossboned Gulliver / Riddled with ghosts') and we 'lie / Deadlocked with them'. 'Deadlocked' because we are both locked in to the past and are stuck, held fast in the embrace of our coming death.

This poem celebrates no living tradition for the individual to inherit. The past here is both dead and therefore unalterable and also terribly alive, pursuing the living with a malicious smile – that 'granite grin'. Sylvia Plath is here expressing her personal obsession with death but attempting to convince us of its generality. As she explores this obsession with its intimations not of mortality but of the living being controlled by the dead, she moves further and further into her own deepest feelings until she writes finally and with a dark calm of her own fate: 'Fixed stars govern a life'.

The burden of her sense of an inherited identity which is smothered in the 'incense of death' is also experienced in 'The Manor Garden', the opening poem of the volume although actually written three years after 'All the Dead Dears'. In the garden of a country house during autumn she contemplates the coming birth of her child. It is a meditation heavy with the sense of that child's inheritance. The birth is foreshadowed not by the coming of innocence into the world but by the weight of a family history, 'Two suicides, the family wolves, / Hours of blackness'. This highly selective history is entirely negative, and the all-pervading emotion here even dominates the imagery describing the garden. It is a barren, dying history the child inherits and which is reflected in the autumnal decay of the garden:

The fountains are dry and the roses over.
Incense of death . . .
A blue mist is dragging the lake.

Even nature witnesses the imminent birth of an ambiguous mixture of pain and hope as the 'small birds' converge 'with their gifts to a difficult borning'. As with 'deadlocked' which ended the

159

previous poem, 'borning' is a pun on which the whole theme
pivots. It suggests birth both in the sense of coming into the world
and in the sense of 'borne' as having to sustain the responsibility
of the inheritance of a history of pain and suffering.

Both these poems so far considered commence with a scene or
event in the outside reality and within a single opening stanza
have moved to establish that subject in terms of the poet's own
situation and history. The outer world is incorporated into her
own moods and emotional responses, and the focus for each
poem's concern then becomes not the world but the poet's view of
her world. This is basically achieved through the *enactment* of her
view within the poem's metaphorical development which creates
both her highly idiosyncratic perspective on outer reality and the
feelings associated with it. Sylvia Plath has a striking gift for the
metaphorical extension of an idea (see the unusually playful
'Metaphors') and in making these metaphors central to her
poems' development she is able to create a strong climate of
feeling without explicitly arguing for her perspective. This cir-
cumvents any rational doubt a reader may have concerning her
themes by crushing him under the highly charged weight of the
emotions whose authentic expression cannot be doubted. This
highly personal perspective is seen most clearly in the title poem of
the volume.

'The Colossus' speaks directly of her sense of herself and her
destiny as shaped by the inheritance of a particular relationship
with her father. The father-figure is identified with the huge
Colossus of Rhodes, the giant statue that stood by the harbour,
but which appears in the poem as ruined. The poem is addressed
to the dead father and recounts the fruitless attempt by the poet to
gain a meaning for her own life from attempting to rebuild her
image of her father:

> Thirty years now I have laboured
> To dredge the silt from your throat.
> I am none the wiser.

She crawls 'like an ant in mourning / Over the weedy acres of your
brow' and at night she squats 'in the cornucopia / Of your left ear'.
Her days are 'hours . . . married to shadow' spent trying to wrest a
sign from this impossible oracle of the dead. The notion of her

father as a ruined giant and the daughter's obsession and desperation are the emotional centre of 'The Colossus'. This diminished
sense of her own significance finds perfect expression in the
description of her scrambling over the statue's surface searching
for a way to clean and restore it and care for its repair. But no
loving care can breathe life into a marble statue and a desperate
awareness of this breaks into these lines:

> No longer do I listen for the scrape of a keel
> On the blank stones of the landing.

This seems to suggest a turning of her back on the possibility of
any sign from without her own psyche. 'The Colossus' confirms
the increasingly self-absorbed search for meaning. It marks the
beginning of her engaging with a personal myth, the setting out on
the task of which Ted Hughes spoke. The obsessiveness and
immensity of that task and its doomed nature are caught perfectly
in this poem's image of the futile attempt to glue together the ruins
of the Colossus. It is as if the poet has no active sense of herself and
is unable to throw a meaning over her own life without first
reconstructing the image of her dead father.

These poems express a threat and menace hanging over the
poet's sense of identity as a result of her inability to assimilate her
past, and it is the consequent need to probe that past and reorder it
that makes her increasingly withdraw into her own psyche. It is
thus not surprising to discover that when she looks out on the
natural world she should experience it as harsh and unresponsive
to human needs. In poems like 'Hardcastle Crags', 'Blue Moles'
and 'Mushrooms' the life of landscapes, animals and plants is
experienced as totally, frighteningly non-human.

'Hardcastle Crags' is concerned with a woman who walks out
at night beyond the village and on to the moors in order to escape
her own mood and the 'dark, dwarfed cottages' and the 'dream-
peopled village'. The opening which describes the woman walking along the 'steely street' has a hard, pushing rhythm. Her
isolation and her angry mood of alienation from the people
around her are caught in the explosive imagery of fireworks:

> Flintlike, her feet struck
> Such a racket of echoes. . . .

> . . . she heard the quick air ignite
> Its tinder and shake
>
> A firework of echoes. . . .

The 'k' sound crackles and explodes through the lines. But this forceful presence is soon diminished as she pushes on beyond the houses and up into a wilder moorland landscape. Now the energy is transferred to nature which, in contrast to the human sleepers, is wakeful and restless: 'the incessant seethe of grasses / Riding in the full / Of the moon, manes to the wind.' It is 'tireless, tied' like an energy reined in but always capable of abandoning its restraints. The anger of the woman is dwarfed by the impact of such boundless energies. The wind pares the walker down and presses its voice to her ear. The moonlit landscape is utterly indifferent to human mood or emotion:

> All the night gave her, in return
> For the paltry gift of her bulk and the beat
> Of her heart was the humped indifferent iron
> Of its hills, and its pastures bordered by black stone set
> On black stone.

'The whole landscape / Loomed absolute' and no relation with it is possible. Thus shut out, the woman concludes with a recognition of nature's astonishing strength and endurance which contrasts with her own, and she turns from its 'humped indifferent' hills unable to draw a support or meaning from it that can strengthen her own identity. It is the same threat suggested by the image from 'All the Dead Dears' in which a malevolent universe grinds the human skull down to the bony form of rocks. This same image lurks behind these lines in 'Hardcastle Crags':

> . . . the weight
> Of stones and hill of stones could break
> Her down to mere quartz grit . . .

But even the much tamer, more civilized landscape of the meadows around Cambridge which is described in 'Watercolour of Grantchester Meadows' retains elements of a hidden threat to the possibility of human love and tenderness. Although it is an apparently innocuous 'country on a nursery plate' with its 'spotted cows', lambs jambing the sheepfolds, the comforting confines of a quiet river where 'nothing is big or far' and appears to be the idyllic spot for the university undergraduates in their 'moony indolence of love', the poet nevertheless sees through it to the hidden yet very real presence of inevitable suffering which is suggested in the final comment:

> unaware
> How in such mild air
> The owl shall stoop from his turret, the rat cry out.

A whole group of poems, which includes 'Frog Autumn', 'Mushrooms', 'Blue Moles' and 'The Thin People', reveals the menacing presence in the life of even the slightest forms of nature. Entering 'the soft pelt of the mole', the poet shares these creatures' black and solitary underground life of grubbing after the 'fat children of root and stock'. It seems the moles too are involved in the gross eating game which permeates the life of the universe, even down in the darkness beneath the surface of the earth. In 'Mushrooms' these plants grow out of that dark, subterranean world and multiply and spread in a grotesquely meek and insidious way until their many millions 'inherit the earth'. In 'The Thin People', a phantasmagoria of macabre presences, the dead yet active 'grey people', menace our dreams in their 'thin silence' until finally breaking through into our daylight world.

Nature provides no consolation for man haunted by the shadowy presences of his past and the macabre and threatening creations of his inner life. Taken together, these poems produce a sense of an unspecific yet all-pervading threat, a climate of fear and danger.

This feeling of being threatened is connected with the experience of being unable to give a positive significance to a sense of self. The poet is menaced by the fear of meaninglessness as we can observe in the flow of sympathy she expresses for the suicide whose source of despair in 'The Suicide Off Egg Rock' is his burden of selfhood. For the subject in this poem it is a world without meaning in which he is trapped, 'that landscape / Of imperfections his bowels were part of'. Driven by his despair to the edge of the sea, the suicide stands under a hot sun 'like a damnation' in which the beat of the sun on the water echoes the beat of his blood with its reiterative pointlessness of 'I am, I am, I am'. The suicide's burden is his inability to escape from himself, from an identity which is mere *existence* without meaning or significance. The poem describes his 'body beached with the sea's garbage' and he can think of himself as having no more purpose than a mere breathing machine whose mechanical functions he casts off as he walks into the waves in a state of complete alienation from life.

Few poems in this volume escape this sense of a hostile or indifferent world. A cautious note of optimism may be heard perhaps in 'Black Rook in Rainy Weather', which shows a belief in the possibility of sudden moments of positive illumination which can for a time throw a light of meaning and significance over life; or in 'Ghost's Leavetaking' where the familiar sense of menace is held at bay with an unfamiliar lightness and deft humour; or, again, in 'Sculptor' where the artist is celebrated for his power to defy death and meaninglessness by using his art to give life 'a solider repose than death's'. But the struggle to assign significance to experience or to create a positive sense of identity rarely lasts long. The moments of illumination are brief, and over the vast majority of poems the light flickers and fails and we are plunged into a death-haunted darkness. At the heart of this darkness is the 'fear / Of total neutrality' ('Black Rook in Rainy Weather'), a numbing meaninglessness in which neither the self nor the world is experienced as positive. In 'The Disquieting Muses' the poet herself is in no doubt about the source of her poetry – the company she keeps is death itself.

The most explicit attempt in this book to render the poet's sense of incompleteness of identity is 'Poem for a Birthday'. It is the longest poem, made up of a sequence of seven poems, and is placed at the end of the volume. It is not an easy poem to understand because the progression of ideas is entirely metaphorical and the images and symbols proliferate. It is a non-literal description of the state of mind of someone recovering in a mental hospital after an attempted suicide. It expresses the emotional and psychological responses of the patient to her rehabilitation through ECT (electro-convulsive-therapy). This treatment is intended to lift an acute depression and to help the patient regain a sense of life and purpose.

Like 'The Manor Garden', this poem begins by counterpointing the autumn scene and the patient's inner life. It is a time for both season and patient when 'the fruit's in, / Eaten or rotten'. The opening poem of the sequence describes the patient's life as vegetating and mouldering among the 'cabbageheads' of her fellow inmates. An atmosphere of dryness and deadness is created through the images of a fusty mummy's stomach (suggesting the hollow core at the centre of the patient's sense of herself), the dead heads of flowers and the rattle of dry hydrangeas. The experience of ECT ('they light me up like an electric light bulb') only serves to increase her dependence on the doctors, and she remains cut off both physically and mentally from any sense of reality. The following sequence of poems explores this sense of alienation and emptiness through a train of metaphors and symbols. Many of these (in, for instance, the mole images of the second poem) suggest the patient's desperate desire to grope through the darkness towards some sign or indication of the direction which her life should take to give her a much-needed sense of meaning. But as the sequence develops, the images become harsher and fiercer and the self-loathing at the heart of the patient's sense of her identity grows explicit:

> I housekeep in Time's gut-end
> Among emmets and molluscs,
> Duchess of Nothing,
> Hairtusk's bride.

The rapid trail of images that spills across the poems creates a sense of some expressive improvisation by a patient gripped with a bitter sense of emptiness.

By 'The Stones', which is the last of the sequence, this sense of sterility is complete. She is reduced to the condition of stones in 'the stomach of indifference, the wordless cupboard'. Surrounded by the machinery of recovery she feels she is in 'the city of spare parts' and is acutely aware that the doctors are trying to create a superficially new self for her. But she is wiser than they. It is impossible to create an individual's sense of meaning, however many parts of his body may be replaced. The core of the self cannot be changed. In the desperate conclusion of the poem it is clear that the patient cannot experience the healing power of love.

She rejects the nurses' professional expressions of love and is incapable herself of that giving which is the genuine part of love and which is the only thing that would attract the returning love of another:

> Love is the uniform of my bald nurse.
>
> Love is the bone and sinew of my curse.
> The vase, reconstructed, houses
> The elusive rose.
>
> Ten fingers shape a bowl for shadows.
> My mendings itch. There is nothing to do.
> I shall be good as new.

The 'bald nurse' reminds us of the disquieting muses (who have 'stitched bald heads') and who are close to the sources of the poet's sense of meaningless existence. The vase is her body which, however it may be repaired, can hold only the shadow of the rose whose genuine beauty is so elusive. No authentic sense of love is more possible now than before. The final assertion is the bravado of the damned. The patient knows that her old feeling of emptiness remains behind, whatever new mask she is given. The poem ends on a chilling note of irony.

It is a devastating poem with which to close the book. There is an extraordinary intensity of feeling released in the flow of highly charged images. And although some of the details of the symbols remain obscure the general tenor of the poem is quite clear. The theme is the poet's sense of a lack, or loss of a positive experience of selfhood. While at one level this is expressed as the experience of hospitalization, at another it is recorded as a crisis of personal identity. David Holbrook has pointed out[5] that the first part of the poem is entitled 'Who' but without the expected question mark behind it. This is because the patient cannot answer the question as to her identity. She has no sense of herself as a positive, meaningful and loving person. This lack of a sense of being is the shadow that falls across all the poems in this volume.

The techniques and styles of the poems in *The Colossus* reveal great craftsmanship. A wide and inventive vocabulary gives precision and insight to the exploration of ideas and feelings. It is not so much a matter of the unusual word as the care taken in searching for exactly the most appropriate word (see, for example, 'spumiest dove' in 'Point Shirley'). The diction is also frequently chosen as much for its sound as for its meaning. This can be seen very clearly, for example, in a poem like 'Sow' which is a descriptive *tour de force*. The last eight stanzas of this poem, in particular, rely upon the sound as much as the meaning in creating a sense of the pig's hideous bulk and fat fecundity. Here, as elsewhere in this volume, the diction is often rather literary. But this gives a richness without overflowing into any kind of ostentation. It provides an elegance, but that elegance is controlled by the sheer energy and gusto of the inventive metaphors which are the heart of many poems and this preserves them from becoming merely flamboyant.

Sylvia Plath's particular gift for creating lively and original metaphors which combine the description of a subject with the feelings that subject creates in the poet may be seen in these examples chosen at random. She describes two foetuses preserved in a hospital:

> In their jars the snail-nosed babies moon and glow.

Or describing the early-morning view of a river:

> The blue water-mists dropping
> Scrim after scrim like fishnets
> Though fishermen are sleeping.

Or a description of the sea eating at Point Shirley:

> And I come by
> Bones, bones only, pawed and tossed,
> A dog-faced sea.

This last example shows the typical interweaving of an idea in a metaphor. Bones are literally found among the detritus on a beach, but they also suggest an extension of the image of the sea eating away at the cliff like a dog gnawing a bone. Bones also suggest the dead, and in this poem the poet is remembering her dead grandmother's house by the sea. The way the sea plays with apparently solid structures of land also creates a sense of the way the elemental powers of the universe play with human lives for their sport. The fact that the images grow out of a description of action and movement rather than out of some stationary object is also typical of many of the most original metaphors in these poems.

A minority of poems in this volume employ traditional metres in their rhythms. Most use a free-stress pattern or a syllabic count (the line length being determined in this case by the need for an equal number of syllables rather than the number of stresses). Yet the poems never become slack or garrulous. This reflects the hard work the poet put into writing and rewriting them. She worked them up slowly and carefully in contrast to the rapidity and relative ease with which the *Ariel* poems were to be written.

Ariel: the dialectic of death

The poems collected in *Ariel* were written mainly in the last year or so of Sylvia Plath's life and they came with a speed unusual for her. They have an intensity and energy which suggest she had really broken into a part of her sources of feeling that required the most urgent release. Alvarez has written: 'She was systematically probing that narrow, violent area between the viable and the impossible, between experience which can be transmuted into poetry and that which is overwhelming.' In 'Kindness', one of the very last poems she wrote, her own awareness of the dangerous sources of her poetry is expressed in two lines which capture both a sense of release and a hint of the final tragic outcome: 'The blood jet is poetry, / There is no stopping it.' The heart of *Ariel*'s poetry is life-blood indeed; there she moves into a fully mature and individual style which is expressed in a voice that rises out of her deepest, most personal concerns.

Death dominates this volume. To whichever poem we turn, by the time it has reached its conclusion we have been made to peer not just into the dark depths of some generalized expression of man's mortality but into the very stare of the poet's private dark angel. Death here is always an active agent, but he is also an ambiguous presence who is not necessarily seen as destructive. He appears in all guises: he is transmuted into a landscape of isolation and comfortlessness, 'a heaven / Starless and fatherless, a dark water' ('Sheep in Fog'); as a personal suit of clothing for the poet, 'Black and stiff, but not a bad fit' ('The Applicant'); as the terrifying attractions of a perfectible skill and black aesthetic in which 'Dying / Is an art' ('Lady Lazarus') or, finally, death is present everywhere from 'the atrocity of sunsets' to the barren moon or the 'great abeyance' of the sea. In 'All the Dead Dears' from the earlier volume Sylvia Plath wrote of the 'hag hands' of the past, her personal dead, dragging her with overwhelming force into their world. The poems in *Ariel* exist largely to explore that force. They dive deeply into the world behind the mirror of that poem and disturb a sea of images that flows over the whole book in a macabre, vivid, continually expanding life which drowns the reader in a shadowy below-surface world where death is a darkness that can both hide and reveal everything. By the last poem we are ready to accept that the whole of life and death is manipulated by the unreflecting light of the stars below the pool's surface:

> From the bottom of the pool, fixed stars
> Govern a life.

This highly personal obsession could become an embarrassment or a bore to the reader, yet it does not. Why? There are two particular reasons. In the first place the astonishingly various moods and occasions of death itself (from the obviously frightening to the strangely seductive nature of a final resolution), which have been indicated above, give a range of tone and a variety of unexpected insights. But the second reason may be even more important. This lies in the astonishing vigour and electric energy of the language. Both deny the mawkishness and ultimately stultifying air with which such death-laden verses might have been choked in the hands of a less original poet.

The style of this volume is less literary and aureate than *The Colossus*. The poems are lyrical but are made of a toughness that accommodates dissonant voices. Those voices are basically conversational, but they are never quiet and detached; they range over passionate feelings, at times angry, at times despairing, at times blustering and buoyant, but always with absolute conviction. The individual poems are pushed forward not so much by a narrative as by the motive power of the images of feelings and perceptions. It is an organic style, the form of the poems developing from the material handled in them, which is unlike the more traditional rhythmic line of *The Colossus* with its carefully constructed stanzaic frames. In these poems line length is determined by syntax or meaning rather than strict metre, and the stanzas are brief two- or three-line images in many poems. This form itself contributes to the sense of urgent, improvisatory explorations of quickened feelings that gives this poetry its energy. Often these poems gain their curves of energy from a dazzling display of metaphor and symbol which swing in and out of the lines creating a poetry not of statement but of image.

Alvarez has pointed out that these poems were written for the ear rather than the eye. Their patterns are to be heard. The speaking voice follows the short, sharp breathings of image, of exclamation and question, of stinging statement and so on.

The image base of the poems and the fact of their being written particularly for the ear may be seen by examining part of 'Elm' and by indicating some of the varied uses of the moon image in this and other poems in the volume.

These are the last lines of 'Elm':

> Clouds pass and disperse.
> Are those the faces of love, those pale irretrievables?
> Is it for such I agitate my heart?
>
> I am incapable of more knowledge.
> What is this, this face
> So murderous in its strangle of branches? –
>
> Its snaky acids kiss.
> It petrifies the will. These are the isolate, slow faults
> That kill, that kill, that kill.

Only the first line here is a simple descriptive statement and even in this the sound is important because the lingering sibilants prefigure the building up of the 's' sound through 'irretrievables' and 'so murderous in its strangle of branches' to the final climactic venom of 'its snaky acids kiss'. The whole has a tone that is a long way from the detached observations of a calm meditation. We are in the middle of an active process of deep and disturbed emotional response. The questions and the conclusive 'I am incapable of more knowledge' combine to destroy any sense of a careful, rational compilation of ideas and replace it with a series of images (clouds, tree, moon), unimportant as pictures of the external world but crucial as symbols carrying the sense of the poet's self tied to its fears, dissatisfactions and 'voice of nothing' which lies at the centre of her identity and which is the meaning of this poem.

It is in such ways that the imagery of these poems focuses their themes and is itself continually moving, responsive to the accelerating power of the feelings generated by the subjects of the poetry. Yet there is rarely any loss of control. Only infrequently do the images become esoteric or private. Normally they arise from nature or from the domestic scene and they are employed to fuse external events with the feelings within the poet. Gradually, poem by poem, a handful of recurring images accrete related meanings until they begin to construct a personal mythology: the moon, the sea, journeys, the mirror, yew and elm trees, blood, poppies, colour and lack of colour, bees and ghostly presences. The precise meaning of such images changes from poem to poem but overall they are connected in a skein of associations. It is partly this that gives the collection an atmosphere of continuity, of creating a complete landscape of one particular mind. If a single image is traced across the whole book these interconnections become visible. Tracing the moon, for instance, reveals a constellation of meanings that associate it with sterility and despair (the 'O-gape of complete despair'), with 'something beautiful, but annihilating', with a light that is borrowed, reflected and cannot be its own source. Through this compound-symbol Sylvia Plath expresses her sense of fruitless isolation, a cold, solitary and meaningless existence. Together these various images combine to become the contours of a mindscape:

> This is the light of the mind, cold and planetary.
> The trees of the mind are black. The light is blue.

Ariel creates a highly personal world in which every route seems to lead to death. Two particular routes emerge: on the first there are poems concerned with the poet's sense of identity and her relationship with others; on the second there is a group of poems bound together by their shared sense of the closeness of death itself and of a strange belief in it as a kind of possible rebirth.

Those poems exploring a sense of identity convey an acute loss of meaning and alienation from reality, revealed particularly in

171

the fear of relationships. There are poems that give a sense of dissolving self ('Tulips') and are written out of experiences of illness which become a sign both of alienation from everyday realities and of the possibility of death as a release from the burden of identity ('Berck-plage'). There are also poems which express the nature of personal relationships (as in the sequence of poems connected with bee-keeping) and mother–child relationships in particular ('Morning Song', 'The Night Dances', etc.).

'Tulips' was written in March 1961 and is therefore one of the earliest poems in this collection. Ted Hughes has said that this was one of the first poems to be written very quickly. In its form it reflects some of the careful patterning of the poems from the previous volume, but its content places it close to the final poems.

It is constructed in seven-line stanzas with each line usually consisting of two phrases balanced on either side of a caesura. This creates an effect of statement or assertion being immediately balanced by qualifications, or an illustration of that statement. Randomly chosen lines illustrate this effect:

The tulips are too excitable, it is winter here.

I am learning peacefulness, lying by myself quietly.

I am nobody; I have nothing to do with explosions.

I have let things slip, a thirty-year-old cargo boat.

They have swabbed me clear of my loving associations.

And I have no face, I have wanted to efface myself.

This effect reflects the way in which the state of mind of the poet in this poem is built up. The lines express both what she feels and explain and explore the consequence, as she experiences it, of those feelings. The essence of these feelings is the desire for the peace of non-existence, but as she sinks into an acceptance of her sick state, hugging her illness to her as a means of escape from life's commitments, she is disturbed by the presence of a gift of tulips. These vivid flowers contrast with her sick state and call her back to health and to a life of relationships and commitments.

The first half of the poem expresses the desire for freedom from any human claims, from all feeling and any reciprocal relationships. As a patient she is reduced to anonymity and welcomes this: 'I have given my name and my day-clothes up to the nurses'. The hospital room with its white walls and cleanly sheeted bed and quiet atmosphere suggests a winter snow scene. This creates a sense of frozen emotions, a lack of feeling which the patient greets as a calm peace. That it is not a calm peace but a withdrawal, a rejection of the outside world, is made evident in the patient's annoyance with the fact that she cannot completely ignore her surroundings:

> They have propped my head between the pillow and the sheet-cuff
> Like an eye between two white lids that will not shut.
> Stupid pupil, it has to take everything in.

She refuses to move outwards and makes no connection with her nurses (who are reduced to 'white gulls', each identical and anonymous) or with her possessions ('I watched my teaset, my bureaus of linen, my books / Sink out of sight') or even with her family whose photograph by the bed has 'little smiling hooks' that catch on to her skin but which cannot make real contact. 'They have swabbed me clear of my loving associations,' she declares, and in her antiseptic freedom she regards herself as having attained a release from the obstructions and impurities of relationships: 'I am a nun now, I have never been so pure.' But what does such a purity amount to? It is the purity of a peace that is all-embracing, 'so big it dazes you', but it dazes because it is death itself:

> It is what the dead close on, finally; I imagine them
> Shutting their mouths on it, like a Communion tablet.

It is a peace described in terms of nothingness, of hands empty and upturned, denying all giving. It is stasis, not contentment.

After the desire for such peace is established, the second half of the poem returns to the tulips and only now does the meaning of their first description become clear. 'The tulips are too excitable' and are called 'explosions' because they are seen to represent life, health, energy and are tokens of a caring relationship – all of which the patient wishes to reject. Their redness contrasts with the sterile white of the hospital. They are described in aggressive terms as demanding presences, loud noises in the patient's newly acquired quiet, as dangerous animals. The hyperbole of the descriptions reflects the depths to which the patient has sunk in her reversal of all the usual perspectives. In the poem's contrasts of life and death, living colour and sterile white, relationships and commitment and the purity of independence and detachment, etc., it is the second of each pair of terms which has proved the most attractive to the poet. The temptation to retreat from life is all but overwhelming. Although gradually the patient becomes aware of the connection between the 'bowl of red blooms' and her own heart and she returns slowly, painfully to life and health, we are left not totally convinced of her power to sustain the recovery:

> The water I taste is warm and salt, like the sea,
> And comes from a country far away as health.

The unusual perspective of this poem leaves the reader with a feeling of having glimpsed a nightmare world in which everything has been turned upside-down and in which the stasis of death has been mistaken for contentment, the inevitability of nothingness misread as the boundlessness of peace.

In 'Fever 103°' illness is again used to convey the experience of the 'purification' of identity by the abandoning of the external world. In this poem the fires of hell and high fever are fused in a symbolic purging of the sin of existence. But whereas in 'Tulips' the poet retains a consciousness finally that it is a *sick* state that she desires to perpetuate, in this poem there is no outer framework of normal relations and healthy expectations within which to place the experience of sickness. This poem is purely an enactment of that sick state and the positive possibilities the sick poet believes to be inherent in that state.

The poem begins by asking 'Pure ? What does it mean?' but the answer is no rational explanation. Instead the remainder of the poem accelerates through a series of images that realize both the sensation of fever and the underlying psychic disturbance of the poet. A raging fever is likened to the fires of hell ('The tongues of hell') but even the fat Cerberus, the dog that guards the gates to hell, cannot lick clean the taint of sin that is associated with the body (an association made not just because the body is sick in illness but because the body represents the fact of existence-in-the-world). In a remarkable development of the fires image, the burning body produces 'scarves' of smoke which are blown in the air 'like Isadora's scarves, I'm in a fright / One scarf will catch and anchor in the wheel.' The meaning of this last allusion is clear when it is remembered that the dancer Isadora Duncan died in a bizarre accident when her long exotic scarf was caught in the wheels of an open car and strangled her. The love that is invoked in the lines alluding to this incident is deliberately ambiguous. It is both an expostulation to the lover and itself the scarf which binds her in a relationship which she is afraid may strangle her or bind her to the wheel of death-in-life. The 'sullen smokes' continue to rise and drift through the following stanzas changing into the fires of Hiroshima and becoming entangled in an image of adulterous love suggested by the allusion to the film *Hiroshima, Mon Amour*. Then the flame is transmuted into an image of her body in which the raging fever is like a light flickering on and off in a delicate, fragile paper lantern. The fever burns without a flame and continues for three days giving her a sense of purity in which the touch of relationship becomes a suffering:

> I am too pure for you or anyone.
> Your body
> Hurts me as the world hurts God.

Her assumption of divinity suggested here has been hinted at in the reference to the three-day suffering, and this prepares us for the final audacious image in which the hell fires turn into heavenly ones and her sense of sin is finally burnt from her as she ascends from the earthly shackle of her bodily identity:

> I
>
> Am a pure acetylene
> Virgin
> Attended by roses,
>
> By kisses, by cherubim. . . .
>
> (My selves dissolving, old whore petticoats) –
> To Paradise.

The way in which these later poems are built around a metaphorical development of the central ideas is explicit in this example. Here narrative has been completely superseded by the expression of a complex state of feeling in a welter of image and symbol. This image flow and the obsessive internal rhyming on the word 'sin' give in this particular poem a tremendous sense of the power of the speaker's obsessions. At the heart of this matrix of feeling is the experience of a sense of nothingness as a state of purity and of escape from ties with others. It differs from 'Tulips' in that here there is no return to earth and reality.

'The Moon and the Yew Tree' is the poem which perhaps most successfully articulates the sense of utter desolation at the centre of the *persona* who presides over *Ariel*. Yet despite the despair which is felt in the poem, the reader carries away from it a sense of a terrible beauty born out of the superb control and dark lyrical grace of its execution. This is because the scene described in the poem is the perfect embodiment of the state of mind that is expressed through it.

It begins as a description of a moon seen through the branches of a yew tree in a churchyard. The blue-black light of the sky which illuminates the tree, the clouds and stars is the light of the mind of the poet and these colours modulate throughout the poem. In the moonlight the scene is a cold blue, 'cold and planetary'. Under it the poet suffers a sense of the world's pain, 'The grasses unload their griefs on my feet as if I were God'. There appears to be a sense in which she feels expected to bear the burden of the world's pain and to give it meaning. This she feels unable to do: 'I simply cannot see where there is to get to.' The light of the moon admits of no relief ('The moon is no door'); it is the 'O-gape of complete despair.' The church bells ring but the poet hears no resurrection in their tolling. The traditional explanations no longer carry meaning. It is not the Virgin Mary but the moon who is the spiritual mother. The blank, black meaninglessness of the night sky darkens any possibility of a saving tenderness such as the church represents. Only the clouds 'flowering / Blue and mystical over the face of the stars' hold any possibilities of redemption. But the last twist of the knife occurs in the description of the moon's cold light entering even the church and blanching the warm, redeeming colours of the Virgin's statue into that all pervasive cold, planetary blue. All that remains is 'blackness and silence'. The church with its '*cold* pews' and effigies '*stiff* with holiness' (my italics) is a rigid and dead tradition which can offer the poet no support for the weight of the world's pointless suffering.

It is a chilling yet beautiful poem. Its beauty lies in the way each detail of the natural scene works both to create that scene and to carry the meaning of the poet's emotions. It is a perfect example of T. S. Eliot's 'objective correlative', a description of a scene that re-creates the feelings of the poet. For the reader, if not the poet herself, 'the icy world is delineated with a strength which to some extent denies the apparent despair'.[6] These poems reveal an inability to give any positive significance to the experiences of life and express the consequent break-up of the sense of personal identity. Many of the other poems express similar experiences, including poems that comment on marriage. Marriage is a vicious circle of misery: 'A ring of gold with the sun in it? / Lies. Lies and a grief.' In 'The Applicant' marriage is seen in bitter terms as a cover-up, an attempt to heal a wound of inner emptiness that is doomed to failure. This is a somewhat maliciously conceived poem but it clearly expresses a sense of false, empty, inauthentic existence. This sense of a disintegrating self that no relationship can heal is clear in this line from 'Elm': 'Now I break up in pieces that fly about like clubs.' In 'Death & Co.' she reduces her sense of self to a mere carcass awaiting the butcher death, and in 'A Birthday Present' there is a clear cry for some revelation of meaning to counter the nothingness of everyday existence 'Filling my veins with invisibles, with the million / Probable motes that tick the years of my life.' 'Getting There' sees living as a train journey into a battle zone in which the poet is dragging her wounded body among a thousand other wounded bodies. They all lack identity and have been reduced to the level of a mere animal need to survive. 'Pumped ahead by these pistons, this blood / Into the next mile'. The landscape of the journey is an inferno reminiscent of the mid-European battle zone of the last war. The train's destination is death and in the last lines there is again the implication that death is a kind of innocent state, a condition of purity otherwise unknown to man. In this poem the poet's personal state of mind is generalized to a universal human condition.

One sequence of poems which is concerned with the relationship between the poet and others and her attitude to her self is the
successful group of poems about keeping bees. It is successful for
the same reason as is 'The Moon and the Yew Tree': there is in the
bee-keeping rituals a suitable concrete metaphor for inner feelings. It is particularly apt because the poet's father – whose loss is
expressed in these poems as being connected with her sense of a
loss of personal identity – was an expert on the life and habits of
bees.

'The Bee Meeting' concerns the poet's introduction to keeping
bees as she attends a meeting of villagers who are to remove a
future queen from the hive. This necessitates the destruction of the
old queen, and the poem intertwines the account of the episode
with the poet's state of mind, a state of fear and alienation as
glimpsed in the first line where she meets the villagers. Their
identity is hidden by their protective clothing. The rector, mid-
wife, sexton and others remain in the background throughout the
poem. She has no real relationship with them and feels vulnerable,
'nude as a chicken neck', because she has no protective clothing:
'does nobody love me?' She is isolated and frightened and,
although they give her the necessary clothes, she remains with
these feelings because she is ignorant of what is going on and
unable to relate to the others who remain anonymous figures in
their shapeless clothing. It seems to her that the whole episode is
like an operation that she is being asked to join in. The hive is
the body. A sickly pallor covers the scene (even the hawthorn
has blood clotting the tendrils). Slowly she comes to realize
that it is her body they operate upon, that she is co-operating
in the destruction of the old queen, the sense of her own
identity.

In 'The Arrival of the Bee Box' the delivery of her own hive is
the subject. Now the hive seems like a coffin which imprisons not
the dead but the terrifyingly alive swarm that both repels and
attracts her as it dins with the noise of 'unintelligible syllables'.
She begins to be afraid for the power that rests in her as the one
who must unlock the hive. Her responsibility over life and death is
one she cannot escape from in the end.

Taken with 'Stings' and 'Wintering', these poems form a
dramatic sequence recording the feelings of fear, isolation and

uncertain identity. The bees, as a reality outside herself, are a mysterious source of both sweetness and danger. They are also herself in her task of recovering a sense of identity – creatures who are prepared to kill to protect their hive, in the same way as she has expressed the possibility of death as means of recovering her lost sense of meaning.

The only relief from this dark vision occurs in a small group of poems dealing with her relationship with her children. 'Morning Song', which opens the book, celebrates the joy felt at the arrival of a new baby. It is built around images of rising, of delicate hopes (sounds, breath, clouds, balloons), images which reflect the mother's happiness and the baby's fragile life. But even here the affirmative feelings are immediately qualified. The child's cry is 'bald' (we have seen that the associations this word has in Sylvia Plath's poems suggest a lack of relationship and love) and the images of balloons, clouds, etc., indicate vulnerability and insubstantiality of being. The mother also experiences her own sense of insubstantiality by the very presence of the baby,

> I'm no more your mother
> than the cloud that distils a mirror to reflect its slow
> Effacement at the wind's hand.

In 'The Night Dances' the mother watches her child dancing in its cot and feels its movements 'travel / The world forever'. These movements are the beautiful gifts of innocence and create a blessing which momentarily falls upon the mother to give her a brief sense of fullness of being which lightens 'the black amnesias of heaven'. This light can never be destroyed and will nowhere be forgotten. Yet the word 'nowhere' has an ambiguity that hints that perhaps the blessings land on nothing and that they are too insubstantial to wipe away the black amnesias for long:

> These lamps, these planets
> Falling like blessings, like flakes
>
> Six-sided, white
> On my eyes, my lips, my hair
>
> Touching and melting.
> Nowhere.

In 'Poppies in October' another kind of gift is celebrated, the gift of unexpected beauty in nature when some late poppies flower. Yet the underlying feeling that is awakened in the poet is her questioning of whether she is worthy to receive such gifts:

> O my God, what am I
> That these late mouths should cry open
> In a forest of frost, in a dawn of cornflowers.

In 'Nick and the Candlesticks' the mother nurses her child by candlelight. In the dark she imagines she is a miner underground in a cold world of bats, stalactites and dark pools. Then the baby jolts her into a realization that these are the horrors of her own mind and need not be part of his world. She has decorated the room for him, 'hung our cave with roses', and in the final religious image of the poem the child becomes the source of strength in which the haunted mother can rest:

> You are the one
> Solid the spaces lean on, envious.
> You are the baby in the barn.

In these poems about her children (including 'Balloons', 'You're' and 'Letter in November') there are moments of affirmation and love. But they are brief, delicate and vulnerable. Despite the assertion of the above lines, they do not provide the strength to overcome the dark powers expressed in the poems about death.

It is the poems which deal directly with death – and, in particular, the temptations of suicide – that form the second group of poems in the volume. Strangely, in this reverse world of *Ariel*, these poems partake of the most positive tones in the book. Here there are no qualms; the flight into death is celebrated as the means whereby a fragmented sense of identity can be unified in a totality of meaning.

The poem that particularly expresses the exhilaration of this flight is the title poem of the collection. At the superficial level 'Ariel' is about riding a horse. But the destination of this journey is the same as in 'Getting There', only now the experience of facing death is neither generalized nor full of horror but instead is solitary and full of excitement and anticipation. Ariel was the

name of an actual horse Sylvia Plath rode but it is also the name of
Shakespeare's non-human creature with his magical powers.
There is an element of the non-human in this *tour de force*. It is a
poem completely expressive of the exhilaration of movement and
speed. It re-creates the urgency and delight of riding a galloping
horse across moorland. This is achieved both by the way the
surrounding landscape is itself made active in the description,
from 'the substanceless blue / Pour of tor and distances' at the
beginning to the 'dew that flies' towards the end; and also by the
complete merging of horse and rider:

> God's lioness,
> How one we grow,
> Pivot of heels and knees!

The movement is hurried forward through the short, punching
rhythms and through placing the stress on verbs of urgent action
('Splits and passes', 'Hauls me through air', 'Flakes from my
heels', etc.). The horse is present only in its movement; it is not
described at all. The description is entirely of the rider's sense of
complete identity with horse and landscape: 'I / Foam to wheat, a
glitter of seas.' The moment in which the poet at last seems able to
relate to her surroundings and to affirm her sense of existence
appears, ironically, only in this extraordinary flight towards destruction. That it is a destructive flight, despite the excitement,
becomes evident in the closing lines. The thrust forward, the
relentless momentum, does not cease but shoots away to merge
into a universal energy:

> . . . at one with the drive
> Into the red
>
> Eye, the cauldron of morning.

The rising sun ought to suggest the living energy of morning and
hope, but here it is a bizarre affirmation. The flight is called
'suicidal' and the 'Stasis in darkness' of the opening line, the only
still point in the whole poem, is completed at the end as the birth
of a new day sees the rising of death. This poem leaves no doubt of
the welcoming rush towards it.

The most famous poems in the volume are 'Lady Lazarus' and

'Daddy' which are both about this move towards death and the embracing of suicide as a kind of rebirth of identity. With the excellent analyses of both poems that are now widely available[7] it seems unnecessary to provide yet another detailed account. Nevertheless it is important to point out some of the distinctions of these two poems.

'Lady Lazarus' is one of the most original conceptions of this poet, and 'Daddy' is one of her most powerful. It is these two poems in particular, with their very public display of deeply private obsessions, that has led some critics to speak of Sylvia Plath as being a 'confessional poet' (together with fellow Americans, Robert Lowell, Anne Sexton and W. D. Snodgrass). But although the material of the poems appears to invite readers to probe aspects of her autobiography, they are also attempts to widen the private experiences through the use of imagery drawn from the extermination camps of the Second World War and to suggest that the poet's private sufferings are not discontinuous with the effects of mass murder and the attempt to expunge the identity of a whole race.

'Lady Lazarus' is about the suicidal tendencies of the poet and the fact that she has made previous unsuccessful attempts to kill herself.

> I have done it again.
> One year in every ten
> I manage it —

It is a disarming opening: it appears casual, almost offhand, as if letting the reader in on a juicy bit of gossip (an idea she will round on a little later in the poem). The comment on her attempts at suicide also implies a certain naturalness about it. But as the poem develops we are persuaded that the naturalness is an appearance developed from great skill, and she identifies her perfectionism as a poet, her dedication and absorption in her craft, with the obsession with self-destruction. The effect is to convince us of the underlying seriousness with which she views the possibility of suicide and at the same time to make it clear that *she* regards it as a creative act. It is this realization as it breaks upon the reader that frames the poem and distances the peculiarly inverted world of the poem from the reality of the world the reader knows.

Dying
Is an art, like everything else.
I do it exceptionally well.

I do it so it feels like hell.
I do it so it feels real.
I guess you could say I've a call.

The tone of this is deliberately ambiguous. On the one hand it has a seriousness and apparent honesty, but on the other the somewhat slangy diction and simplistic syntax strike a flippant, rather exhibitionist note. This ambivalence is everywhere in this poem. It is both an authentic disburdening of deeply personal feelings and also the product of a kind of showmanship. The question must arise as to whether this ambivalence is intended by the poet. Does she recognize these mixed feelings in herself, or does she simply believe she is expressing her obsessive concern with her own death and is the ambiguity sensed by the reader actually a product of the poet's lack of awareness of the perverse, exhibitionist side of her nature?

After the apparently casual opening the following lines use a kind of shock tactic in their fusion of the poet's personal past with the history of the Nazi concentration camps:

> . . . my skin
> Bright as a Nazi lampshade,
> My right foot
>
> A paperweight,
> My face a featureless, fine
> Jew linen.

This repulsive reminder of twentieth-century barbarity is repeated later in the poem. Through this imagery an attempt is made to link all private and public suffering and victimization. Both in the poet's private world and in the public world of recent history death is seen as an assault on identity. The Nazis wished to destroy the identity of a whole race. The poet does it 'so it feels real', to eliminate her old body and self (which is incapable of giving her a sense of significance) in the expectation of creating a new identity that will confer a meaning on her. This is partly the meaning of the phoenix image in the last lines of the poem. A further link is effected between the poet's situation and that of the Jews in the camps through the reference to those objects (lamp-shade, paperweight, linen) made from the remains of the camp victims. The poet also feels herself having become an object to herself, to family, friends and doctors. This becoming an object of unfeeling curiosity also leads to a reference to the callous, inhumanly detached responses of the Nazi guards who were incapable of compassion for their victims. The camp guards and those who treat the suffering poet as an object of curiosity or amusement are described as voyeurs:

> The peanut-crunching crowd
> Shoves in to see
>
> Them unwrap me hand and foot –
> The big strip tease.

This attack on those who can watch the suffering of others with no sympathy or understanding includes the reader of the poem whose response to that throwaway opening stanza may have been a faint excitement at the prospect of the poet's confession of her personal hell.

This poem refuses to be abject or apologetic about suicide. There is just that slight suggestion of the futility of the act in the lines, 'What a trash / To annihilate each decade', but the poem as a whole swings through an arc of changing tones, none of which asks for pardon. It includes the matter-of-fact acceptance, as if it was the most admired thing in the world, of this peculiarly horrific 'talent'; the unpleasantly sensuous description of the after effects of a suicide attempt ('They had to call and call / And pick the worms off me like sticky pearls'); the sardonic attack on the unsympathetic spectators of suffering; the bitter realization of her position as doomed victim ('The pure gold baby / That melts to a shriek') and the angry and revengeful cry of the final stanzas:

> Herr God, Herr Lucifer
> Beware
> Beware.
>
> Out of the ash
> I rise with my red hair
> And I eat men like air.

It is in these changes of tone that the underlying tensions of the poem are controlled and explored. The basic tensions are expressed in the contrast between content and form. The deadly serious subject is expressed in a style that seems, at first, a kind of light verse. The diction is colloquial, almost slang in places; the stanza structure is simple with many end-stopped lines and frequent repetition of words and sounds in a regular internal rhyming pattern. All this contrasts with the dark, complex emotions which are the poem's subject, and the effect is to create a sardonic humour or the impression of some grotesque joke. But by the end of the poem it is a joke that has been bitterly turned against the reader.

In the last lines the poet's attack on the 'peanut-crunching crowd' goes much further. The crowd is joined with all those others who cannot leave the sufferer alone, the doctor who brings round the suicide (and who is likened to the Doktor of the concentration camps who experimented on his victims) and those who would give religious explanations that cannot cure the pain, all of whom are seen as poking and stirring in the ashes of the dead. They are figures symbolizing the crowd who cannot leave alone the suffering victim but who cannot stop the sufferer's pain. The poem becomes a vicious, violent tirade which culminates in the threat of the final lines. The onlookers cannot understand the pain of the victim. Only after the victim's death will they be jolted into a realization of what that victim felt, but by then it is too late to save the suffering or assuage the spectator's guilt. The suffering of the Jews was known about but no one could believe how terrible it was. When they did it was too late. As the images of the poem remind us, all that was left of the victims was the gold of their rings and teeth fillings and the hideous 'cake of soap' made from human fat. It is a terrifying indictment of the callous spectator.

'Lady Lazarus' has undoubted force. As a dramatization of the state of mind of a suicide, it has shocking power. The underlying hysteria is presented and yet held in control by the quick changes of tone. These changes of tone serve to draw in the reader from his early position of a detached observer (which he shares with the crowd of onlookers) finally to awaken him to the intense suffering of the victims in their sense of a loss of identity. Yet despite this power some readers are left wondering whether the poem as a whole is a complete success. Is the final threat in the last stanza meaningful, a matter of genuine insight into the relationship of sufferer and spectator, or is it the boast of a victim who has not fully assimilated her pain into the creation of her art? Is it a cry of desperation rather than of triumph? Do the references to the historical facts of twentieth-century brutality and attacks on the identity of a whole race work to generalize a whole climate of pain in which the poet is partaking by becoming 'an imaginary Jew', or do they appear as a rather forced attempt to give spurious universality and justification to a very personal and private suffering? Each reader must decide for himself. Critics like David Holbrook[8] have argued that the ambivalence of tone, especially in the last stanza, is a sign that the poet here has not achieved complete mastery of her material. Others, like Eileen Aird,[9] argue strongly that the worlds of 'personal pain and corporate suffering' are satisfyingly fused.

'Daddy' is a poem that also explores deeply personal themes utilizing a light-verse, almost nursery-rhyme, style and which presents the reader with similar problems of evaluation. This whole poem rocks to the sound of 'you' (the father-figure that is made the symbol of the mixed feelings of the *persona* of the poem) which is chimed internally throughout the sixteen five-line stanzas. This achieves an uncanny mixture of a half-lighthearted and half-deadly incantation of sound. In the poem the *persona* expresses her sense of pain and longing for her own death as a result of the breaking of her childhood relationship with her father when he died and her subsequent feeling that she can re-create that relationship and the sense of meaning that would flow from it by dying herself. But, as in the previous poem, an attempt is made through the images to generalize the state of mind expressed. The father is seen as part-Jewish, part-Nazi and thus involves in the one figure the roles of both torturer and victim. The *persona* also sees herself as both the lover and the enemy of this composite figure. She inherits and pursues a love that is also compounded of brutality and hatred.

The two forces, persecutor and victim, are brought together because the *persona* cannot completely renounce the brutality which is embodied in the father/lover image without renouncing the love she feels for father/lover figure. The love/hate she feels is the very centre of her emotional life without which she can have neither emotion nor life. In this sense she can be said to co-operate with those that persecute her and, indeed, to connive at her own suffering. As in nursery rhyme, the heroine loves her familiar terrors.[10]

The father-figure dominates the daughter (he is 'marble-heavy' and a 'ghastly statue' – a description that reminds us of the earlier 'The Colossus') and inspires both devotion and revulsion. This explosive mixture leads the daughter to try to obliterate memories of her father, but such feelings are not so easily exorcised. The only way through may be in death. The killing of herself and the death of her persecutor and the reuniting with the figure she loves are all accomplished in the one final act of suicide.

> So daddy, I'm finally through.
> The black telephone's off at the root,
> The voices just can't worm through.

The simple rhythmic qualities of the verse, its nursery-rhyme swing, and sharp, plain language present a horror that is all the more powerful and hypnotically evident in the contrast of form and content. The deliberate light-verse form avoids a lapse into sentimentality on the one hand and a too strident personal justification on the other.

The final poems of the book, written in the last week of Sylvia Plath's life, return again to the sense of failure in relationships, to a breaking up of identity and to the inevitability of death as a personal final solution. These poems have none of the anger or hysteria of the last two we have looked at. They are calm and accepting and their words echo in the reader's memory long after he has relinquished the book.

In 'Edge' she steps over the edge into death itself. In this death the woman's body 'wears the smile of accomplishment'. She has achieved perfection. Even her children are dead with her, folded 'back into her body as petals / Of a rose close'. The moon stares over the scene from 'her hood of bone', a goddess presiding over the final, terrible act. References to Greek tragedy suggest the inevitability of the act, and the whole poem has a tone of stark detachment, a placing of the act in a kind of black aesthetic.

In 'Words', the final poem of the book, the words are axes that echo through the wood of our lives, 'travelling / Off from the centre like horses.' What the words express is the cause of the wound in the tree from which the sap 'Wells like tears'. Then, in a typical sequence of metaphorical transformations, the sap/tears are seen as water in a pool, the pool is disturbed by a falling rock which looks like a skull and then grows calm again, like a mirror:

> The sap
> Wells like tears, like the
> Water striving
> To re-establish its mirror
> Over the rock
>
> That drops and turns,
> A white skull,
> Eaten by weedy greens.
> Years later I
> Encounter them on the road –
>
> Words dry and riderless,
> The indefatigable hoof-taps.

Thus the depths of the self released in the words (including the words of the poem) remain to disturb long after they are uttered. The poem concludes with a sense of the way lives are determined by those words that express the wounds of the self:

> From the bottom of the pool, fixed stars
> Govern a life.

There is also a suggestion that words cannot alter the powers that control our destiny. In the end nothing can change the poet's knowledge of the inevitability of her suicide.

The poetry of Sylvia Plath puts us in touch with an experience of non-being, as Holbrook calls it.[11] Without a glimpse of what lies on the dark side of being, perhaps none of us can adequately value our individual sense of meaning in life. These poems express a collapse of identity, and yet their language, imagery and rhythm have a paradoxical zest and energy of life. The affirmation of meaning that the poet seems denied is bequeathed to the reader in his response to the power of the style of the poetry. If the poet could not escape the pull of death it is a human tragedy we all may mourn. But the poetry, even at its darkest, has a living force which may stand for the rest of us as itself an example to place in opposition to the pull of meaningless existence and the nullity of death. Sylvia Plath herself suggested in 'Sculptor' that only the artist can give a shape of meaning to our visions. Even in his bodying forth of our nightmares he shapes them to last beyond death itself. He upholds our true identity. It is a tragedy that the writer of a poem expressing this belief could not herself feel the sustaining power of her own words and rest accomplished not in the false perfection of death but in the living perfection of an art which is

A solider repose than death's.

6

'I step through origins'

The poetry of Seamus Heaney

The dignity of simplicities

Seamus Heaney began publishing his first poems in the early 1960s and is the oldest of a group of Ulster poets who have produced consistently interesting and valuable poems over the last ten years.

The rural landscape of Heaney's childhood forms the background to many of his poems and is frequently the central subject of the best. His work often reminds us that until recently Ireland has been the only country in northern Europe to retain something approaching a genuinely peasant culture, and the traditions and rituals of that culture, together with the spirit of Ireland's rural history, emerge in many of Heaney's poems. This spirit is related to his own childhood and early family memories. His first book, *Death of a Naturalist*, was published in 1966 and has been followed by *Door into the Dark* (1969), *Wintering Out* (1972), *North* (1975), and *Field Work* (1979).* These titles alone speak of his subjects: nature, the seasons, the countryside and its community, a sense of the past and the dark undercurrent of danger and menace in Irish life, both in past centuries and in the present political instability.

Heaney has proved to be popular with the poetry-reading public, often having an immediate appeal because of his accurate descriptive powers and the clarity of his figurative language. The following lines exemplify this immediacy:

> Clouds ran their wet mortar, plastered the daybreak
> Grey. The stones clicked tartly
> If we missed the sleepers but mostly

* This book appeared too late for discussion of it to be included in this chapter.

Silent we headed up the railway
Where now the only steam was funnelling from cows
Ditched on their rumps beyond hedges,
Cudding, watching, and knowing.

('Dawn Shoot')

The superficial clarity of this poetry, especially in his first two volumes, is something that has aroused disagreement among Heaney's critics and reviewers. All reviewers of *Death of a Naturalist* praised the way the poet created a sense of this rural Irish life, but a difference of opinion arose over the value of such descriptions. Writing in the *Kenyon Review*,[1] David Galler spent a considerable proportion of his review pursuing an argument that sought to make a distinction between descriptive poetry which remains 'exposition' and descriptive poetry with 'complication'. He maintained that description–exposition poems are merely the attempt to give reality to what is described, whereas description–complication poems occur when the poet uses his observation not just to re-create a scene but also to impart a universal significance to the individual particulars of that description. Galler argues that the latter type of poetry (exemplified in Wordsworth) has most lasting value and that Heaney does not achieve this kind of poem. Apart from ignoring the fact that a young poet might be forgiven for not yet writing at the level of the mature Wordsworth, Galler comes close to confusing surface clarity of expression in poetry with banality of theme and ideas. He underestimates Heaney's capacity to breathe a universal significance into his best descriptions (in 'Blackberry-Picking', for example). What Heaney is not doing is setting out to write poems of ideas as such. The source of many of his best poems is a memory of childhood experiences which he then renders accurately and almost physically in a direct language that shuns obscurity of expression. This may be a virtue often underestimated among literary academics and reviewers but which, nevertheless, gives Heaney's work a powerful precision and lucidity.

Death of a Naturalist includes many poems that have the countryside or animals as their subject, and yet it would be a mistake to see Heaney as a nature poet. It is the country experiences, the community and its traditions, the craftsmen and the village rituals that most interest the poet, and his deeper themes are concerned with growing up and maturing in such a rural life. This early volume contains three groups of poems: those directly concerned with his rural childhood, those that re-create the physical presence of animals (usually connected with childhood experiences as well) and a small group of love poems.

It is the first group that provides the more important poems, but a prior comment on the other two groups might be helpful. The poems about animals develop from the poet's boyhood memories of farm life. The animals are domestic (turkeys and cows) or those encountered on hunting or fishing expeditions (like trout); they are not the wild, untamed animals that fill the early poems of Ted Hughes, but Heaney does share some of Hughes's ability to describe an animal with great accuracy and liveliness. Yet Heaney's descriptions are made as from an observer's point of view: he does not try to re-create the presence of the animal from within the animal as Hughes does. It is usually the effect upon the poet-child-observer that is dwelt upon (see 'Turkeys Observed').

The love poems are light and witty, frequently built upon a simple extended metaphor and offering a warm, sunny glimpse of an uncomplicated love. In them even the parting of the lovers cannot be seen as disastrous or final:

> In your presence
> Time rode easy, anchored
> On a smile; but absence
> Rocked love's balance, unmoored
> The days. . . .
> Until you resume command
> Self is in mutiny.

('Valediction')

But the mutiny seems a mild affair, a matter of wit rather than passion, and we have no doubt that she will resume command. Probably the best of these rather delicate poems is 'Honeymoon Flight' which gives us a sense of the lovers' tentatively built trust in their newly married state. This is created through a description of the flight of the aeroplane as it carries them off to their honeymoon. As it flies through turbulence the passengers feel safe only because they trust the crew, and this is used as an image of the trust the lovers have placed in marriage. This simple idea is made effective by the quality of the description of the flight itself, its accuracy and its tone. 'The coastline slips away beneath the wing-tip' and

> Below, the patchwork earth, dark hems of hedge,
> The long grey tapes of road that bind and loose
> Villages and fields in casual marriage . . .

This suggests a connection between the marriage of landscape and community and the lovers themselves. The countryside's patch-work pattern is stitched into the garment of the landscape and drawn together by the 'grey tapes of roads'. The word 'casual' implies a relationship that is easy and natural and suggests the lovers' trust in a marriage which has been launched into a flight that will reveal the pattern of their lives. The tone is tender, the theme and language clear and straightforward. A basically iambic rhythm nevertheless allows secondary stresses on the adjectives in 'dark hems' and 'long grey tapes', and has the effect of slowing down the run of the first two lines so helping create the impression of the slowly turning landscape (suggested, too, by the accumula-tion of long vowel sounds), thus undermining a too stolid rhythm which would have marred the tentative step of the central idea of trust.

The virtues of a simple originality of image and diction can be seen more clearly in the poems about childhood and rural life. Two of the best of these are 'Churning Day' and 'Blackberry-Picking'. 'Churning Day' captures the ancient ritual of farm life in the days before mechanization in its description of the hand churning of milk into butter. It is built on a traditional iambic norm which holds in the details, binding together a strong percus-sive diction that creates a pressure against the steady but forceful flow of plosives. Adjectives and adverbs cluster thickly and this concatenation in the diction suggests the noise and hard work of the operation. This roughness also avoids any suggestion that the poet is writing a 'Country Life' idyll. His intention is twofold: to give a feeling of the hard physical slog of butter making, and to re-create a boy's sensuous observations. It was through his eyes and ears that the boy watched. For him churning day meant not so much the end product of butter but the noise, energy and bustle of

the activity itself. From the opening onwards the poem is alive
with this energy:

> A thick crust, coarse-grained as limestone rough-cast,
> hardened gradually on top of the four crocks
> that stood, large pottery bombs, in the small pantry.

The choice of 'pottery bombs' may be an intrusive feature, but
otherwise the 'k' sounds and the limestone simile perfectly bring
out the quality of a crust on standing milk. As the poem develops
it concentrates its energy increasingly into the verbs ('scoured',
'spilled', 'plunged', 'spattered', etc.), building up a flurry of noise
and activity and of the skilled work of the mother, until by the end
(in a phrase embodying the tiring slog of it all) she,

> . . . set up rhythms
> that slugged and thumped for hours. Arms ached.
> Hands blistered.

This may be a delightful world for the grown man's memory to be
drawn back into, but for those who lived in it then it was a tough,
unceasing life of labour and Heaney preserves the endurance of
the people in the strength of his sounds and rhythms.

The core of the poem, buried within the imitative sounds and
rhythms of the day's work, is the theme of the process of purification and transformation. It is not a meditative or contemplative
poem and, since Heaney, as pointed out earlier, is not primarily a
poet of ideas, this theme is not worked out as a concept. It does
not perhaps achieve the full generalizing power that Mr Galler
thinks necessary for the greatest descriptive poetry. But what
Heaney does do is to look hard and closely at the ritual and seize
the sense of it for the child who plays in the middle of it on the
'flagged kitchen floor'. It is therefore an idea of *the senses*, not of
the mind, and suggests that the churning is perhaps a process of
purification whose effect on the boy and the young man remembering his past is implied but not stated. We experience this idea
through the child's eyes and ears and it is the accumulation of
sensuous detail that matters: the crocks 'spilled their heavy lip / of
cream, their white insides, into the sterile churn.' The child *feels*
more than thinks of the patient process as the mother works on to

the limits of her aching arms and blistered hands so that 'finally gold flecks / began to dance' until in a final, sudden moment 'a yellow curd was weighting the churned up white'. It is not a fanciful poetic image to describe the final butter as 'coagulated sunlight', for the young boy must have seen this as a magic act, a mother's Midas touch, and the startling gold yellow of the butter was a regular miracle for the child. Thus earlier in the poem it is the child's sense of strange power that allows the poet to describe the cow's initial transformation of grass into milk as 'the hot brewery of gland, cud and udder' and the house after churning as stinking 'acrid as a sulphur mine'. Although requiring an adult's knowledge, these images are demanded by the remembered *child's* sensuous response. And thus each constituent of the poem underlines the physical and emotional experience, including movement and sound being picked out in this description:

> And in the house we moved with gravid ease,
> our brains turned crystals full of clean deal churns,
> the plash and gurgle of the sour-breathed milk,
> the pat and slap of small spades on wet lumps.

Mr Galler sees this poem as no more than an accumulation of descriptive details. This is too dismissive and does not take account of the fact that the act of description is valuable in itself when it helps us to see plainly and feel deeply the experience at its heart. His damning of phrases like 'hot brewery of gland', 'busy scrubber', 'churning day' and 'purified' for being 'phrases with mysterious implications' but no depth overlooks the obvious point that each is an altogether accurate description of part of the activity and what mystery the poet sees in them is only an 'implication' for the young boy. Christopher Ricks's comment in an early review is far more justified: 'What is surprising is the dignity with which Mr Heaney invests such simplicities, such as "wet lumps".'

In 'Blackberry-Picking' we have a similar approach to a familiar childhood ritual. Utilizing the same basic rhythm (although with frequent inversions of stress that move it away further from the iambic norm of the two poems), Heaney this time employs greater use of rhyme, particularly assonance and half-rhyme. There is again the attempt to re-create a physical sense of the

activity, and he stresses the appeal of the fruit in its various stages
to eye, hand and tongue:

> At first, just one, a glossy purple clot
> Among others, red, green, hard as a knot.
> You ate that first one and its flesh was sweet
> Like thickened wine. . . .

But in this poem there is a more conscious attempt to see and place
the childhood experience through the conceptualizing of the
adult:

> Like thickened wine: summer's blood was in it
> Leaving stains upon the tongue and lust for
> Picking.

'Blood' and 'lust' might seem to be overdoing it, perhaps falsely
exaggerating the particulars to create a universal significance, yet
the trail of the pickers is smeared throughout with suggestions of
blood, appropriately both creating a sense of the overpowering
desire for the fruit (which makes the pickers endure the most
precarious positions and painful lacerations) and also preparing
for the second part of the poem in which the failed attempt to
store the fruit modulates into the child's first awareness of the
experience of disillusion. Precisely because this idea arises naturally from the description, we feel in the end no overworked
attempt to moralize. The final line both contains an accurate
recall of childhood and raises the subject towards a full-bodied
image of our natural human inclination to hang on to what has
given us great pleasure. Linked, as it is, to the seasons' cycle
('summer's blood was in it') and hinting at the unbridled nature of
our first gluttony for the fruit (berries at the top of the can are 'big
dark blobs [which] burned / Like a plate of eyes' observing and yet
attracting the greed), we are prepared for the terms of the final
disillusion:

> Once off the bush
> The fruit fermented, the sweet flesh would turn sour.
> I always felt like crying. It wasn't fair
> That all the lovely canfuls smelt of rot.
> Each year I hoped they'd keep, knew they would not.

That last straightforward comment on the yearly experience brings the poem to a sharp halt with its final return to the everyday reality, eschewing any portentous symbols yet allowing a wider meaning to arise naturally from the child's experience. The possible moral is there because it *is* part of the growing awareness of this country child. Reality relentlessly tempers his dreams – a theme central to both the first two books.

Growing up

Maturity and the experiences of childhood that hurry it forth are at the heart of several of the finest poems in the early books. The title poem of the first volume and 'The Advancement of Learning' are two very successful evocations of moments of growing up.

'Death of a Naturalist' shares many of the characteristics of the poems already examined. A childhood experience is again conveyed in a vigorous diction, this time riding on a four-/five-stress line which only approximates to an iambic norm.

> All year the flax-dam festered in the heart
> Of the townland; green and heavy headed
> Flax had rotted there, weighted down by huge sods.
> Daily it sweltered in the punishing sun.

An extra syllable in the third line is used to slow down the speed of the rhythm, pulling down its centre of gravity, as it were, and using the caesura of the second line to separate the generalized opening from the particulars following. This prepares 'festered in the heart' (which is emphasized by taking the stress at the end of the line) as a prelude to the theme of the whole poem. That theme is developed tangentially through the evocation of the experience and not by direct comment, according to the procedure of the poems already looked at.

In the first half of the poem the boy collects tadpoles among the flax-dam in order to carry them home to observe 'The fattening dots burst into nimble- / Swimming tadpoles.' His teacher would tell him of the 'daddy' frog and how it was called 'a bullfrog' and 'how the mammy frog / Laid hundreds of little eggs'. It was cosy, domestic, clear and lovely. The frogs were outside him, collected, observed, controlled by him and even used for predicting the weather:

> You could tell the weather by frogs too
> For they were yellow in the sun and brown
> In rain.

But in the second half of the poem comes the decisive experience of 'one hot day when fields were rank / With cowdung' ('rank' and the excretory image indicate the change of tone), and he comes across hundreds of frogs croaking loudly in the flax-dam. They look obscene and threatening and he runs from them, for he sees them as an invading enemy shouting at him in anger. The familiar isolated calls he has heard before suddenly become a huge chorus of 'coarse croaking'. He is utterly revolted by their pulsing life and their apparent abandonment of their previously tame existence. They have become 'great slime kings', no longer tame or domestic or controlled, and he can no longer maintain a detached view. They insist on reminding him that they have a life of their own and one that is unrelievedly physical. The last image of the poem – '. . . and I knew / That if I dipped my hand the spawn would clutch it' – shows how the boy's attitude has changed. The frogs are now on the offensive and control the boy. No explicit statement explores the theme but the presentation of this total image of the experience leaves us in no doubt of the physical quality of a moment when the boy suddenly realizes his youth is turning into manhood. Leaving behind a state of nature, a feeling of at-homeness with natural processes, the language of the second half of the poem is used to create the sense of distaste and fear for the physicality and sexuality of adolescence that the boy is beginning to feel. The description of the frogs shows this clearly enough (I have italicized the words carrying a submerged sexual association):

> The air was thick with a *bass* chorus.
> Right down the dam *gross-bellied* frogs were *cocked*
> On sods; their loose necks *pulsed* like sails. Some hopped:
> The slap and pop were *obscene threats*. Some sat
> Poised like mud grenades, their *blunt* heads *farting*.

The boy's revulsion at his own sexuality, the young adolescent's smutty embarrassment at his body, are projected on to the frogs. In these lines description blends perfectly with 'complication' to create a generalizable theme without over-exploiting the particulars of the description. This poem is a perfect fusion of description and comment in a single experience. The title is given to the whole volume in which the poem appears because the predominant theme of that book is growing up. The community described in the poems may be particular but the experience of maturation is a universal one.

'An Advancement of Learning' takes even further the idea of the menace in an experience of the repulsive side of nature and uses it to reveal the growing power of the maturity in the boy. This is the experience of a slightly older adolescent. While walking along the river embankment, he encounters two rats and recalls his earlier childhood fear of them, remembering he

> . . . used to panic
> When his grey brothers scraped and fed
> Behind the hen-coop in our yard,
> On ceiling boards above my bed.

But on this occasion he stands his ground, refuses to panic and stares the rats out. These rats are real enough to the reader as well as to the poet: 'a rat / Slimed out of water',

> He clockworked aimlessly a while,
> Stopped, back bunched and glistening,
> Ears plastered down on his knobbed skull,
> Insidiously listening.

The presence of the rats has already been prefigured at the beginning of the poem when the river itself is pictured as some slimy, cunning animal in the guise of the colours and reflections of its surroundings:

> The river nosed past,
> Pliable, oil-skinned, wearing
>
> A transfer of gables and sky.

One reviewer criticized the inappropriateness of these lines. But this is a mistaken verdict. A river may 'nose' not just because it is prefiguring the creatures in the poem but because it flows into places, pushes forward and then retreats in small exploring rivulets, and the industrial pollution that floats on so many rivers is imaged in the notion of the skin of oil on the water.

We are reminded again of this polluted river towards the end of the poem when the rat crawls back into its 'natural' habitat of a sewer pipe. The poet-boy sees him off, then crosses the bridge and walks away. For a short time the reader is held, like the boy, staring the experience through, and then is released to continue his progress. The sickening fear of the dark, hidden, repulsive world of the rat is overcome, in the same way that the boy comes through into a balanced recognition of his sexuality and is taken a step beyond the condition in the previous poem.

In some of the poems in the first book Heaney begins that exploration of his own relationship with the past history of his country and his family which is to become a staple theme of the later verse. One of these interesting early poems is 'For the Commander of the "Eliza"'. This is a different kind of poem from the ones so far examined. It is a dramatic monologue built around an actual historical incident – the refusal of a coastguard ship's captain to take on board six men drifting in a small boat as they searched in vain for some way to avoid starving in the potato famines in Ireland in the 'hungry forties'. It is a credible attempt to get inside the skin of an unpopular character who was carrying out orders which, he claimed, gave him 'no mandate to relieve distress'. The 'Six grown men with gaping mouths and eyes' are quickly and deftly pencilled in alongside the expression of the commander's attitude. The scene is described in a predominantly curt, matter-of-fact tone suggestive of a report in the ship's log. It is clear that this style reflects not just that the commander is unable to feel some pity (although he is so limited, as the language he uses reveals in its reduction of suffering humanity to the level of bad odours – 'Next day, like six bad smells, those living skulls Drifted through . . . my ship') but also that he is the representative of the British government whose official stance is: 'Less incidents the better.' This view is underlined in the reprimand delivered to the commander's land-based superior who tried to order famine relief to the area. This poem is an accurate, restrained but nevertheless fierce accusation of the past wrongs done to Ireland, and it succeeds in both explaining the lack of humanity in the political sphere and making us feel the tensions between an official's carrying out of orders and the human being's sense of pity for suffering.

This poem contains the ghosts of an earlier Ireland, a tragic Ireland. In this and 'Docker', a portrait of a riveter with his 'Speech . . . clamped in the lips' vice', we gain glimpses of a more social, political aspect of Heaney's poetry. But in this volume he does not extend these aspects. He is more concerned with feeling his own way back through his personal past towards a community and a landscape that will help him discover his country and shape his sense of identity. Nevertheless 'Docker', written before the later political violence in Northern Ireland, does contain a sad prophecy that the bitter divisions of the past could still break through:

> That fist would drop a hammer on a Catholic –
> Oh yes, that kind of thing could start again. . . .

Two poems in particular concern the poet's relationship with his own family past: 'Digging' and 'Follower'. Both are about the poet's father. 'Digging' is also about the writing of poetry. It is the first poem in the first book and it makes clear the connection between the poet's vocation and his inherited traditions. The subject and situation are simple: sitting writing, the poet hears his old father digging beneath his window and as he watches him his memory recalls earlier childhood scenes of his father digging up potatoes and of his grandfather cutting peat. The poet recognizes that, although he has seemingly abandoned the family farm, he does 'dig' on with his pen, trying to cut down into the soil of a shared existence and throw up a connection between them all. The poem is itself a discovery and a recognition of his past and an honouring of the family tradition of craftsmanship. The qualities of that tradition – its physical and sensuous pleasures in a life lived naturally and in touch with the land – are the qualities that Heaney seeks to preserve in his poems.

The link between the poet's deliberate and conscious attempt to create his own poetic identity and the nature of those family traditions is made explicit in the description of his father among the flowerbeds. He

> . . . comes up twenty years away
> Stooping in rhythm through potato drills
> Where he was digging.

So that

> Between my finger and my thumb
> The squat pen rests.
> I'll dig with it.

The poem is to capture the rhythm of a fast-disappearing tradition and in so doing allow the poet to lay hold on his own sense of self. Thus we begin to realize that *Death of a Naturalist* not only explores the transformation of boy into man, farmer into poet, but also reckons with the gradual displacement of a traditional rural life which was close to natural sources. The whole volume is 'digging' in the sense that the act of writing is an unearthing of the poet's past and the historical roots of a nation. Heaney is uncovering a sense of selfhood and nationhood:

> The cold smell of potato mould, the squelch and slap
> Of soggy peat, the curt cuts of an edge
> Through living roots awaken in my head.
> But I've no spade to follow men like them.

That these living roots are important becomes clearer in 'Follower' in which the poet pictures his father ploughing, 'His shoulders globed like a full sail strung / Between the shafts and the furrow.' This extravagant simile begins a poem which celebrates the strength, expertise and craft of the poet's father. Heaney recalls how as a boy he 'stumbled in his hob-nailed wake' (the sailing image implicitly continued) and how he then wished for nothing more than to grow up and take over his landed inheritance. Then

> I was a nuisance, tripping, falling,
> Yapping always. But today
> It is my father who keeps stumbling
> Behind me, and will not go away.

A follower as a boy, he is now dogged by memories of his father and must in turn follow the family tradition in his verse, straining with his father's energy to capture the craft and expertise of the poet in the tight traditional rhythms and rhymes of the ballad-like form of this poem. The sense of craft is the only remaining link across the generations. Pursuing the past in this way Heaney shows his sense of its durable qualities but also asserts a changing tradition through his own very different vocation.

Entry into the buried life

Heaney's second volume, *Door into the Dark*, continues the search of the family past initiated in the first book and begins to look towards some of the thematic material of the later poems. The evocative title might seem to suggest some kind of move towards the unknown, or death, or into the subconscious, but these poems of rural landscapes, traditional crafts and village communities suggest a slightly different movement. There are two particular, but related ways in which these poems are doors into the dark. In the first there are poems like 'A Wife's Tale' and 'Mother' which develop the technique begun in 'For the Commander of the "Eliza"' and which try to peer into the darkness of the personality of someone very different from the poet and yet someone who has grown from the same tradition as the poet. In the second way into the dark are those poems which look further into the natural processes of country life, into the dark interior of earth, nature, nature's forms and the rituals man has created upon them (for example, 'A Lough Neagh Sequence'). By living within the landscape, being part of it and by seeing through it into the lives of those dependent upon it (the farming and fishing community), the poet explores the rich, dark inheritance of his country. In the final poems of the volume the processes of nature in the peatbogs of Ireland are examined as part of the mysterious, black heart of the country's history and its people's identity.

'The Forge' is a sonnet which celebrates the craftsmanship of a village blacksmith. This is the complete poem:

> All I know is a door into the dark.
> Outside, old axles and iron hoops rusting;
> Inside, the hammered anvil's short-pitched ring,

The unpredictable fantail of sparks
Or hiss when a new shoe toughens in water.
The anvil must be somewhere in the centre,
Horned as a unicorn, at one end square,
Set there immoveable: an altar
Where he expends himself in shape and music.
Sometimes, leather-aproned, hairs in the nose,
He leans out on the jamb, recalls a clatter
Of hoofs where traffic is flashing in rows;
Then grunts and goes in, with a slam and flick
To beat real iron out, to work the bellows.

The precise and unadorned diction of this poem represents as
honest a piece of craftsmanship as the subject it describes. From
first to last, images of sight and sound predominate: sight in lines
1–2, 4–6, 10–11; hearing in lines 3, 5, 9, 11, 13–14. Between
them they encapsulate the setting and the action. But more than
just the particulars of a deftly sketched description emerges with
the central simile of the unicorn. This appears at first because of
the visual metaphor, but the suggestion of the unicorn's horn
reminds us of the unique, rare quality of the blacksmith's craft.
The 'shape and music' of his art is plainly stated and thereafter in
the reference to 'an altar' we perceive the almost religious dedication of the craftsman to his traditional skills. He is a man of few
words who has little regard for the flash of cars that streak by
where his horses used to go. He turns away, with unmistakable
disdain for the modern world, to beat 'the real iron out', and in
that one small word 'real' a disparaging colour is thrown over all
the inferior products of mass production – a doomed disdain for
the world which will slowly, inevitably relieve him of his dedication. The door into the dark is also the way into the oblivion of a
future in which such traditions will be cancelled.

There is no need to make large claims for this short poem; it
does not have a large public or political sweep and in fact does not
explore the dramatic qualities of the social theme it implies. But it
is accurate, it does come alive as it records the last moments of a
dying craft, and after it has been read it lingers in the mind to
recall that even after the last blacksmith has gone 'The anvil must
be somewhere in the centre', if only as an image of the rich

potency of such a dedication to any excellence of a craft, be it smithying or writing.

In 'The Wife's Tale' Heaney takes a monologue form again and applies it to a farmer's wife as she takes out a meal to the menfolk who are bringing home the harvest. The poem begins with her description of the scene as she spreads a linen cloth under the shade of the hedge and listens to 'The hum and gulp of the thresher [as it] ran down'. But it is the poet's voice rather than his character's which talks of the sudden silence and the momentarily loud sound of 'their boots / Crunching the stubble twenty yards away'.

This poem is in four short parts, and in the second part we overhear the raffish banter of the husband as he makes light-hearted fun of his wife and shows off a little to his friends (and yet at the same time we perceive a genuine admiration and pride in his words):

> 'Give these fellows theirs.
> I'm in no hurry,' plucking grass in handfuls
> And tossing it in the air. . . .
>
> 'I declare a woman could lay out a field
> Though boys like us have little call for cloths.'
> He winked, then watched me as I poured a cup.

These lines quickly sketch the established roles of the sexes in the farming community – the man with his strength and disdain of comfort, the woman with her small attempts to add grace and civilizing values to a basic existence. The man's pride in the harvest and his desire to share his good fortune with his wife leads him to tell her to 'Away over there and look' at the results of their labour. Then in the third part the wife runs her hands through the corn 'hard as shot / Innumerable and cool.' After this recognition of the 'good yield' the men turn away from her, her part is done, and she moves away with the unbitter realization of her dismissal from her husband to return to her different role, leaving the men at ease 'spread out, unbuttoned, grateful, under the trees.'

There is in this poem a perfect grasp of relationships in a rural community, and in the careful delineation of their talk and behaviour there is a subtle placing of the value and limitations of

these relationships. It is not romanticized. But it must be added
that the intention of making the poem a tale told by the wife is a
fiction. It is Heaney's voice and a poet's eye that selects the images
and creates the tone. Only in the briefly quoted words of the man
is there the genuine idiom of a character outside the poet.

'A Lough Neagh Sequence' is a long poem composed of seven
short lyrics, each of which describes the fishermen or the eels that
they catch, or the watery landscape of Lough Neagh. It is one of
the most accomplished poems in this collection, and each separate
part gains by being placed together with the other poems even
though each poem is complete in itself. There is no strict development of action or great modulation in tone and mood throughout
the sequence, yet the whole is not long enough for this to be felt as
a limitation. Here is a cycle of thematic material which is not
over-laboured and which gives a sense of completeness and
roundness to the sequence. The themes are not pursued in detail
but appear more as motifs or tropes which are announced in the
first line and then continue to recur like the undertow of the
currents in the Lough – an undramatic but persistent flow. The
theme is: 'The lough will claim a victim every year.' The sequence
is not directly about these victims but about the struggle of the
fishermen to make their livelihood, the life cycle of the eels which
spawn in the Lough and the children who love to catch them, one
of whom was the young poet. In their various ways all are victims
of the lough, not because they drown but because it absorbs them
and they absorb it, carrying it in every step of their lives. It is
present even in the poet's boyhood when in 'Vision' (the last
poem) he remembers having been threatened that

> Unless his hair was fine-combed
> The lice, they said, would gang-up
> Into a mealy rope
> And drag him, small, dirty, doomed
>
> Down to the water.

Yet eventually he is claimed by this water not in this distasteful
way but by his boyhood's years spent in the marshy fields 'at night
when eels / Moved through the grass like hatched fears / Towards
the water'. The brilliant transformation of the opening image of

the rope of lice into the flow of eels in the lines quoted above, and then into 'his world's live girdle' and 'horrible cable' of the following final stanza, firmly claims the poet as 'victim' of the lough, its fishing community, their traditions and behaviour.

The different parts of the poem employ varying forms, from a basic iambic four-line stanza, through three-line stanzas rhyming *abb*, to another rhyming *aaa/bbb* and a freer two-/three-stress line. All of these (but especially the second poem on the spawning of the eels and the fourth poem on the fishermen) create a tight, vigorous pull of feelings which rise at moments to descriptions touched with a sense of vision. One such moment occurs in this description of the eel that burrows in the land during the day and suddenly reappears at night:

> Dark
> delivers him hungering
> down each undulation.

Another such moment occurs in the fifth poem, when the fishermen haul in their catch of eels as they are

> . . . slapped into the barrel numb

> But knits itself, four-ply,
> With the furling, slippy
> Haul, a knot of black and pewter belly

> That stays continually one
> For each catch they fling in
> Is sucked home like lubrication.

The sheer physical presence of this compressed imagery is astonishing.

The sequence as a whole successfully fuses Heaney's love of his rural roots and of the people who still live in the countryside with his sense of awe at the mystery of the dark interior of the land (for which the strange, extravagant life cycle of the eel is an excellent symbol), and shows his talent for bodying forth with physical presence the subject of his descriptions. This poem looks ahead to some of the later attempts to use sequences to tie together a range of different impressions.

A further poem, 'Requiem for the Croppies', takes a historical incident as its source. It is written as if spoken by the rebellious 'croppies' who in an earlier period revolted against the landlords and who lived on the run until, at Vinegar Hill, they were mown down. The closeness of these people to the land is what the poet emphasizes as he describes them on the run and living off the crops – people who, when they died, would sift down to become the very land from which the crops would spring. The political theme and the restrained irony of the idea behind the poem are more evident than usual in Heaney's earlier poetry. But this image of the soil of Ireland literally containing the blood and bones of its past is to become a central symbol in his later poems.

Another later symbol which is first announced in this book is that of the peat bogs and their surrounding landscape (for example, 'Bann Clay' and 'Bogland'). The clay may be 'baked white in the sun' but it hoards all kinds of 'Mesolithic flints', scraps of the past which can suddenly be shovelled up by a boy who is simply involved in cleaning a field drain:

> This smooth weight. I labour
> Towards it still. It holds and gluts.

It is as if the key to the past of the whole race is in the grip of the land. In all senses the soil gives the community its roots and life.

Similarly the peat bogs have the property of preserving intact whatever falls into them. 'The ground itself is kind' and as it keeps

> Melting and opening underfoot,
> Missing its last definition
> By millions of years

it constitutes a 'wet centre' that is bottomless. This provides the last image of this book. It is as if we had come in by the door of the old rural life and had fallen out down a shaft into the bottomless dark pit of the land itself.

Door into the Dark confirms the adroit skill of handling image, rhythm and language that was revealed in the first book, but it adds a deepening theme. These poems develop a tautness of line and a spareness of language which is no less rich nor vibrant than the earlier book but which also opens up a depth and resonance that set 'the dark echoing'. At their best these poems rise beyond mere observation towards an emotional exploration and evaluation of a subject which has increasingly moved from the identity of the poet to the nature of Ireland herself.

The heart of a land

More space has been devoted to the first two books than will be to *Wintering Out* and *North*, not because they are considered better or more important but simply because they are easiest for a new reader to assimilate and form the indispensable groundwork for a full appreciation of the poet's aims in the later work. This work leads away from the personal and narrower confines of the poet's own past and towards the wider, public inheritance of the country's history. It is felt by Heaney to be an inheritance that is deep and sometimes violent. Certainly in poems written after 1970 there is an increasing recognition of the political troubles of Northern Ireland (although some of the most political poems have not yet been collected into book form). Yet it is not simply the acknowledgement of the facts of social division nor the terror of the Troubles that makes *North* important. It is important because in this volume, as in parts of the previous one, Heaney relates past and present, his personal past and the country's history, in order to get beneath the dangerously oversimplified political perspectives on Ireland and its people. He maintains the poet's traditional role of guardian of the word-hoard, that deep repository of a people's reality and their dreams. Through this commitment to a continuity of past and present explored in the language of people and place, Heaney begins to discover an identity for himself that acknowledges his own part in a strife-torn land but which does not take the easy way of identifying himself with that side of history to which his birth would align him. The ground (literally in the poems about the soil of Ireland) on which he has chosen to stand is beyond, or rather beneath, the normal divisions and inevitably exposes him to the ridicule and hatred of those on any side who believe salvation lies in being partisan. It leaves him to appear as either enemy or deserter. It is not an easy stance but he draws his courage from the fact that ultimately it is the only stance that can include the whole of Ireland – the only possibility for resolution.

The strain of this lonely task is seen in *Wintering Out*, where

many poems, although not overtly political in subject, are about
the estrangement and isolation that the poet feels ('Servant Boy',
'The Last Mummer', 'The Wool Trade', 'Shore Woman' and
'Bye-Child'). In them the poet identifies with various conditions
of alienation in others, and they seem to reflect a suggestion that
he is circling round some deep centre in himself which he has not
yet clearly traced, touched or understood. In other poems that are
concerned with places and the language of the names of places
(the words that begin to put him in touch with the 'word-hoard')
there is also this feeling of a search for some stable centre. A glance
at 'Servant Boy' and 'The Last Mummer', together with a closer
look at 'Gifts of Rain', may make this link between people and
place clearer.

'Servant Boy', consisting of five unrhymed four-line stanzas, is
an uncomplicated poem which communicates a sense of the bitter
independence concealed by the docile competence of the servant's
outward behaviour. He works on a farm or great house which has
its own outhouses and chicken runs. In the poem he is seen
collecting eggs and wandering through the stables and into 'the
back doors of the little / barons' to bring 'the warm eggs'. He is an
'Old work-whore, slave- / blood' who must be at the beck and call
of his masters and yet who has still learnt to hug to himself a free,
private self that he keeps safely from the knowledge of his masters: he 'kept your patience / and your counsel'. He is pictured
'wintering out' at 'the back-end of a bad year', and the poem
swings round the contrast between his cold, outcast situation and
his role as the delicate bearer of 'warm eggs'. Parallel to this
dark/light and cold/warm contrast is the poet's relationship with
the boy with whom he clearly identifies:

> . . . how
> you draw me into
> your trail. Your trail
>
> broken from haggard to stable,
> a straggle of fodder
> stiffened on snow,
> comes first-footing
>
> the back doors of the little
> barons. . . .

The association of 'first-footing' with New Year rituals suggests the boy is more than just a servant in the poet's eyes. He is an isolated figure, outside his society; yet he has kept his heart and mind clear, untrammelled by the condition of slavery to which that society has reduced him. In fact that society, unknown to its masters, is utterly dependent on the slave's ability to keep the eggs warm – to bring its source of life and sustenance. As such he becomes an image of the poet who feels unable to identify with any one part of his society and who is trying to discover and restore the sources of life beneath his country's divided powers.

Historically a mummer is an actor who roamed the country or appeared at Christmas and the New Year to act out the rituals of the season in a traditional 'automatic style' and with a 'curiously hypnotizing impressiveness', according to Thomas Hardy. In Heaney's 'The Last Mummer' we have a poem of light, clear two-lined verses with a minimum of punctuation and the lightest of regular stress beats, which allows the mummer to move rapidly through the poem. He appears almost as a ghostly memory, an insubstantial creature and creator of dreams and visions who wanders the countryside and 'Moves out of the fog / on the lawn, pads up the terrace' to the great house, 'beating / the bars of the gate' to demand entrance to perform the regular rituals that will remind the inhabitants of his magical powers. He takes on a mysterious, unanchored form in this poem, being close to nature and the repository of the language of all communities:

> His tongue went whoring
>
> among the civil tongues,
> he had an eye for weather-eyes
>
> at cross-roads and lane-ends
> and could don manners
>
> at a flutter of curtains.

Protean, he takes the shape of any part. He is magic – 'His straw mask and hunch were fabulous' – and he could escape the politicians and their attendant strident divisions of opinion by the cunning of his craft as entertainer and magician who can manipulate reality for the conviction of all sides. He is master of all realities:

He came trammelled
in the taboos of the country

picking a nice way through
the long toils of blood

and feuding.

He leaves the poet dreaming of 'a line of mummers', precursors of
the poet who 'untousled a first dewy path / Into the summer
grazing.' Again the poet is identifying with someone apart from
his society who nevertheless performs an indispensable service for
that society through their deep allegiance to the secrets of the
country's traditions. It is this that gives him the power to thread a
path through the blood and feuding.

Through these poems Heaney expresses his being forced as an
artist away from his community and yet, because the roots of his
art lie in the life of that community and its traditions, he believes
he must continue a search for some way to remain fiercely independent so that he can play the true servant to his community as
the magus who can create the community's dream and make 'dark
tracks' between its members and the deep springs of their lives.

Some of the other poems in this collection concern themselves
with the names of places: 'Anahorish', 'Toome', 'Broagh'. The
language of the place-names is identified with the tongue of the
land and the speech of the poet:

Anahorish, soft gradient
of consonant, vowel-meadow,

after-image of lamps
swung through the yards
on winter evenings.

We begin to see in this poem the use of names, of language as
metaphor and symbol for Ireland and its past. We begin to register
Heaney's fusing of place, people, politics, past and poetry. On its
own this poem does not go so far. Here the 'place of clear water' is
no more than an after-image of the past community which burns
gently, if not brightly, in the syllables of the present name. But in
'Gifts of Rain' we have the explicit handling of this extended
metaphor of language-history. It is not a poem of statement, but a

vigorous description of the land lashed by storm, written in a
loose-limbed stanza pattern which, being more open than
Heaney's previous style, seems able to catch the downpour of a
cloudburst and rush it on through the runnels of the poem as it
rises to a swift flood that gives a sense of the movement of the
water. In it there is no clutter of adjectives and adverbs to describe
the man working through the downpour and experiencing himself as part of the elements:

> So
>
> he is hooped to where he planted
> and sky and ground
>
> are running naturally among his arms
> that grope the cropping land.

The rain 'world-schooled' the poet's ear, and turning to the
farmers, he becomes aware of his distance from those who crop
the land and of his need to reawaken some sense of continuity
between himself and the past, the people and the land.

> I cock my ear
> at an absence –
> in the shared calling of the blood
>
> arrives my need
> for antediluvian lore.
> Soft voices of the dead
> are whispering by the shore . . .

As he listens to the water of 'the Moyola harping on / its gravel
beds' he is visited by a vision of 'The tawny guttural water' as it
seems to him to spell itself, and he sees it 'bedding the locale /
in the utterance'. The swollen river breathes 'through vowels and
history'. In this looser, freer style of line with its pared-down
language, Heaney is beginning to transpose description by exposition into a truly metaphorical, symbolic level of meaning where
the meaning cannot exist apart from its image in the poem, in just
the same way as he comes to believe that the meaning of the voices
of the dead cannot be separated from the living waters of the
Moyola. He is developing a technique that will defeat clumsy

commentary. The poems will not mean, but be. So it is in another poem about a place that he says

> My mouth holds round
> the soft blastings,
> *Toome, Toome,*
> as under the dislodged
>
> slab of the tongue
> I push into a souterrain

and thus he speaks the land, becomes 'sleeved in / alluvial mud'. In 'Broagh', too, he speaks a language that is composed of the place, and the poetry and place interfuse to capture the land's identity and make it his own.

In *Wintering Out* he writes out of this land, the people and places that he has always spoken of, but the need to know them becomes more and more acute as he increasingly writes out the memories of his own childhood. 'A Northern Hoard' and 'Traditions' make it clear that there is a search now for a way back from the personal poems of his own past towards the past of a whole country. The urgency of this search is revealed in the dedicatory poem written after he had seen a new prison camp for the internees. Seeing this he feels that 'we hug our little destiny again'. Ireland's new troubles remain the same as the old ones and Heaney suggests the poet's task also remains the same. The poet must use his craft to bring an order to the chaos of divided feelings, to grasp and hold both sides of the struggle, to speak for the past, dead Ireland and in so doing to create a new song out of the deeper destiny of the country that links past and present to reveal its 'coherent miseries'.

It is *North* that really begins to provide the sense of that centre to his identity around which Heaney seems to have been circling. In it he pursues the honing of his style begun in the previous volume and in the clean, clear sweep of these poems the continuities and coherences really begin to be gathered up.

The title poem presents the poet looking out over the Atlantic from 'a long strand, / the hammered shod of a bay' from where he hears 'the secular / powers' of the sea and can look north towards Iceland. Standing there he is well placed geographically and metaphorically to look into the cold heart of northern Europe. His mind fills with the 'violence and epiphany' of the Norsemen who linked Iceland, Greenland, Scandinavia and Ireland, and he remembers the tombs, monuments and relics of that warrior race scattered between Orkney and Dublin in museums and in

> ... the solid
> belly of stone ships,
> those hacked and glinting
> in the gravel of thawed streams.

These memories crowd together and link war, travel and trade, 'thick-witted couplings and revenges', whose memory incubates spilled blood. The past is redolent with the same violent revenges as the present. But to the poet these northern histories and legends, landscapes and hatreds, travels and tongues, are all contained in that 'long strand' which is the essence of Ireland. The Atlantic that bore the longboats with their 'swimming tongue ... buoyant with hindsight' is to the poet a source of 'secular powers' which can replace the religious bigotry that is at root of the long history of violence because that ocean *precedes* all religious differences. The land was there before man. The poem ends with the 'longship's swimming tongue' pronouncing invocation and command:

> 'Lie down
>
> in the word-hoard, burrow
> the coil and gleam
> of your furrowed brain.
>
> Compose in darkness.
> Expect aurora borealis
> in the long foray
> but no cascade of light.
>
> Keep your eye clear
> at the bleb of the icicle,
> trust the feel of what nubbed treasure
> your hands have known.'

The poet is to dig down into the past, beneath even the violent history, to close with the earth and sea that clutches and drowns remnants of the past (wrecks, flints in pebbles, bodies preserved in the peatbogs – each of which have poems to themselves elsewhere in the latest volumes). He must cling to what he already knows, to what the land preserves; he is to search out the 'word-hoard' of this ancient language.

The form of this poem is sparse and ribbed compared with the heavier, more opulent language of the earliest poems. The lean line and free rhythm (a basic two-/three-stress system) are given more power by the diction. From the metaphor of the rocky shore ('hammered shod of a bay') to the cool, bright light of the aurora borealis, we are presented with a pattern of imagery that suggests cold, hard edges and which captures the landscape and its climate, the nature of the Norse raiders and the poet's determination.

The 'word-hoard' is explicitly stated in this poem, and it begins to call up threads from other poems, such as 'Anahorish', which have also used the language metaphor to connect place and past with the poet's task. This metaphor becomes dominant as a symbol over this whole volume. The poet speaks, but the land, its history, objects and people speak through him in each poem.

A further symbol of continuity is developed in 'Tollund Man' in the previous book and in *North* is firmly established as a controlling metaphor in several of the best poems. These are about the peat bogs' peculiar power to preserve whatever falls into them. They are full of relics of Ireland's past, including bodies (usually of those who have been murdered or have otherwise met a violent end). This natural phenomenon links the landscape with the people and with the rural past of Heaney's own family who, like many rural families, cut peat for themselves and to make a living. Of this image Heaney has written: 'So I began to get an idea of the bog as the memory of the landscape, or as a landscape that remembered everything that happened in it and to it.'[2]

It is impossible to describe the sharp, physical sense of the bogs and their buried 'treasure' except by quotation:

> My body was braille
> for the creeping influences:
> dawn suns groped over my head . . .

the seeps of winter
digested me. . . .

I knew winter cold
like the nuzzle of fjords
at my thighs –

('Bog Queen')

The grain of his wrists
is like bog oak,
the ball of his heel

like a basalt egg.

('The Grauballe Man')

These bodies of people killed by violence who yet remain, preserved permanently in the horrible attitudes of death –

I can feel the tug
of the halter at the nape
of her neck, the wind
on her naked front

('Punishment')

– are perfect images for Ireland's troubles past and present, and
for the persistence of the violent past in the present. In 'Punishment' Heaney proposes this most explicitly as he writes of his
sympathy for the young girl who was hung as an adultress and
who was one of the bodies discovered in the bogs. He acknowledges that, although 'I almost love you', if he had lived at the
time of her trouble he would have remained silent at her fate, even
if he knew it was wrong, and would not have been prepared to
take sides to defend her. In the same way he cannot speak out
directly to plead for those girls branded as traitors in modern
Ireland because they have fallen in love with British soldiers. He
has been unable to speak when they have been punished by being
tarred-and-feathered by sectarian groups:

I who have stood dumb
when your betraying sisters,
cauled in tar,
wept by the railings,

> who would connive
> in civilized outrage
> yet understand the exact
> and tribal, intimate revenge.

Here we begin to understand what Heaney is trying to do in these images of continuity. His isolation – his sense of being outside and yet connected still to Ireland's troubles (victim and yet also related to the perpetrators of the violence) – is seen in this poem, and in this whole volume, as a necessary stand for the artist. The poet's imagination (his mummer's power to enter into the lives of the many) takes him through his family past to the dark peat core of Ireland where he experiences life as both invader and invaded, revenger and victim. It prevents him from taking sides, 'and in the process someone is betrayed' by this 'artful voyeur' who must accept his own punishment by standing fast to the 'word-hoard', even though he suffers the derision of those who condemn him for not making a plainer political response. The artist's role, Heaney insists, is to stand on all sides and to accept 'the mire and complexities' of the blood of a whole people.

All the poems that dig after ancient Ireland, the island of the north, of Viking inheritance, especially those about the bogs, are gathered up in 'Kinship'. In this taut and controlled poem the language is simple but penetrating, a statement predominantly of noun and verb:

> I love this turf-face
> its black incisions,
> the cooped secrets
> of process and ritual. . . .

On this land of his kin he declares 'I step through origins'. It is ground that is 'outback of my mind' and provides him with a 'centre [that] holds / and spreads'. The 'melting grave' of the bog is 'vowel of earth', contains 'mutations of weathers / and seasons' and though 'sour with the blood' of Ireland's past it is 'the goddess [who] swallows / our love and terror.' It is the land he feels closest to, it is the land that literally preserves all that falls into it, and the poet chooses to stand there and, paradoxically, stands firm by allowing himself to be sucked down into its dark interior.

Whether this is a real resolution or whether it is only a fiction depends upon the individual's response. For some readers a fiction – the imaginative reconstruction of a world connected with reality but not synonymous with it – may be the only kind of resolution possible in a deeply troubled world and the only way left for preparing the ground for the growth of a new and solving insight.

North is an ambitious book. It is written in a quiet but persistently penetrating tone, a hard but not colourless style. It is far from the luxuriant growth of the first book in terms of technique but it was nevertheless prepared for in those previous volumes. The early poems of childhood and growing up provided Heaney with the first strong foundations on which to feel what it was to be a poet in Ireland. From these he learnt to trace his origins further and further back into his country's past. That is why the two tender dedicatory poems of *North* remain directed at his family and his family's native countryside. Heaney has talked of his poetry as the revelation of identity:

> . . . poetry as revelation of the self to the self, as the restoration of the culture to itself; poems as elements of continuity, with the aura and authenticity of archaeological finds, where the buried shard has an importance that is not obliterated by the buried city.[3]

He has set himself a daunting task in attempting to do this. In the dedicatory poems he writes of 'our anonymities' (the common experiences which are shared by all but which are rarely spoken of) and the preservation of these which is the essence of any true culture. In the last poem of *North* he hints, through characteristically rural imagery, at the object of his task and its gains and losses (a 'wood-kerne' is a footsoldier (usually a peasant) who has taken to the woods to escape capture):

> I am neither internee nor informer;
> An inner émigré, grown long-haired
> And thoughtful; a wood-kerne
>
> Escaped from the massacre,
> Taking protective colouring
> From bole and bark, feeling
> Every wind that blows . . .

7

Three new poets

Douglas Dunn, Tom Paulin, Paul Mills

There are a number of poets whose work has achieved promi-
nence only in the last few years. It is still too soon to be sure which
of these will produce the most lasting poetry. With poetry as recent
as this any reader must rely upon his own taste and judgement to
guide him in his choice of reading. It is also unprofitable to
attempt to group new poets or to try to distinguish trends among
those who are still at the beginning of their literary career. We
should be grateful that there continue to be new poets emerging
who have the talent, dedication and originality to produce
worthwhile work. In this chapter there is no intention of providing signposts 'to the most promising young poets'. Instead three
poets, with rather different styles and concerns, whose work is of
interest to the author and for whom he seeks a wider audience,
have been asked to introduce their own poetry.

1 Douglas Dunn

Douglas Dunn, a Scotsman, is the oldest of the three poets, born in
1942. He first reached a wide audience in 1969 when he published
Terry Street, which arose from a period he spent as a student
living in Hull and consists of poems about the way of life of the
inhabitants of a run-down street in part of that city. The book
enjoyed considerable critical acclaim as a first collection and has
been followed by several other interesting volumes: *The Happier
Life* (1972), *Love or Nothing* (1974) and *Barbarians* (1979).
Douglas Dunn is now a freelance writer who still lives in Hull
and is the editor of a number of anthologies of poetry, has

220

Douglas Dunn, Tom Paulin, Paul Mills

written plays for television and radio and is a regular reviewer of poetry.

Terry Street was welcomed for its sensitive and realistic portrait of what one reviewer called 'the surfaces of humdrum urban living'. These pictures of day-to-day living proceed from an honest, yet rather indirect viewpoint, which works by the slow accretion of a series of images until the whole spills over into a meditative embrace of their subject. The later books have widened the scope of Dunn's poetry, particularly in some of the longer, rather ironical poems about his sense of himself and his childhood which are some of the best poems in *The Happier Life*. In some of the latest poetry there is a wry sense of humour which combines with his gifts of social observation to produce a moving and forceful poetry.

Douglas Dunn made the following response to a request to give a brief account of the development of his work:

Over the years my writing has tried to keep a promise with a Scottish, rural working-class background. It is a promise I don't remember making. What the precise nature of that promise is, I also don't know. I am certain it is more than a social or political gambit; and I am sure it means more to me than an act of sentimental fidelity. Nor is it an example of one of these manic, wished-for but impossible returns of an uprooted Scotsman. To persevere with the art of poetry is to pick up a bet you make with yourself. Nationality and background are involved in the bet I made.

My first book, *Terry Street* (1969) was mainly about a working-class street in Hull, a real street, where I lived for about two years, and which has since been demolished. These poems were never intended as a 'scenes from working-class life'. Some reviewers saw the book as such. The reason why they did may be that they had never been in such a street, let alone lived in one. It just happened that I wrote a fictionalized version of what was around me. I have never self-consciously *chosen* to write about a particular subject in my life. An explanation of why I wrote about Terry Street, and a way of understanding the moods of these poems, is that I felt myself a stranger in the street and town in which I lived. In the community of accents and attitudes Hull represents, I still feel as if I'm not at home.

No deliberated plan went into *Terry Street*. Events, people and environment, and the stories they made, came into my head and I wrote them down. My *persona* was much like that old poet in Browning's 'How it Strikes a Contemporary' –

> He took such cognisance of men and things,
> If any beat a horse, you felt he saw;
> If any cursed a woman, he took note; . . .
> So, next time that a neighbour's tongue was loosed,
> It marked the shameful and notorious fact,
> We had among us, not so much a spy,
> As a recording chief inquisitor,
> The town's true master, if the town but knew!

Except that, of course, I wasn't.

At that time, my ideas of poetic technique were vague and uninformed. I could talk the hind end off a horse on the subject of Ben Jonson's classicism, or the 'rough verse' of John Donne's *Satyres*; but the matter of contemporary poetic style is a more formidable set of problems altogether. Before I went to university at the age of twenty-four, my reading had been wide and wild, but a means of coming to grips with a technique of writing I could actually *use* had always eluded me. Three years in which I did nothing but read the canon of British literature before 1900 was a boon to me – thank you, Government – although whatever decision I made about poetic technique arose less from what I read, and more from a confrontation of what I lived and saw and felt with an overrated sophistication I got from books. These were my inhibitions of the time – avoid the classical pantheon like the plague; write not about childhood; write not, certainly, about daffodils; never speculate on infinity from insufficient evidence; maintain a moderate degree of clarity, at least; do not invent when reality is good enough and lying to hand for the making of images; show more than you tell; do not push subjectivity too much into the foreground of the poem. . . . But I suppose that, like other poets of my generation, I found it easier to know what I should not do, and strenuously difficult to discover a *positive* programme of aesthetic values.

It took me until 1966 to realize that free verse wasn't a joke. Before that I'd thought of it as a contradiction in terms, publicized by those who were too lazy to apply a little elbow grease or who had avoided the Presbyterian work ethic. Attempts at free verse made me feel guilty. Writing almost exclusively in metre – that is, before *Terry Street* – even when I was writing about second-hand subjects, was an apprenticeship which I am glad I underwent. If nothing else, I was practising something on nothing, instead of nothing on nothing. It was also preparation for what I am inclined to believe is the most crucial problem in contemporary British poetry.

> That a specimen of free verse can be found displaying a complexity and profundity comparable to those of such poems as Hardy's *During Wind and Rain* . . . I do not believe; nor do I believe that such a poem can ever be composed . . . I believe that the nature of free verse is a permanent obstacle to such a composition.

Thus Yvor Winters in his book *Primitivism and Decadence*. There is no denying that he has a point. Winters's belief and an essay like Edmund Wilson's 'Is Verse a Dying Technique?' are useful stimulants on the subject of the uses and values of free verse and formal verse.

In *Terry Street* I was unaware the problem existed, and, I suppose, I wish I still knew nothing of this issue which has Balkanized poetry. But it can hardly be side-stepped. It must continually be thought out, rethought, understood and revised while at the same time refusing to lose track of the truth that poetry does not necessarily inhere in its forms, but in the imagination which uses language and forms.

I feel it is vain to refer to my own poems, and probably it gives the show away completely to quote one. It is like writing about myself writing about myself. If nothing else, though, I can illustrate my own confusions and vulnerability before the awkward aesthetic issues which present themselves before any attempt to write contemporary verses.

A Removal from Terry Street

On a squeaking cart, they push the usual stuff,
A mattress, bed ends, cups, carpets, chairs,
Four paperback westerns. Two whistling youths

In surplus U.S. Army battle-jackets
Remove their sister's goods. Her husband
Follows, carrying on his shoulders the son
Whose mischief we are glad to see removed,
And pushing, of all things, a lawnmower.
There is no grass in Terry Street. The worms
Come up cracks in concrete yards in moonlight.
That man, I wish him well. I wish him grass.

A family, therefore, is seen leaving one of Terry Street's 'terraces', pushing their belongings in a large hand-cart. Technically, the lines are formed by flattening iambic pentameter. Some lines, several phrases and parts of lines are precisely iambic; but the impulse of the poem is descriptive, and I suppose it was the weight of observation and narrative and the presence of people and objects – 'Four paperback westerns' and 'Two whistling youths' – which made it unnatural or undesirable to sustain the iambic rhythm of the classic English line throughout.

The last line of the poem is intended as ironic. That man, and his lawnmower, setting off for a new place, perhaps a better place, and perhaps some grass for him to look after, moved me; and yet I also saw this vignette as an image of vanity, of that man's touching faith in progress, and of my own unjustifiable cynicism in an environment which perfectly embodied the shame and wormwood of British society. The last line of the poem is also as perfect a pentameter as I can make one. It's in two sentences – pretty Shakespearian, eh? One line of exact form – it's an attempt to dignify a subject which otherwise disrupted whatever sense of form I had to begin with. For I did wish him grass. I still do. He deserves better than his belongings and aspirations suggest.

Since *Terry Street*, I have written many poems in metre and verse, and many in free verse of various types with various degrees of detachment from the accredited metrical norms. In my own experience, traditional forms can inhibit imagination. Metre sometimes feels too specific, too much of an instrument for the exclusion of uncertainty. For that reason, I keep my options open. *The Happier Life* (1972) and *Love or Nothing* (1974) contain a variety of poems with different formal justifications.

By the winter of 1974, with three books behind me, I began to realize I had written a number of poems which, to my mind, suggested a continuity, or a subject I had been opening up to myself without knowing too much about it. 'Ships', 'Landscape with One Figure' in *Terry Street*; 'Guerrillas' in *The Happier Life*; and 'Clydesiders' and 'The Competition' in *Love or Nothing*, offered me the attitudes of *Barbarians* (1979). Short, sub-lyric forms began to look unattractive, and I was discontented with the cult of the delicate touch. If there are several poems in *Barbarians* that look as if they were written by someone who was not feeling that discontent, then it's because I'm incorrigible, or not incorrigible, as the case may be.

My political convictions are substantially the same now as when I wrote *Terry Street*, but in that book they were submerged in the material of the poems. They were far from the reason for having written them. By temperament, I'm unwilling to be a 'political poet'. There are times, though, when everyone is led to go against the grain of what they expect of themselves. My imagination has tried to encompass political feeling – I don't like it, but imagination often does what the conscious mind may not particularly want it to do.

Barbarians is 'about' psychologies of class, racial and national superiorities – distempering, recalcitrant subjects. It is largely written in metre for the reason that someone in the *persona* of a barbarian would be expected to write them in grunts. A reversal of the standard myth of barbarism is obviously implicated in this stylistic ploy. The style of the book hopes to portray a gesture of affront to readers who might be expected to approve of a metrical way of writing, while finding the meaning of *Barbarians* disagreeable.

At a poetry reading, it was suggested to me – no, I was *told* – that the way I'd written *Barbarians* was a footling and dishonest compromise with forms associated with bourgeois culture. Ordinary people, this man said, could be invited to read poems only when they could see they had nothing to do with the poetry they read at school. His point of view strikes me as political and literary madness, while it is also, to me, offensive. *His* accent was middle-class; but he was legislating an attitude to poetry for the kind of people *I* come from.

Apart from the strategy of writing *Barbarians* in a way that certain readers would recognize as *verse* (while they were choking on what the poems *say*), there is another reason for their formalized appearances. Where I come from is a region noted for work, whether you take the industrial history of Clydeside, or its agricultural life (about which I'm better informed). Anything jerry-built or done in a hurry not only looks like it, but, in the best traditions of the west of Scotland, is an affront to its maker's self-respect. (This, of course, is not meant to suggest that free verse is inherently slipshod.) I consider it an obligation to make my poems as best I can, in the belief that the people I come from expect the best I can give them. To write for only one section of what could possibly be a wider audience would, however, be perverse; but, if you can fulfil an expectation, then you are halfway towards one day surprising it, which it is the delight of poetry to do. I write for anyone who cares to pick it up and read it. Certainly, I don't write for myself, although I have standards I try to satisfy.

But it would be unwise to expect even personal ideologies fully to condition a poem. There are always factors of personality, experience and imagination – not to mention talent – which deflect what and how you *want* to write into the result you learn, after as much revision as you can give it, that it's what you're stuck with. Poems emerge from half-understood truths and hazy overlaps of meaning which are discovered in the act of writing them. You might begin with a word, a phrase, or a line, and find they lead you into a poem which wasn't what you thought you had in mind. It is like being granted a daughter when you wanted a son, or vice-versa, when all along you knew a child of any gender would please.

I can illustrate this by saying that at one time I thought I had finished *Barbarians* and had nothing else to do but send it to my publisher. About a year later, when the book was in the press, I found myself writing three more poems which should have been in the title sequence of that book. They are more ambitious metrically than the others, longer, more substantial, and, because of their conspicuous formality, make the metrical strategies of the book as a whole much clearer. Two of them, 'John Wilson in Greenock' and 'Tannahill', appeared in *Akros*, December 1978, and the third, 'Green Breeks', was published in *New Edinburgh Review*, No. 45 (February 1979).

Poetic techniques are partly explained in the context of the literary politics of the time. Poets are often anxious to be seen proving their decisions and choices about style and subject. A lot of poetry is gestural. Its arm-waving and 'look-at-me-writing-like-*this*' posturing semaphore are a means of showing that you, too, participate in convictions of style, life, literature, politics and morality. Personally, I'd rather not bother, but from earlier remarks it's obvious that I do. Where it becomes necessary to draw the line is when you notice more energy is going into the alignment of your work with trends rather than into the effort to write poems pure and simple.

While I was writing the poems in *Barbarians*, I was also working on other poems which have entirely different formal procedures. One of these, 'The Jazz Orchestra', appeared in *Stand*, Vol. 16, No. 1, and another, 'Le Chemin. A poem-film, starring Jean-Paul Belmondo', appeared in *Stone Ferry Review*, No. 1 (1978). Two others, 'Straight, no Chaser' and 'Dead Lady', are much longer and are unfinished – depositories, perhaps, of a practical theorizing of techniques as well as of their subjects – alcohol in one case and Europe in the other. These poems are uncollected. In fact, they would make a book in themselves. Although I believe it to be both possible and legitimate to write in updated traditional styles *and* in ways which derive from modernism, I still feel timid before the opportunity to present these two different stylistic extremes in one book. Convinced that difference does not necessarily mean opposition, I'm also aware that in many minds that's exactly what it does mean. I used to feel that the two ostensibly different approaches to a poetic my work perhaps represents amounted to a portrayal of confusion, or of dithering about where, stylistically, my imagination belongs. But the more I write, the more I consider an internal debate about what does or does not constitute an authentic contemporary poetic style is creative rather than disabling. Indeed, I see a generosity of styles in the work of contemporary poets with whom I flatter myself at feeling some degree of affinity – in Derek Mahon, for instance, whose imagination is one of the most interesting in contemporary poetry; in Seamus Heaney, who writes both a plain, realistic verse and a denser, more impacted and mysterious kind of poem altogether; in Michael Longley's work, Tom

Paulin's, Paul Muldoon's (although Muldoon is more stylistically consistent), in Hugo Williams's and in Tony Harrison's.

2   Tom Paulin

Tom Paulin was born in 1949 in England but grew up in Belfast. In the last three years he has emerged as one of the most interesting of an important group of Ulster poets whose work has been published against the background of political violence in Northern Ireland. Paulin's poetry frequently deals with aspects of his Irish background or uses Ulster for its setting, but the themes of the poems have a more universal significance than this localized subject matter might suggest. This significance is seen particularly in the themes of justice and responsibility which dominate the finest poems in his first collection, *A State of Justice* (1977). Before the appearance of this book, poems by Paulin had appeared in a variety of periodicals, as well as in *Poetry Introduction 3* (1975). In 1976 he was a recipient of the Eric Gregory Award, and he received a Somerset Maugham Award in 1978. He currently lectures in English at the University of Nottingham and is author of *Thomas Hardy: The Poetry of Perception* (1975).

The poems in *A State of Justice* are composed of scenes, situations, events and narratives taken from memories of childhood, from aspects of life in Ulster and from stories the poet has gathered from the lives of his family and friends. They frequently begin as descriptions of people and places, or as narratives, and develop into an exploration of personal and social states of being, often ending in an image that expresses that state with almost symbolic force. The predominant idiom is colloquial and the style, although capable of expressing an idea with force, is usually deliberately low-keyed. But the calm surface tone of this unforced style moves on a groundswell of unease and unresolved tensions. These tensions centre on the idea of justice. The state of justice is both personal and political, and many of the poems examine the pull between natural justice and institutionalized justice: between justice as a human desire for equity and the politicizing of that desire with its consequent danger of interpreting justice as retribution. The individual is caught between his need for a fair order and the danger that the state will exploit this in a partial and dogmatic

justice. It is a tension which takes on an urgency and importance
in the work of a writer conscious of the political unrest in Ulster.
In an interview for this book, Tom Paulin talked about this
tension and about the concerns of some of the poems from *A State
of Justice.*

Settlers

They cross from Glasgow to a black city
   of gantries, mills and steeples. They begin to belong.
He manages the Iceworks, is an elder of the Kirk;
   She becomes, briefly, a cook in Carson's Army.
Some mornings, walking through the company gate,
   He touches the bonnet of a brown lorry.
It is warm. The men watch and say nothing.
   'Queer, how it runs off in the night,'
He says to McCullough, then climbs to his office.
He stores a warm knowledge on his palm.

   Nightlandings on the Antrim coast, the movement of guns
Now snug in their oiled paper below the floors
   of sundry kirks and tabernacles in that country.

Paulin: I suppose the conflict's between two forms of action. The
poem is about my maternal grandparents who emigrated from
Glasgow to Belfast in 1912. My grandfather was manager of an
ice and cold storage firm; he was a businessman and an elder of
the Presbyterian church. My grandmother was a cook in the
army set up by Lord Carson to fight the British army in order to
keep Ulster British. Some years ago I heard a family story – at
least I think I did – of how my grandfather would come into the
yard of his works in the morning and see the lorries lined up – it
would be early in the morning. Sometimes, when he touched
the bonnet of one of the lorries, it would be warm, and this
meant that it had been used during the night to transport guns
which had been landed on the Antrim coast. The guns were for
the Protestant Ulster Volunteer Force or 'Carson's Army'. He
pretended not to know this, but the fact that he says 'Queer,
how it runs off in the night' shows he does know and he's
turning a blind eye.

King: Letting them know he knows?

Paulin: Yes. He's colluding with them and encouraging them. But because he's also in a position of authority and bound by a system of laws he ought to prevent the gun-running, but he doesn't. I've tried to get this over in the form of the poem which looks like one section of ten lines with a three-line coda. In fact, it's fourteen lines with a line missing – fourteen lines or a sonnet. The missing line was something like 'A blind eye turned to the knowledge he has', and I cut the line in order to enact this. The last three lines are about the way the guns were stored under the floors of churches, parish halls, mission halls.

King: The last three lines make us conscious of what is unspoken, a tacit acknowledgement that's emphasized by the physical gap between the lines. The man has become identified with the act of rebellion and yet cannot come out into the open with his knowledge. Let's turn to two other poems which, in different ways, embrace a sense of unresolved conflicts: 'Fin de Siècle' and 'States'.

Paulin: Yes, there is a conflict in 'Fin de Siècle'. It's meant to have a kind of Jamesian situation – it's set in the park of a country house – and I wanted to present the girl as a symbol of pure knowledge. She's upper class, while the man's, say, working class and provincial. He and the girl are like a pair of platonic lovers whose situation is controlled by some sort of universal force, an absolute, which prevents them from ever marrying. I think that what I was getting at is the way history strives towards a social ideal – a good and just society – and never achieves the ideal. Roughly, the man is history and the girl is the ideal. She is too pure because her ideal consciousness is detached from the practical world. She is one extreme; the man is the opposite extreme.

King: Innocence and experience?

Paulin: Well, not in the usual sense, because the girl's purity is so intense it's corrupt, and the man's bound by a kind of purity too. The lovers will never have a real relationship.

King: Why not?

Paulin: They're victims. They come from different social classes. It's meant to be like a situation in a nineteenth-century novel. They can only admire each other at a distance – the class system forbids them to marry.

Douglas Dunn, Tom Paulin, Paul Mills

The beeches in the green demesne,
The dovecote by the summer-house,
Will never tell how when a culture sends
A hopeless man to love a drifting girl,
Then never lets them touch or kiss,
Its selfish flowers have begun to stink.

'States' comes out of innumerable night journeys by boat between
Ireland and England. It's very strange, travelling between two
countries in complete darkness and seeing the lights of distant
cities and towns, the lights strung along the coast. The whole
complex organization of society, of law and order, is reduced to
a pattern of cold lights on complete blackness.

States

That stretch of water, it's always
There for you to cross over
To the other shore, observing
The lights of cities on blackness.

Your army jacket at the rail
Leaks its Kapok into a wind
That slices gulls over a dark zero
Waste a cormorant skims through.

Any state, built on such a nature,
Is a metal convenience, its paint
Cheapened by the price of lives
Spent in a public service.

The men who peer out for dawning
Gantries below a basalt beak,
Think their vigils will make something
Clearer, as the cities close

With each other, their security
Threatened but bodied in steel
Polities that clock us safely
Over this dark; freighting us.

King: Who's speaking in the poem?
Paulin: I'm addressing a shadowy figure who's travelling back

to Belfast. He's wearing an army jacket – a functional garment that matches the functional appearance of the ship. The ship is compared to a public convenience, and by this I really mean the state – it's a well-worn idea, the ship of state. Its public security is bought at the expense of individual lives.

King: What I'm not sure of is what weight to give to the very fine ending. As an image it is powerful, with the clock image suggesting both orderliness and keeping things safe, and with also, to my mind, the suggestion of the ticking of a time-bomb – a coming danger.

Paulin: I don't know about the ending – it's a kind of empty gesture. What worries me is that the state is just like a cattle boat. It's indifferent to its human cargo, but it can also be hostile to various individual members of society. You can worship the state too much – like a conservative anarchist. I'm trying to sort out my feelings about the state in this poem. Obviously it's necessary to have an organized state. I wouldn't quarrel with that idea. But it's sometimes important to quarrel with the notion of the state, because, unless the state is in tune with everyone's needs and ideas (which it never can be), then its existence is hostile, a blunt instrument that can be used against us.

King: The phrase 'freighting us' in the poem has a sense of carrying us safely, like a cargo, yet placing us in a dangerous position, a knife-edge that carries us towards death.

Paulin: There's a play on 'fate'.

King: This poem seems to suggest more than does 'Settlers' that the state, or the Law with a capital 'L' (as you call it in other poems), is an instrument of repression, or if not exactly that then at least a possible threat.

Paulin: It depends on the state. But certainly I was thinking about Ulster here, and of the state being repressive – which it once unjustly was and which it now has to be.

King: How far is it any state and not just Ulster? In 'Under the Eyes' you talk of the machinery of state as a 'set of scales that squeezes out blood'. Is the state's justice always bought at such a high price?

Paulin: I believe this must be true of any state. It's because the

existence of a state depends on a Benthamite equation between
individual happiness and liberty and the greatest happiness of
the greatest number. So every state is bought at the price of
individual lives and suffering. Again, the title of the book
glances at a different kind of state – Hobbes's state of nature
where man's life outside society is, in those famous words,
'ugly, nasty, brutish and short'. So does justice exist in nature?
Is it created by man to control his own nature? Isn't justice a
rational cruelty? I wish I knew the answers.

A Just State

The children of scaffolds obey the Law.
Its memory is perfect, a buggered sun
That heats the dry sands around noon cities
    Where only the men hold hands.

The state's centre terrifies, its frontiers
Are sealed against its enemies. Shouts echo
Through the streets of this angry polity
    Whose waters might be kind.

Its justice is bare wood and limewashed bricks,
Institutional fixtures, uniforms,
The shadows of watchtowers on public squares,
    A hemp noose over a greased trap.

King: In 'A Just State' you seem appalled by the idea of a fixity of
things gone hard and unyielding.

Paulin: The poem started with an account of a visit to Pakistan.
The atmosphere of the country reminded me a bit of the North
of Ireland. I hate the idea of living in a theocracy and I detest the
notion of vindictive justice.

King: Law with a capital 'L' in the poem?

Paulin: Yes. Protestant Fundamentalists worship the Mosaic Law
– an eye for an eye, measure for measure.

King: What do you mean by 'the children of scaffolds'?

Paulin: I'd read about some students leading a right-wing demon-
stration in a Muslim country. To be young and right-wing – it's
like a contradiction in terms.

King: Your phrase 'a buggered sun' and the image of the men holding hands (which is a common sight in Muslim countries) suggest the heat and stasis of that kind of culture.

Paulin: I hope so. It's also about a state of mind – a very masculine mind. That mind is limited, narrow and vindictive – the mind of a hangman.

King: Not all the poems in this volume are directly political, but even in the more personal poems there is a social theme. Let's take 'Young Funerals'.

Paulin: This poem is about the street where I lived when I was a child. It's off the Ormeau Road in Belfast. Two children who lived in the street died and in the days before the funerals – and for days afterwards – the blinds in their houses were kept drawn. I'd to pass one house on my way to and from school and I always tried to avoid walking directly past it. I'd cross the road in order to avoid the atmosphere of misery that clung to that house.

King: Again the idea of crossing over?

Paulin: Yes – I live in England and so you could say I'm avoiding Ireland and what's happening there.

King: You've a more recent poem, 'Surveillances', which is concerned with this, haven't you?

Surveillances

In the winter dusk
You see the prison camp
With its blank watchtowers;
It is as inevitable
As the movement of equipment
Or the car that carries you
Towards a violent district.

In the violet light
You watch a helicopter
Circling above the packed houses,
A long beam of light
Probing streets and waste ground.
All this might be happening
Underwater.

And if you would swap its functions
For a culture of bungalows
And light verse,
You know this is one
Of the places you belong in,
And that its public uniform
Has claimed your service.

King: A number of your poems tell a story. What is the situation behind 'Newness'?

Paulin: Briefly, it's set in County Antrim, one of the great centres of the Ulster linen trade. The period is about the end of the last century, when the trade was at its height. An old woman is thinking back to that time, to her wedding night. In the morning she hears the workers going to the mill. She remembers how her husband held her hands as they washed in a bowl of water – you know the old-fashioned sort that have a ewer and are often decorated with a design of wild roses.

King: And the ending?

Paulin: Oh, it's meant to be happy. For once softness triumphs over all that hardness we've talked about.

Newness

Cool to our bodies, the fresh linen pleats
And valances that met our eyes then.

He pressed my hand, my lover, my husband;
Held them both underwater in the wide bowl.

It was still night when I heard
The tramp of clogs to the mill.
Frost on the cobbles, I thought;
Hard wood is worn by the stone,
So is stone by the softness of feet.

3 Paul Mills

Paul Mills was born in 1948 and has published two collections of poetry, *North Carriageway* (1976) and *Third Person* (1978). He is a freelance writer who has held several creative writing fellowships and is currently Gregory Fellow in Poetry at the University of Leeds. *North Carriageway* reveals a poet of linguistic sensitivity and originality, particularly in descriptions of landscapes and the countryside. A celebration of the intense pleasure in the atmosphere of places, particularly coastal landscapes and rocks, is everywhere apparent in this volume. Many of the poems concern the escape of the individual into the living energies of natural landscape and the revitalization of the human emotions through this. But there are also poems about people and events. History is seen as process and the poems relive that process, a process burdened by pressures for both destruction and release. Poems like 'Stormclouds' and 'Rain' are concentrated visualizations of the natural scene and yet are employed to give a sense of the cleansing and relaxing of human energies as well as the natural ones; they body forth the renewed strength of peace that occurs after a storm or any violent experience has passed. The poems frequently see human personality in terms of landscape, or rather landscape is interpenetrated by human form and feeling in a way that creates a strong sense of the continuum of man and nature and what Ted Hughes calls 'the elemental energy circuit'.

Third Person is a deliberately cooler book. There is an intended flatness in these descriptions of the torments involved in the break-up of a relationship. They are poems of acute observation of those small, subtly shifting and potentially violent rearrangements of relationship between a couple. A sense of loss and the gradual, not always successful, building up of new, stronger hopes pervades the entire collection. A tentative, hesitant free-verse style charts the breakdown and recovery of the possibility of faith in relationship, in a painfully self-aware attention to the future. The typical style and tone are caught in these lines from the end of 'An Accident'. Observing a road accident and its victims, the watching couple realize that it could be their own future they are looking at, even though they are quick to deny they would be hurt by it. The last lines bring home a sense of the pull between honesty and faith that is at the back of much of the poetry in this volume:

> We let the narrow road squeeze us together,
> Another mile, another. Another hour,
> A year. Each moment is always

Douglas Dunn, Tom Paulin, Paul Mills

The one place we daren't stop for,
Daren't think about, so we go on
Staring forward together.
We say what's happened still can be averted.

Paul Mills has written an introduction to his poetry to which he gives the title 'An Island':

To say anything meaningful about one's own poems overall is really like trying to land a boat on an island, admittedly in this case a small island, but still one which has several possible landing-places, varieties of coastline, none of which can show at first glance the overall shape of the interior, some places where it would be treacherous to put ashore, others where it may even be too safe. Unfortunately, of course, there is no well-trodden, straight road from the mainland; at least it doesn't feel that way. In fact, it feels that the work of many poets now is well represented as islands, inhabited by the one man or woman poet and a few others if you're lucky, who believe the journey was worth it after all, and, if you're very lucky, have stayed and are still investigating. Some of them perhaps think they can find on that particular bit of land similarities to the real country, the imaginative world, in which we all live. Yet an island is a separate, an individual place with its own customs and conditions, even its own kind of language. Parts of it will look strange, parts of it familiar, at the same time. From a visitor's (i.e. reader's) point of view, it would be satisfying to be able to offer a neat blend of strangeness and familiarity: too much of the first and no people would bother to come at all; too much of the second and they may as well stay at home. But the fact is that the island exists in all its personal lineaments and one has no choice about its particularities. All that matters in the long process of writing is to bring it to definition.

That I choose to explain myself in this way is not an accident. Many of the first poems I wrote had for their subject matter this coastal scenery. I had written others before I got hold of anything in poetic terms which I knew had a special meaning, but that point at which suddenly, out of the flat seas, solid territory unfolded and gathered up was the primitive upheaval which marked a

237

beginning. The reason may have rested in psychological forces and changes – in fact, at that time one of the books I read and took to heart contained C. G. Jung's essay, 'The Spiritual Problem of Modern Man' – but what I wrote about was rock, the sides of cliffs, precipices, caves, a sense of the damp interiors of chalk hillsides, and of the arrested pressure visible in rock. One can look at the surface of sea where the wind forms bands of small ripples, and see the same patterns in the sand, and again in the fossilized sand-ripples in Torridonian rock of 400 million years ago. The same pattern is both very old and very immediate: a ripple can be rock or water, fixed and fluid. Nor is it an accident that the Old English word for rock is the direct ancestor of our Modern English word 'cloud', and understandably so. Appearances make metaphors obvious and natural. In natural forms, the presence of a central, obsessive energy system or pattern creates resemblances between one substance and another, regardless of size or age, and it was the nature of that system and our containment in it which interested me. Form or fixed shape was the outcome of force, matter of fluidity, land-mass out of the sea and tide and wind, all flowing; yet at the same time these manifestations – flow and arrest – were separable one from the other. As an example, something of the treachery of that separation was what I was after in the poem 'Cape Cornwall'. The 'warning', a fog-signal sounding offshore, accompanies the speaker as he climbs on the cliff-face.

Cape Cornwall

Walls, wires, fields, and a crumbly road
Show up beyond me the misty space
While a warning drones through the fog.
A big insect. A deep chord
On the keyboard of the sea, untraceably slow
Music in a vast room.

Some without footholds, long floors of rock
Tilt into foam or cloud. To a gull
Or a bat, this edge is not their world's.
I must be a lizard to survive –
Entering its alert stealth and ease,
Growing comfortable with this atmosphere,
Body homing round jut and crack, carefully.

And now, tensed, balanced, gripping, holding
My weight down to the centre of ledge then ledge
Which it takes one step to remove –
Just shifting my treacherous strength
To make a fulcrum of nothing

How big is the inch my foot reaches
Down towards and finding, clenches?
What surprised yell must I not hear
To stay on, how quick not turn my head
To be bumped over full in the face
By the crystal breakage of crushed stone teeth
Somewhere to which side of me?

A red admiral blown out helplessly
Into the Atlantic that eats England
That ends here, shows how much easier it is
To be that careless stumbling wave failing wave
That I could reach by stepping into air
To become nothing,
That wave that falls back into the sea,
No longer in danger of becoming anything.

Since experience continues beyond the fixed moment and is unpredictable, loaded with possible disasters, it threatens to destroy the attempt to fix moments in words, and some of my early poems such as this one represent that attempt together with a sense of that threat. I was trying to find the right words for the atmosphere of places – in this case, of a misty brackish outcrop west of Land's End.

At the same time, I was aware of anxiety, even of a sort of paralysis, the effort to cling to one spot, not daring to move or give way to movement, a feeling of vertigo. To risk an action that just comes from himself, or to move by instinct like the sea – the speaker is trapped between. In the poem 'The Green Room' a room has been decorated in such a way that it is intended to harmonize with the details of the view seen through the window. The landscape has been invited, in a sense, into the interior of a house. The elderly woman seems happy with this arrangement, but the young man her visitor is not. He feels clumsy and

239

awkward, out of place. The fear he expresses merely stands in for an unspoken fear.

The Green Room

Raising the blind, she said –
'We like the landscape and the room
To blend.' The summer sunlight
Cushioned itself quietly
On the cooled surrounds.

Inside and outside – green, the carpet
Smoothed into a fitted lawn,
The walls into a costly screen of trees,
Beyond, the sea, kept at a distance
As colourless as sky.
'Even the weather' – I observed,

But watched the silence
Grow into disquiet, and wondered
How the trees behave, if at night
Something comes knocking

On the glass, or in the eye
Of a storm, if the white ornaments
Uncoil, fly into the static sea
Behind their heads, its huge walls
Of water about to burst.

The wind blew a clumsy leaf
Across the floor. 'Do you find what
You do rewarding then?' – she asked,
And did not taste rain in the teacup,
Her special blend, but drained
Into her skull, a second cup.

The presence of landscape wasn't always so threatening in these poems, but often regenerative. I wanted to write poems which dealt not only with concepts but with sensation, sensation of an unresolved sort, aroused to the point where something had to be done about it, some verbal equivalent had to be found. The result, often, were poems which tried to evoke a sense of the past, of early civilization in the countryside, or even landscape seen as an empty stage where only spirits existed. Maybe that is one area more suitable for poetry than for prose fiction, whose subject matter is usually confined to the period within living memory at the time it is written: that is one of its differences from poetry. But it seemed presumptuous to write about the present until one had formed some account of the past or at least taken personal possession of some of it, even though the present would be the ultimate target; and by the past I mean its general mentality, scientific and religious processes – far too huge a subject for one small book of poems. And what actually came were a few jotted perceptions.

The literary influences on my work bear little relation to each other so far as I know, but what I usually am looking for are new poetic structures; in fact, before writing a poem I normally have some idea of its shape and probable progression, as if without a strong sense of form and structure it would be impossible to say anything. I like the way that Herbert and Donne, even Jonson at times, can fill out an idea by supporting it with one image and letting that image grow. Ted Hughes's third book, *Wodwo*, published in 1967, was valuable to me when I started, mainly in expanding my sense of possibilities of form. The sentence: 'A cool small evening shrunk to a dog bark and the clank of a bucket – / And you listening', for example, was a discovery. But the employment of much older devices – repetition, and parallel sentences which diverge only in one or two words – can in subtle degrees control the meaning while keeping the syntax simple, as in the following poem from *Third Person*.

Procris

Now she is wearing a blue gown
Covering her ankles
And red sandals
And a necklace
Decorated with shells. Now she is smiling
Wide, a glistening ocean

Now she is gazing out of the door.
Now her blank eyes slant to the side.
Now she is wearing a secret smile
Which sometimes she changes
For a secret numbness.

Now she is asleep, like Procris
Under the hands of Pan
Who has found a leopard
In the form of a young girl, asleep,
Pillowed on her hands.

But now she is trying to cover herself up
With sleep. Now trying
To struggle out of her dreams.
Now she is clenched.

The door opens and she comes into the room.
Not here. She sits down, she smiles.
Not here. Now she is wearing a new face.

Third Person is a kind of verse novel with a present-day setting
and a good deal of reported narrative. What I attempted was a
poetry of direct statement, maximum simplicity combined with
maximum subtlety, compression of meaning into almost artless
syntax. The locations of the plot, which concerns two married
couples, provide metaphors through which the themes are
advanced. The style is all presentation, at the beginning, of a
recognizable environment – motorways, sitting-rooms, rivers
inside cities. The subject is not the phenomena of mountains and
cliffs, seascapes and caves, but more of interior nature, sex, the
self; yet the question is the same, of whether or not its direction
and force can be trusted, of how much value can be placed in it.
Third Person is intended to finish with a marked advance towards
a more supple, reinvigorated world – a world created again, fluid
and refreshed – in response to a few poems where the self speaks
quietly to itself that it *is* valuable.

But there is a paradox here which I must explain. To live one's
life with any degree of real contentment it will be important at
times to think of oneself as something valuable – to value that
individual self which we have to look after and not squander or
deceive – as Stevie Smith insists in her poem 'Valuable' – but, as
far as art is concerned, nothing could be further from the truth.
Nothing could be further from the truth even though art is about
that very thing, the self. In my view, art exists because somebody
has refused to believe in any of the other explanations for what a

person consists of. That centre which we call a person is not a numeral or a series of inhibitions and phobias, not a divorce, a class, a political movement or a profession. It is something which nevertheless longs to hear what it is and to be valued by a wiser authority than simply other people, other opinion. Art tries to give a true explanation and a true value, but who, then, is the artist? Isn't he a person just like us? For some he has to be, otherwise they couldn't believe what he says. The existence of a wiser authority is a matter at present of longing and also mistrust – understandably so – and it will take some time before people can act again in the wisdom of unknowingness – which is a matter of trust, finally.

But as for the artist, he harbours the same attitude towards himself which other people generally have towards him, generally one of suspicion. To him, his experiences and feelings are not important just because he happens to be the owner of them: the temptation is to imagine that because *I* have felt something, that must make that thing, *ipso facto*, a good subject for art. All I need to do is have interesting experiences; in fact (so the illusion goes), my experiences are always interesting because *I* had them. Again, these are the words of the interfering 'I', and in writing a poem, maybe in creating any work of art, that 'I' must be silenced. In the business of the actual writing, arranging the words in a system of vital tension, each one taut as a wire in a piano so that together they achieve a precise sonority, in letting imagination speak, one is sliding the weight out of the interfering 'I' and into the feeling or experience so that the feeling will become a thing in itself, objectified, and with a life of its own. An artist puts all his being into his art, so as, paradoxically, not to be discovered in it. His experience, partly or wholly, has been transformed. The island, ideally, exists where we land to find its creator not there and we are free then to make it our own.

Notes

Chapter 1 – *Philip Larkin*

1 C. Ricks, 'A True Poet', *New York Review of Books*, 28 January 1965.
2 A. Brownjohn, *Philip Larkin* (Longmans, 1975).
3 D. J. Enright (ed.), *Poets of the 1950s* (Kenkyusha, Tokyo, 1955), p. 77.
4 P. Larkin, *All What Jazz?* (Fontana, 1970).
5 'Philip Larkin Praises the Poetry of Thomas Hardy', *The Listener*, 25 July 1968, p. 111.
6 P. Larkin, 'Big Victims: Emily Dickinson and Walter de la Mare', *New Statesman*, 13 March 1970, p. 368.
7 J. Press, *A Map of Modern Verse* (Oxford University Press, 1969), p. 253.
8 H. Peschmann, 'Philip Larkin: Laureate of the Common Man', *English*, 24 (Summer 1975), p. 51.
9 Brownjohn, op. cit.
10 'Four Conversations: Philip Larkin', *London Magazine*, November 1964, pp. 71–7.
11 D. Timms, *Philip Larkin* (Oliver & Boyd, 1975), p. 89.
12 Ibid., p. 97.
13 Peschmann, op. cit.
14 A. Thwaite, 'The Poetry of Philip Larkin', *Phoenix*, 11/12 (1973–4).
15 'Four Conversations: Philip Larkin', op. cit.
16 C. Bedient, *Eight Contemporary Poets* (Oxford University Press, 1974).
17 Timms, op. cit., p. 131.

Chapter 2 – Charles ~~'otes~~

1 C. Tomlinson, 'The Miu. ~~VII~~, 2 (April 1957).
2 'Charles Tomlinson in Conversatie', *Essays in Criticism*, 5, 1 (1977).
3 C. Tomlinson, 'Some American Poets: A *Nation Review*, *Contemporary Literature*, XVIII, 3 (1977). Record',
4 Ibid.
5 M. Kirkham, 'A Civil Country', *Poetry Nation Review*, ɔ, (1977), p. 42.
6 *Poetry Nation Review*, op. cit., p. 35.
7 Ibid., p. 37.
8 A. Alvarez, *Beyond All This Fiddle* (Allen Lane, 1968), chs 1, 3, 5.
9 *Poetry Nation Review*, op. cit., p. 40.
10 Ibid., p. 47.

Chapter 3 – *Thom Gunn*

1 Interview in *London Magazine*, December 1977.
2 This phrase is taken from J.-P. Sartre, *Being and Nothingness*, trans. H. E. Barnes (Methuen, 1958).
3 F. Grubb, *A Vision of Reality* (Chatto & Windus, 1965).
4 M. Dodsworth (ed.), *The Survival of Poetry* (Faber, 1970).
5 *London Magazine*, op. cit.
6 Ibid.
7 Ibid.

Chapter 4 – *Ted Hughes*

1 *Poetry Book Society Bulletin*, Autumn 1957.
2 Ted Hughes, 'Myth and Education', in G. Fox and G. Hammond (eds), *Writers, Critics and Children* (Heinemann, 1977); reprinted in *The Times Educational Supplement*, 2 September 1977.
3 Ibid.
4 K. Sagar, *The Art of Ted Hughes* (Cambridge University Press, 1975), p. 2.

on Magazine, January 1971:

5 Interview with H⸍
   'Ted Hughes ar
6 Sagar, op. ci⸍
7 Ibid., p. 9
8 Ibid., p⸍
9 Ibid, op. cit.
10 Hⁿiew in *London Magazine*, op. cit.
11 ⸍ Lodge, 'Crow and the Cartoons', *Critical Quarterly*, Vol. 13, No. 1 (Spring 1971).
13 Interview in *London Magazine*, op. cit.
14 E. Homberger, *The Art of the Real* (Dent, 1977).
15 A. Thwaite, *Poetry Today 1960–1973* (Longmans, 1973).
16 Sagar, op. cit.
17 This chapter was written before the publication of the second, enlarged edition of K. Sagar, *The Art of Ted Hughes* (1978) and I should like to recommend Mr Sagar's scholarly essay on *Gaudete* as taking much further some of the points raised here and adding many valuable new ones.
18 Hughes has more than once emphasized his own Celtic ancestry.
19 Anthony Hecht's words, quoted in I. Ehrenpreis, 'At the poles of poetry', *The New York Review of Books*, 17 August 1978.

Chapter 5 – *Sylvia Plath*

1 In N. Hunter Steiner, *A Closer Look at Ariel* (Faber, 1974).
2 M. L. Rosenthal, 'Poetry as Confession', in M. London and R. Boyers (eds), *Robert Lowell: A Portrait of the Artist in His Time* (New York, 1970).
3 J. Wain, 'The New Poetry', in London and Boyers, op. cit.
4 A. Alvarez, review of *The Colossus* in *The Observer*, 18 December 1960.
5 D. Holbrook, *Sylvia Plath: Poetry and Existence* (Athlone Press, 1976).
6 E. Aird, *Sylvia Plath* (Oliver & Boyd, 1973).
7 Both poems are interestingly but differently dealt with by Holbrook, op. cit., and Aird, op. cit. A very favourable account of 'Daddy' is to be found in C. B. Cox and A. R.

Jones, 'After the Tranquilized Fifties', *Critical Quarterly*, Vol. 6, No. 2 (Summer 1964).
8 Holbrook, op. cit.
9 Aird, op. cit.
10 Cox and Jones, op. cit.
11 Holbrook, op. cit.

Chapter 6 – *Seamus Heaney*

1 D. Galler, review of *Death of a Naturalist* in *Kenyon Review*, 29 January 1967.
2 Introduction to his poems in F. Finn (ed.), *Here and Human* (John Murray, 1976).
3 Ibid.

Selected reading

Recommended critical reading for individual poets does not include articles.

Place of publication is London unless otherwise indicated.

General surveys and criticism

Alvarez, A., *Beyond All This Fiddle*, Allen Lane, 1968.

Bedient, C., *Eight Contemporary Poets*. Oxford University Press, 1974.

Davie, D., *Thomas Hardy and British Poetry*. Routledge & Kegan Paul, 1972.

Dodsworth, M. (ed.), *The Survival of Poetry*. Faber, 1970.

Fraser, G., *Vision and Rhetoric: Studies in Modern Poetry*. Faber, 1959.

Grubb, F., *A Vision of Reality: A Study of Liberalism in Twentieth-Century Verse*. Chatto & Windus, 1965.

Hamilton, I., *The Modern Poet*. Macdonald, 1968.

Hamilton, I., *A Poetry Chronicle: Essays and Reviews*. Faber, 1973.

Homberger, E., *The Art of the Real Poetry in England and America Since 1939*. Dent, 1977.

Martin, G. and Furbank, P., *Twentieth-Century Poetry: Critical Essays and Documents*. Open University, 1975.

Press, J., *Rule and Energy: Trends in British Poetry Since the Second World War*. Oxford University Press, 1963.

Press, J., *A Map of Modern Verse*. Oxford University Press, 1969.

Raban, J., *The Society of the Poem*. Harrap, 1971.

Rosenthal, M. L., *The New Poets*. Oxford University Press, 1967.

Selected Reading

Schmidt, M. and Lindop, G., *British Poetry Since 1960*. Carcanet Press, 1972.

Thwaite, A., *Poetry Today 1960–1973*. Longmans, 1973.

Anthologies

Alvarez, A. (ed.), *The New Poetry*. Penguin, 1962; rev. ed. 1966.

Bold, A. (ed.), *Cambridge Book of English Verse 1939–1975*. Cambridge University Press, 1976.

Conquest, R. (ed.), *New Lines 1*. Macmillan, 1956.

Conquest, R. (ed.), *New Lines 2*. Macmillan, 1963.

Hobsbawm, P., and Lucie-Smith, E. (eds), *A Group Anthology*. Oxford University Press, 1963.

Horovitz, M. (ed.), *Children of Albion*. Harmondsworth, Penguin, 1969.

Lucie-Smith, E. (ed.), *The Liverpool Scene*. Donald Carroll, 1967.

Lucie-Smith, E. (ed.), *British Poetry Since 1945*. Harmondsworth, Penguin, 1970.

Macbeth, G. (ed.), *Poetry 1900 to 1965*. Longmans, 1967.

Robson, J. (ed.), *The Young British Poets*. Chatto & Windus, 1971.

Summerfield, G. (ed.), *Worlds*. Penguin, 1974.

Individual poets

Philip Larkin (b. 1922)

The North Ship. Fortune Press, 1945; rev. ed. Faber, 1966.

The Less Deceived. Marvell Press, 1955.

The Whitsun Weddings. Faber, 1964.

High Windows. Faber, 1974.

All What Jazz? Fontana, 1970.

Jill, a novel, 1946; rev. ed. Faber, 1964.

A Girl in Winter, a novel. Faber, 1947.

Bedient, C., *Eight Contemporary Poets*. Oxford University Press, 1974.

Brownjohn, A., *Philip Larkin*. Longmans, 1975.

Day, R., *Philip Larkin*. Unit 28, Open University: Twentieth-Century English Poetry Course, 1976.

Dodsworth, M. (ed.), *The Survival of Poetry*. Faber, 1970.
Rosenthal, M. L., *The New Poets*. Oxford University Press, 1967.
Timms, D., *Philip Larkin*. Oliver & Boyd, 1973.

Charles Tomlinson (b. 1927)

Relations and Contraries. Hand and Flower Press, 1951.
The Necklace. Fantasy Press, 1955; new ed. Oxford University Press, 1966.
Seeing is Believing. Oxford University Press, 1960.
A Peopled Landscape. Oxford University Press, 1963.
American Scenes. Oxford University Press, 1966.
The Way of a World. Oxford University Press, 1969.
Written on Water. Oxford University Press, 1972.
The Way In. Oxford University Press, 1974.
The Shaft. Oxford University Press, 1978.
Bedient, C., *Eight Contemporary Poets*. Oxford University Press, 1974.
Edwards, M., 'Charles Tomlinson', in M. Dodsworth *et al.*, *Donald Davie, Charles Tomlinson, Geoffrey Hill*. Unit 31, Open University: Twentieth-Century English Poetry Course, 1976.
Rosenthal, M. L., *The New Poets*. Oxford University Press, 1967.

Thom Gunn (b. 1929)

Fighting Terms. Fantasy Press, 1954; rev. ed. Faber, 1962.
The Sense of Movement. Faber, 1957.
My Sad Captains. Faber, 1961.
Positives (with Ander Gunn). Faber, 1966.
Touch. Faber, 1967.
Poems 1950–1966: A Selection. Faber, 1969.
Moly. Faber, 1971.
Jack Straw's Castle. Faber, 1976.
Bold, A., *Thom Gunn and Ted Hughes*. Oliver & Boyd, 1976.
Dodsworth, M. (ed.), *The Survival of Poetry*. Faber, 1970.
Rosenthal, M. L., *The New Poets*. Oxford University Press, 1967.

Ted Hughes (b. 1930)

The Hawk in the Rain. Faber, 1957.
Lupercal. Faber, 1960.
Wodwo. Faber, 1967.
Selected Poems 1957–1967. Faber, 1972.
Crow. Faber, 1972.
Season Songs. Faber, 1976.
Gaudete. Faber, 1977.
Cave Birds. Faber, 1978.
Remains of Elmet. Faber, 1979.
Bedient, C., *Eight Contemporary Poets*. Oxford University Press, 1974.
Bold, A., *Thom Gunn and Ted Hughes*. Oliver & Boyd, 1976.
Dodsworth, M. (ed.), *The Survival of Poetry*. Faber, 1970.
Rosenthal, M. L., *The New Poets*. Oxford University Press, 1967.
Sagar, K., *The Art of Ted Hughes*. Cambridge University Press, 1975; rev. and enlarged ed. 1978.
Thurley, G., *The Ironic Harvest*. Arnold, 1974.
Walder, D., *Ted Hughes; Sylvia Plath*. Unit 29, Open University: Twentieth-Century English Poetry Course, 1976.

Sylvia Plath (1932–1963)

The Colossus. Heinemann, 1960; rev. ed. Faber, 1967.
Ariel. Faber, 1965.
Crossing the Water. Faber, 1971.
Winter Trees. Faber, 1971.
The Bell Jar, a novel. Faber, 1960.
Johnny Panic and the Bible of Dreams. Faber, 1977.
Aird, E., *Sylvia Plath*. Oliver & Boyd, 1973.
Alvarez, A., *The Savage God*. Penguin, 1971.
Holbrook, D., *Sylvia Plath: Poetry and Existence*. Athlone Press, 1976.
Newman, C. (ed.), *The Art of Sylvia Plath*. Faber, 1970.
Orr, P. (ed.), 'An Interview with Sylvia Plath', in *The Poet Speaks*. Routledge & Kegan Paul, 1966.
Rosenthal, M. L., *The New Poets*. Oxford University Press, 1967.

Steiner, N. Hunter, *A Closer Look at Ariel*. Faber, 1973.
Walder, D., *Ted Hughes; Sylvia Plath*. Unit 29, Open University: Twentieth-Century English Poetry Course, 1976.

Seamus Heaney (b. 1939)

Death of a Naturalist. Faber, 1966.
Door into the Dark. Faber, 1969.
Wintering Out. Faber, 1972.
North. Faber, 1975.
Field Work. Faber, 1979.
Buttel, R., *Seamus Heaney*. Lewisberg, Bucknell University Press, 1975.

Douglas Dunn (b. 1942)

Terry Street. Faber, 1969.
The Happier Life. Faber, 1972.
Love or Nothing. Faber, 1974.
Barbarians. Faber, 1979.
Ploughman's Share, a play. BBC, 1978.
Scotsmen by Moonlight, a radio play broadcast BBC Radio Scotland, June 1978.
Sneak's Millions, a play. BBC, forthcoming.

Tom Paulin (b. 1949)

A State of Justice. Faber, 1977.
Poetry Introduction 3. Faber, 1975.
Thomas Hardy: The Poetry of Perception. Macmillan, 1976.

Paul Mills (b. 1948)

North Carriageway. Manchester, Carcanet Press, 1976.
Third Person. Manchester, Carcanet Press, 1978.
Nine Psalms. Limited edition, Moira Press, 1978.
Herod, a play. Rex Collings, 1979.

Index to poets
and poems cited in the text

Index